THE SECRET MINISTRY
OF AG. & FISH

Also by Noreen Riols

Eye of the Storm
My Unknown Child
Only the Best
When Suffering Comes
Laura
Katharine
To Live Again
Before the Dawn
Where Love Endures

THE SECRET MINISTRY OF AG. & FISH

My Life in Churchill's School for Spies

NOREEN RIOLS

MACMILLAN

First published 2013 by Macmillan
an imprint of Pan Macmillan, a division of Macmillan Publishers Limited
Pan Macmillan, 20 New Wharf Road, London N1 9RR
Basingstoke and Oxford
Associated companies throughout the world
www.panmacmillan.com

ISBN 978-0-230-77090-4

A CIP catalogue record for this book is available from the British Library.

Printed and bound by CPI Group (UK) Ltd, Croydon, CR0 4YY

Visit **www.panmacmillan.com** to read more about all our books
and to buy them. You will also find features, author interviews and
news of any author events, and you can sign up for e-newsletters
so that you're always first to hear about our new releases.

To Jacques and our children,
Olivier, Hervé, Marie-France, Yves-Michel and Christophe

Contents

Foreword

A few years ago, I was researching my book, *A Brilliant Little Operation*, about Operation Frankton, the top-secret raid on German ships in Bordeaux harbour in 1942. I'd grown up on the extraordinary story of the 'Cockleshell heroes'. Indeed, without them I would never have served in the Special Boat Service, which was formed in the aftermath of their exploits. But what I discovered was that, at the same time as the marines were carrying out their attack, an SOE team of six British officers was a hundred yards away in a café about to do the same thing. I was intrigued and wanted to find out more. In the course of uncovering this extraordinary story, someone suggested I should contact Noreen Riols, one of the few people still alive who was actually involved in the SOE. I fell in love with her immediately, read her previous books and told her that she should write another about her life. She replied she was already doing just that – and here it is!

Today, Noreen is a charming white-haired grandmother with a remarkable twinkle in her green eyes, and a wonderfully witty raconteur. But in the 1940s, still in her teens, she was a key member of SOE. As one of the few surviving members of F Section, her knowledge of the organization and its operations was crucial in helping me understand exactly how Operation Frankton came about.

Perhaps it is her nature, perhaps it is the training which filters into the operative's DNA; Noreen has always downplayed her role in SOE. She is being far too modest. Without people like Noreen the SOE would not have achieved what it did. Her primary, although not unique, task was to be a decoy girl (she is the last living decoy) – testing potential agents, deploying clandestinely to France, on their cover stories. This was vitally important because if they got it wrong they, and others, would die. Noreen played other roles in the organization, including the delivery of the weird and wonderful coded messages that were broadcast by the BBC every evening to tell agents that operations were 'on', training new agents in the not always gentle art of espionage, despatching them off on their missions and helping to debrief them on their return. She and the others worked tirelessly and often at personal cost.

SOE was acknowledged by no less a man than Eisenhower as having played a key part in the winning of the war on the western front which began in France on D-Day. Without it, and all those who worked for it, the Second World War might have ended very differently. I am, therefore, delighted that Noreen has finally agreed to write a memoir of her experiences during the war. Like her, it is witty, vivid and unsentimental, and it is also a story of remarkable courage and determination.

Paddy Ashdown, *May 2013*
Lord Ashdown of Norton-sub-Hamdon

Acknowledgements

Very special thanks to my dear friend Elspeth Forbes-Robertson, who, with endless patience, answered my calls for help and correction, researched and always promptly came up with the right answer and also checked the finished manuscript at least three times in order to detect any 'lapses of memory' on my part; to my great friend Lizzy Buchan, who not only introduced me to my agent Andrew Lownie, for which I shall be eternally grateful, but also 'pushed' me to write this book; last but certainly not least, to Georgina Morley and her wonderful team at Pan Macmillan, whose help and enthusiasm brought these pages to life; and, as always, to Jacques, my husband, who has encouraged and supported me throughout. To all of them, a very big thank you.

SOE Organization

War Cabinet
The 'father' of SOE, Winston Churchill,
ensured his War Cabinet was in close,
almost daily contact with his 'Secret Army'.

Minister for Economic Warfare

Head of SOE
General (later Sir) Colin Gubbins

SOE Western Europe	**SOE Germany–Eastern Europe**	**SOE Asia**
Section headed by Robin Brook		

F Section (1940)	**RF Section (1941)**
Headed by Colonel Maurice Buckmaster. It was the largest country section. All F Section organizers were British trained. When necessary, they recruited local French agents 'in the field'.	Headed by the British. It helped set up and liaised with General de Gaulle's organization, the BCRA, supplied equipment for missions and trained all the agents the BCRA sent into France.

At the end of the war, SOE had 13,000 agents in Europe and Asia.

Prologue

In June 1940 France fell, and a great slice of Europe was now in German hands. With Soviet Russia as his ally, Hitler was confident that the collapse of Britain was imminent and that a German invasion of the island would be a mere formality. But he hadn't bargained for the bulldog spirit of Winston Churchill, that visionary who had predicted the threat of German aggression seven years earlier. At that time, he and Anthony Eden had been lone voices crying in the wilderness, for the most part ignored or scorned by the British parliament. But in May 1940 Neville Chamberlain, who had naively believed Hitler's promises of non-aggression, was forced to resign and Churchill succeeded him as prime minister. Almost immediately he defiantly declared, 'We will never surrender.' His determination fired and inspired the British nation throughout the war.

Churchill understood from the very beginning that this war was going to be different from any other war Britain had ever fought. Only he had the foresight to see that the soft-shoe approach of MI6, the official intelligence service, would no longer be effective. The gentlemanly warfare Britain had always fought was not possible: that age was over, and only ungentle-manly schemes would succeed. Influenced by the German infiltration of agents into Europe during the 1930s – which had been so successful that almost every foreigner in Britain was suspected of being a 'fifth columnist' – Churchill called upon his close advisers to immediately organize such an 'army', a subversive guerrilla force, responsible directly – and only – to him. The Special Operations Executive, also known as Churchill's 'Secret Army', was born, and its first leader, Hugh Dalton, was instructed by Churchill to 'to set Europe ablaze'.

Its founding was not the subject of parliamentary approval. Its budget and its very existence were secret: indeed secrecy became SOE's code, and its officers used aliases when attending government or other business meetings. SOE was a shadow world in which truth, as Churchill said, had to be protected by a bodyguard of lies. This secret army was to cover every occupied European country and, working behind the Germans' back, carry out acts of sabotage and disrupt their means of communication. It would be Churchill's 'fourth fighting force', along with the Navy, the Army and the Air Force. To be sure of victory, Churchill needed an army of 'bandits', to use MI6's derogatory name for the SOE. And they were right: we were trained to be bandits.

SOE was destined to fight a war on three fronts. It had not only Germany as an enemy, but also General de Gaulle and MI6. Often in a war there are 'minor' wars being fought beneath the surface. The enmity – often bitter, even destructive – between SOE and General de Gaulle could be described as one of these 'minor' wars.

As the only woman survivor in France of SOE's F (for France) Section, I am often asked to share my memories with various audiences in both France and England. I always accept these invitations, since I consider it not only my duty, but also my privilege to tell the story of the courage and dedication of so many unsung heroes and heroines, many of whom I knew personally, who fought clandestinely for France, and for freedom.

When SOE's secret files were opened to the public in the year 2000, the media and many historians were drawn to the subject.

Since then, I have been interviewed by both print and broadcast journalists, all eager to know, from a former recruit, what happened 'in the shadows' during the war years.

Countless stories have been written and many films and documentaries made on SOE operations in occupied Europe. But, as far as I know, very little has been told of how these operations were organized back in England. I was part of them, sharing many tense moments with agents not only before they were infiltrated behind the lines into enemy territory, but also on their return from these missions. One of the highlights of my time in SOE was having the opportunity to meet so many men and women, both pilots and agents, who were totally dedicated to their high-risk missions, and to witness their amazing achievements, mostly unknown outside the 'racket', and, even today, often unrecognized.

According to a Latin motto, 'spoken words vanish, but written words remain'. Since a number of friends and journalists have asked me to record my secret experiences within SOE, I have finally yielded to these requests – and this is my story.

Many of those who have heard my story ask me what happened afterwards. At their insistence, I have also recalled my life in war-torn England – and my post-war experience working for the BBC World Service. There I found a similarly elite and fascinating group of people as those I had known within SOE and, as I had done during those war years, I learned so much in both those inspiring environments.

My narrative is therefore divided into two parts: the war years and SOE in Part 1 and the post-war dream – and reality – in Part 2. The book ends seventy years after the war began with a ceremony of remembrance at Valençay, a small town in the Loire Valley. Each year, on 6 May, we gather there in front of the memorial erected to commemorate and honour the memory of the 104 F Section agents, fifteen of them women, who did not return.

Through this annual commemoration, we hope to pass the flame on to the next generation and so keep alive not only the memory but, through that memory, the spirit of those young men and women who gave their lives so that we might live in freedom today.

PART ONE

*Secret Lives and Loves
in War-torn Britain*

Chapter 1

My mother thought I was working for the Ministry of Ag. and Fish. She died in 1974, just before her eightieth birthday, without ever learning the truth, and she wasn't the only one, because all those who worked for SOE, Churchill's Secret Army, were subject to the Official Secrets Act. It wasn't until sixty years later, in 2000, that the British government opened these secret files to the general public. Immediately the media in all its forms pounced on the few survivors still upright, and the questions they most frequently asked me were: 'How were you recruited?' 'Why were you recruited?' 'Who suggested you?' I'd really like to know! Even after all these years, I still haven't the faintest idea who recruited me, or why.

I was a pupil at the French Lycée in London at the time. Like all young people of my generation, on reaching the ripe old age of eighteen I received my call-up papers. I remember breathing a sigh of relief when one morning I saw the official envelope with the government stamp lying on the front-door mat, because, not having done a scrap of work at school, I knew I didn't have a hope of passing my final exam. This was my get-out clause. In 1940 practically the entire school had been evacuated to the Lake District, and the Lycée handed over to the Free French Air Force to serve as their HQ. Only one class of sixteen- to eighteen-year-olds was left *in situ*, closeted in a far corner of the building away from the roving eyes of young Frenchmen who now stalked the corridors. I fell into this category. So, since the arrival of those young men, my studies had been sadly neglected. I'd spent my days roaring round South Kensington on a motorbike clinging ecstatically to the muscular waist of a Free French airman. The place was bursting with them and we pupils were very few – twenty-four girls and one boy! The young Frenchmen didn't have a great deal of choice. Nor could they afford to be too choosy. They had serious competition from the Polish Army, also stationed in South Kensington, not far from the Lycée. The Poles were terribly dashing in their square caps, long grey overcoats almost sweeping the pavement and high black boots, bowing and clicking their polished heels all over the place. The Frenchmen rather paled in comparison.

Dear myopic Madame Gautier was one of my teachers at the Lycée. I thought she was about a hundred at the time, but realize now that she can't have been more than fifty. She always wore a woolly hat, scarf and gloves and a thick tweed overcoat in class whatever the season, declaring she would never get used to the English draughts. Sitting behind her desk on the raised podium, she used to stare in bewilderment at the rows of empty desks in front of her and sigh, 'Oh là là, là là. Où sont-elles passées, toutes ces filles?' ('Where have all the girls gone?'). She didn't know it, but we were of course perched on those motorbikes, clinging for dear life to Free French airmen, who were driving us at a crazy rate round the streets of South Ken. Only a few 'swots' and Wilhelm, a plump, good-natured German-Jewish boy, remained in class.

Another teacher, Madame Laurent, used to prowl between

the desks, noisily sucking sweets. She had a malicious acid tongue and often humiliated me in front of the class, sneering at my clothes, which were too 'English' and lacked French 'chic'. Her husband had abandoned her and run off to the Lake District with the gym mistress when the school was evacuated there. We thought her sad situation highly amusing and used to mock her behind her back. Teenage girls can be very cruel.

Volatile Madame van Gravelange was a White Russian, brought up in Romania and married to a Dutchman. She taught us German – in French – and never seemed to know which language she was speaking. She was very dramatic. Rolling her eyes heavenwards and with much waving of arms, she often shrieked, 'Noreen, you make me take the 'air out of me.' I never discovered whether she meant air or hair!

Poor homesick Señor José Maria (the rest is unpronounceable), who sighed for his native Spain, was only interested in teaching girls who were short and dark with liquid brown eyes. I was then tall and blonde, so was relegated to the back of the class and totally ignored, though I did learn to sing 'La Paloma'!

Madame de Lisle was a kind of school administrator who always wore a fashionable hat both indoors and out. I never saw her without it, though I suppose she must have removed it to go to bed.

And our lovely, gentle *directrice*, a single woman in her forties – what we called in those days a 'maiden lady' – had adopted an orphaned French baby. Suzanne used to sit in her pram in the courtyard, fussed over and petted by us all, until the day a bomb fell. After that, she disappeared. I don't think she was hurt, merely badly frightened, but her adoptive mother must have either sent her to the country for safety or kept her with her in her office.

The bomb fell very near the Lycée, and part of the school was hit, but I certainly didn't realize the danger, nor was I particularly frightened. After the air-raid warning sounded I had been on my way down the stairs to the shelter in the basement when I heard the ominous drone of approaching enemy bombers. Instead of hurtling down the stairs to relative safety, I stopped on the half-landing and gazed out of the large window, fascinated. I don't know what I was hoping to see. Luckily a French airman with more common sense than I saw me, leapt down the stairs and threw himself on top of me. We both crash-landed in a heap on the floor just as the bomb fell on a nearby building and the window above us shattered into a thousand pieces, most of which fell onto our flattened bodies.

I remember getting up, rather dazed. I don't think I even thanked him for saving me from what could have been a very disfiguring if not fatal accident. I just tottered down to the entrance hall in time to see the *proviseur* (headmaster), Denis Saurat, being carried on a stretcher to a waiting ambulance. It was mid-morning, and we were all sent home. But I didn't go home. Delighted to have an unexpected free day, I spent the afternoon wandering around London, returning home later than I usually did, full of my adventures, to find my mother, who had heard on the lunchtime news bulletin that the Lycée had been hit, frantic with worry. The telephone lines to the school had been down, and she had been unable to obtain any news of me. Naturally she thought the worst. When I was late home, her fears had been confirmed, and she was about to scour the local hospitals, convinced that I was one of the casualties. I almost had been! I shudder now to think what dreadful injuries I might have sustained had it not been for the airman's rapid intervention. But at the time I couldn't understand what all the fuss was about.

I regretfully left this idyllic situation when my call to salute the flag gave me the choice of working either in a munitions fac-tory – an idea which did *not* appeal – or joining the armed forces. Deciding that if I couldn't beat 'em I'd better join 'em, I marched to the recruiting office to enlist in the Women's Royal Naval

Service, as a Wren – partly because I come from a naval family, but mainly because I liked the hat. I found it most seductive, and one's legs were shown off to much better advantage in sheer black stockings than in the thick woolly khaki or dull blue ones issued to the unfortunate women recruits to the Army or Air Force.

When I went to sign on, however, a vinegar-faced woman told me tartly that the only vacancies in the Wrens were for cooks and stewards. My hopes took a rapid plunge. This was not at all the future I had fantasized over. The idea of spending the rest of the war making stews and suet puddings was not the glamorous image I intended to present to the waiting world. Vinegar-face seemed to gloat over my crestfallen appearance. 'It's either that or a munitions factory,' she threatened. Her voice, like an umpire's whistle, rang a death knell in my ears. The future looked very bleak. I knew there was no point in arguing, so I asked for time to consider. She sighed exaggeratedly and glanced at the clock on the wall. 'It's almost lunchtime. Make up your mind and come back at two o'clock,' adding menacingly, 'Otherwise I'll put you down for a factory.'

Like a beaten dog, I slouched from the room and out of the building and teetered glassy-eyed down the street, convinced that, because of her decision not to allow me to lead my country to victory, there was now no hope for Britain.

'Hey there, you look as if you've lost half a crown and found sixpence.'

I raised my eyes. It was my friend Tilly. I immediately cheered up. She had been at the Lycée with me and was great fun.

'What's up?' she smiled, linking her arm in mine and propelling me along Holborn.

I told her of my tragic situation. She was sympathetic, but didn't seem to find it as dramatic as I did. In fact, she laughed, which didn't help.

11

'Come and have a cup of coffee in the canteen. We can talk it over.'

'What canteen?' I asked suspiciously, envisaging the British Restaurants the government had patriotically set up and which served cheap, unappetizing meals and grey stuff in thick white cups referred to as 'coffee'.

'The BBC, down the road at Bush House. I'm on my way there now. I work in the German section. The French Section is just across the corridor, I'm sure they'd give you a job.'

My spirits immediately rocketed. I hadn't thought of the BBC. What an opportunity. Blow the hat.

Settling me at a formica-topped table in the BBC World Service's underground canteen with a cup of coffee, which looked and tasted like coffee, and a currant bun, Tilly disappeared to make enquiries. I was fascinated. All around me interesting-looking people were jabbering away in a variety of languages. They seemed very friendly and smiled at me as they passed with their trays. The canteen was crowded, and a young Norwegian asked if he could share my table. He and I were getting along very nicely, practically on first-name terms, when Tilly returned.

'Mission accomplished,' she announced, her dark-brown eyes shining. 'One of my friends is secretary to the head of the French Section. She spoke to him about you, and he can see you now. I'll take you up.' She linked her arm in mine again and made for the lift. 'It'll be fun having you around,' she smiled. Tilly was always smiling. 'This is a great place to work.'

I thought the Norwegian looked disappointed when I got up to leave. I was too. Never mind, I consoled myself, I'll meet him again when I'm on the staff.

I got the job. To start immediately. All I needed was the approval of the Labour Office.

Euphoric, I raced back to the Labour Office, clutching the papers the Head of the French Section had given me, requesting that I be allowed to take up employment there. But the office was just closing.

'Come back at two o'clock,' Vinegar-face snorted, firmly locking the door behind her.

Believing I had won, I was prepared to wait and savour my victory. Drifting into the nearest British restaurant, I was served a lump of indifferent cottage pie and some soggy cabbage by a WVS volunteer who called me 'luv'. (The Women's Voluntary Service was a band of worthy middle-aged ladies who wore a grey uniform with an unflattering flat hat and valiantly served their country.) Having demolished my cottage pie, I still had almost an hour to waste, so I attacked a treacle pudding, and even drank a cup of tepid grey coffee.

I was waiting on the doorstep when Vinegar-face returned and unlocked the door. I followed her impressive silhouette – she was built like a battleship – and sat down triumphantly in front of her desk, deciding to be magnanimous. After all, I had won – or so I thought. She took no notice of me. She disappeared behind a curtain to make herself a cup of tea, returning with it steaming in her hand, but didn't offer me one. I didn't care. My beautiful future was stretching out before me. I could put up with her acid remarks for a few minutes longer. When she finally stopped slurping, she looked up and jerked her head in my direction. I passed the papers across the table for her to sign. She glanced at them and slashed a red pencil across the application with the word 'refused' written in caps. I gasped.

'Not a reserved occupation,' she snapped, and handed them back to me.

'I don't understand,' I spluttered.

'It's . . . not . . . a . . . reserved . . . occupation,' she enunciated, syllable by syllable, obviously convinced I was a halfwit. 'I should have thought what I said was perfectly clear.' She sighed deeply before dredging up a few more syllables. 'You . . . can't . . . work

'. . . for . . . the . . . BBC,' she ended triumphantly and paused to gloat over her victory before dealing her final blow. 'It'll have to be a factory.'

'But *why* can't I?' I snapped back, seeing her select an ominous form from among the pile on her desk. It had something about 'munitions' written across it as far as I could make out, since I had to read it upside down. The milk of human kindness I had decided to pour out on her now disappeared down the drain with remarkable speed. '*Why* can't I? My friend from the Lycée is already working there. If she can, *why can't I?*' I was now beside myself with anger and disappointment. She looked at me coldly. 'She's doing in the German Section exactly the same job as I would be doing in the French,' I fumed. That last remark was my undoing.

'Ah,' she trumpeted, her false teeth leaping to attention like recruits on parade. 'An enemy alien.'

'Tilly an enemy alien,' I shot back. 'What nonsense!'

'What nationality is she?' she barked.

'Nationality?' I stammered. 'Well, I suppose she's British.' We had been such a hotchpotch of nationalities at the Lycée, nobody ever thought about it.

'You *suppose*,' she said sarcastically, 'but you don't *know*.'

'It never occurred to me to ask her. She speaks English as well as I do, I assumed . . .' My voice trailed off, terrible doubts about Tilly slithering into my mind. I began to wonder how many more of Hitler's personal friends had crept into the Lycée. Then reason came to the rescue, and I cheered up. Not Tilly! It wasn't possible. She was far too jolly.

Vinegar-face had her pen raised ready to despatch me that very afternoon to a factory.

'Tilly was born in Germany,' I panted earnestly, forcing a smile and hoping to awaken a spark of human kindness in her. But her spark, had it ever existed, had gone out. 'Her parents sent her to England to live with a family in '33 when Hitler came to power. She's Jewish,' I added lamely, and immediately realized I'd said the wrong thing. Vinegar-face's eyes narrowed. She was certainly a member of Oswald Mosley's Fascist gang. I could see her sporting a black shirt and marching resolutely behind him carrying a banner, her arm raised in a Nazi salute.

'In other words, an enemy alien,' she sneered.

I shrugged and gave a deep sigh. 'If you say so,' I ended wearily, abandoning any further attempt to placate her.

'Can't have such people in the armed forces,' she sniffed, as if Tilly were a bad smell. '*That's* why she's allowed to work at the BBC. But it isn't your case.'

Her pen, held aloft until then, descended. 'If you still haven't made up your mind, I'll put you down for a factory.'

She had insulted my friend and destroyed my dreams, and I suddenly saw red.

'I will *not* go to work in a factory,' I shouted, getting up and stamping my foot to emphasize my determination.

The door opened and a city gent, wearing a bowler hat, with a copy of *The Times* tucked under his arm, walked in. He raised his eyebrows enquiringly in my direction. I was by now puce with rage. Vinegar-face, taken off her guard by my out-burst, was staring at me, her mouth gaping open like a question mark, obviously not expecting what had appeared to be a nicely brought-up young lady to behave like a Marseilles fishwife.

'I've been offered a job in the BBC French Service,' I exploded, 'and *she* says I've got to work in a factory. Well, I *won't*.' My feet may have given a few more stamps to emphasize that my decision was irrevocable.

His lips twitched. He seemed to find the situation amusing.

'I'll take over this case, Miss Hoskins,' he said, holding out his hand for my file, which Vinegar-face had been gleefully mas-sacring since our morning meeting. 'Come with me, young lady,'

15

he smiled and, leading the way down a long corridor, entered a small office, tucked at the far end, and motioned me to a seat.

'Now then,' he said, sitting down at his desk and looking carefully at Vinegar-face's Victorian scrawl. 'I see you have just left the French Lycée.'

I nodded, wondering what was coming next. 'So you speak fluent French?'

'I'm bilingual,' I replied, now on the defensive.

He continued to study my file. Then, putting it aside, he began asking me a great many questions that had nothing to do with the warship I had expected to be invited to command, jumping backwards and forwards between English and French like a demented kangaroo. He seemed surprised that I was able to keep up. After a few more linguistic gymnastics, he made an incomprehensible telephone call, scribbled on a piece of paper and told me to go to this address, where someone was expecting me. The address meant nothing to me. But, relieved to be out of Vinegar-face's clutches, I took the paper and, with a final triumphant smirk in her direction, stalked from the building. My smirk was wasted. She didn't even look up. She was too busy destroying another candidate's hopes.

My mystery destination turned out to be the Foreign Office, and the room I was to find a windowless broom cupboard filled by an Army officer. The room was so small that he and I were practically rubbing noses across his desk while he asked me a lot of bewildering questions which had nothing to do with the Navy. It was the beginning of a series of weary wanderings, answering questions which, to my mind, were completely off the mark. I felt like one of the lost tribes of Israel trailing behind Moses on an aimless ramble from one desert to another. This tour of London didn't appear to be getting me anywhere, and I was becoming seriously concerned, wondering when I was going to be given my seductive hat.

My final port of call was Norgeby House, a large building in central London, at 64 Baker Street. I knew the building well, but thought it was just another government ministry. The plaque on the wall outside read 'Inter-Services Research Bureau', which didn't mean a thing. I think that was the idea. Like the hordes of people who passed by every day, never had I imagined or even suspected that this was the Headquarters of SOE, the Special Operations Executive, the official name for Churchill's Secret Army, which he created in July 1940 after General de Gaulle's radio appeal to the French in occupied Europe to join him in London and continue the fight against Hitler. I wonder if I even knew of the existence of such an army. I certainly didn't realize, and doubt whether any of the other thousands of passers-by did either, that behind those innocuous-looking walls representatives from every occupied European country were busy organizing acts of sabotage and the infiltration at night of secret agents behind the lines into enemy-occupied territory, by fishing boats, feluccas, submarines and parachutes.

The officer who received me must have approved because, after a few more questions, he picked up his telephone, spoke briefly and told me to go a certain room, where Captain Miller was expecting me.

The said captain may have been expecting me *then*, but when I arrived in his office five minutes later, he'd forgotten! He stared at me as if I'd dropped in from outer space, and without any further introduction suddenly barked, 'No one, but *no one*, must know what you do here. Not your father, your mother, your sister, your brother, your fiancé . . .'

I tried to tell him that I didn't have a fiancé and not to worry about my father asking questions, since he was floating about on a submarine depot ship somewhere between Trincomalee and Mombasa. We didn't see him for four years. My little brother was at school in Yorkshire and not in the least bit interested in his big sister's antics, and my mother had moved to Bath, relieved that her offspring had now left the Lycée and was away from the clutches of those wild French airmen. Had she got wind of my last paramour, whom my classmates had nicknamed Tahiti, she would most certainly have stayed in London.

I never did discover who else wasn't supposed to know what I was about to do because before Harry, the officer I thought was interviewing me, had time to tick off a few more members of my family on his fingers, a very tall Irish Guards officer, who must have been about six foot six, exploded into the room like a bomb, making strange squeaking sounds. Some sort of crisis must have occurred – not an unusual occurrence, I was to learn – because Harry, apparently understanding the squeaks, threw up his hands in horror, sending the papers on his desk flying in every direction, and the two of them roared off down the corridor to join other hyperactive members of this strange organization.

I was abandoned to a major sticking coloured pins in a map on the wall, who now turned round. 'Don't talk and don't ask questions,' he said briefly. 'The less you know the less you can reveal if the worst happens.' And he went back to his pins.

I was beginning to wonder what could be worse than the madhouse I seemed to have been trapped in. It turned out to be a German victory, and we were all apparently on their 'hit list'. But I wasn't to learn that until much later.

I would also learn that Harry and his Irish chum had recently returned from 'the field', the codename for enemy territory – everything was in code – and were still slightly on edge. That was putting it mildly. It turned out that the Irishman had been shot in the throat while escaping, hence the strange squeaking voice, which made him sound rather like a ventriloquist's doll. But at the time I was unaware of these details and was convinced I had been lured into a lunatic asylum run by the Crazy Gang.

A young girl in uniform, slightly older than I, was sitting

unperturbed at her desk, studying her finger nails. I looked across at her. 'Is it *always* like this here?' I ventured.

'No,' she reassured me, getting up and collecting the papers the two officers had scattered in every direction in their precipitous departure. 'It's usually worse!' She sighed. 'You'll get used to it.' She was right. I didn't have any option. I had entered the hidden world of secret agents on special missions.

Nothing in life is all bad. Not even in a war. And lighter moments often interspersed the tragedies that went to make up our daily lives in SOE. Otherwise, I think it would have been difficult to cope with the tensions and dramas we lived with every day, not only between SOE's walls, but in the wider world of wartime England. There were some good times, even some amusing times. As the French say, in life there are *les hauts et les bas*, and, strange as it may seem, comical incidents often happened during the air raids.

Living in London, we rarely had a good night's sleep. If ever we did finish early we often spent the rest of the evening and most of the night in an air-raid shelter, sitting huddled around the four sides like terrified patients in a dentist's waiting room, listening to the bombs thumping overhead, or hunched on the dirty platform in the local underground station, surrounded by picnickers, sleeping bags, crying babies and buskers, listening to impromptu 'choirs' roaring 'We're gonna hang out the washing on the Siegfried Line' – a popular song which was slightly out of date after June 1940, but we sang it all the same – or 'Roll out the Barrel', whiling away the time, waiting for Hitler's Luftwaffe to stop dumping bombs on us and fly back home.

The morning after a raid, we got up, picked our way through the rubble and continued as usual.

For those who were less sociable there was always the cellar, if one's house happened to have one. I remember having dinner with a friend at her parents' house in Hampstead when an air raid caught us unawares, so we all trooped down to the basement. At about four o'clock in the morning the 'all clear' sounded, and we settled down to sleep, for what was left of the rest of the night, on the various mattresses scattered about the cellar floor. Half an hour later, just when we had all got nicely off, my friend's mother shot up in 'bed' and announced, 'I shall never get to sleep with that clock ticking.' We had had a particularly ear-splitting night – bombs raining down non-stop, the ack-ack guns booming in our defence – and, now that it was quiet, the tick of the alarm clock was keeping her awake!

The Morrison shelter was the brainchild of the fiery, red-headed government minister Herbert Morrison. The corrugated-iron Anderson shelters, which had been hastily assembled in suburban back gardens after the Munich crisis in 1938, were soon found to flood every time it rained, leaving their occupants up to their knees or waists or entirely submerged in water, depending on their size and age. Instead, the new Morrison shelters were erected inside houses. They were enormously heavy cast-iron structures, secured to the floor, and took up an entire room, leaving no space for any other piece of furniture.

They were slightly less noisy than spending the night on the platform of the local tube station or in one of the municipal air-raid shelters, marginally more private (though not much) and were supposedly made to resist any assault. The only danger, when cowering under them, was that if the house collapsed on top, there was more than a chance that the occupants would be buried alive. In most homes the Morrison shelter replaced the dining-room table, there not being room for both. The family not only sat around it for meals, but also squashed themselves under it as soon as the air-raid siren sounded. They were very chummy structures, but could get rather crowded if guests who had come for the evening were caught by an air raid. Then everyone squeezed under the table together, and it was a case of when father turns we all turn, except that in most houses there was no father. He was either in the armed forces, on duty firefighting or standing on a high roof scanning the sky for approaching enemy planes. If he were too old for any of these activities, he patrolled the streets wearing a tin hat and being officious, blowing a whistle and yelling, 'Put that light out,' if anyone dared to smoke a cigarette outside, or leave a chink in the blackout curtains.

These inside shelters were often erected on Saturdays by volunteer Boy Scouts, and one was expected, as a thank you offering, to put money into their 'Prisoner of War Box', which they rattled hopefully everywhere and anywhere at every opportunity. When home from school on holiday, my little brother used to help put up Morrison shelters. He also, without fail, positioned himself outside the bathroom door when any guest to our house went in and noisily rattled his box when they came out saying loudly, 'Don't forget the prisoners of war,' to the intense embarrassment of my sixteen-year-old friends. It's amazing how a horrible little boy can later metamorphose into a charming young man. Once full, these boxes were emptied at a central depot, and the money used to provide comforts for our prisoners behind barbed wire in Nazi Germany. My little bro's concern and patriotism were praiseworthy, but at times highly embarrassing. And I almost strangled him on more than one occasion.

Another of my little brother's contributions to the war effort, when home from school for the holidays, was to organize his friends into a window-cleaning brigade. Carrying ladders, buckets and cloths, Geoffrey would marshal his troops at our house at 8 a.m. and set off. They were always in demand since, apart from there being no other window cleaners available during the war (it was not a 'reserved occupation', so they were all working in munitions factories or serving in the armed

Chapter 2

Looking back, I cannot help wondering whether during the war there hadn't been some collusion between the Labour Office, the Lycée and SOE. It's the only explanation I can find for the strange way my entry into this secret organization came about. SOE desperately needed people fluent in foreign languages, something the Brits are not famous for. And where better to find them than at the French Lycée?

Recruitment was usually by word of mouth. For obvious reasons, it wasn't possible to put an announcement in the newspapers. Citizens of occupied countries who had escaped and made their way to England, in the hope of continuing the combat, were first sent to the Royal Victoria Patriotic School in Wandsworth, the London Reception Centre. Many resented this, but it was necessary for security reasons, since not all escapees were loyal patriots, nor even always from the country they claimed to have escaped from. German agents frequently posed as refugees and they had to be weeded out, as did other enemy aliens. At the Patriotic School, after being questioned over a few days as to their sympathies, those deemed suitable for recruitment to SOE were sent, without being given any explanation, to Wanborough Manor, a country house near Guildford. At Wanborough, they were again questioned, closely watched to determine whether they could hold their drink and what their relationships were with other prospective candidates, and given various psychological tests to determine whether they were 'agent material' or not.

If they were considered unsuitable, they were either returned to their squadrons or units, if that's where they had come from, or dispersed among the different allied forces in England with none of them being any the wiser! Those who passed the test were asked whether they were prepared to be infiltrated behind the lines into enemy-occupied countries as Allied spies. Those who agreed were sent to begin their long training – six months, or eight to nine if they were to become radio operators. The French refugees would be interviewed by a Colonel Bodington, who would go to Wanborough to offer them the choice of joining SOE or General de Gaulle's Free French unit, the BCRA (Bureau Central de Renseignements et d'Action).

It was F Section that I now joined. F for France was the largest country section, which from 1941 was headed by the now legendary Colonel Maurice Buckmaster, or 'Buck', as we affectionately called him. He was a major when I started, and I remember drinking champagne in his office out of Army-issue cups when he got his red tabs. He was democratic, generous, warm – most of the time with twinkling blue eyes. But the twinkle could disappear in a flash and quite without warning when something displeased him. He had a lot on his plate, it is true, but when Buck flew off the handle and 'blew a fuse' it was best to keep out of his way. But the explosion never lasted long and, like a bowl of soapsuds, his temper would rise swiftly to the surface, froth over and as rapidly subside. And the twinkle would come back into his amazing blue eyes, as he patted his pocket, searching for his pipe.

The Section was staffed by English, French and, like my children, 'half-and-halfs'. It was an everyday *entente cordiale*. We didn't have any set hours. We worked throughout the night when necessary. Weekends didn't exist, we took a day off when we could, and as for holidays, I don't remember ever having any. I suppose I did, but they must have been very fragmentary and spasmodic. Strangely enough, I don't ever remember feeling exhausted, or even particularly tired. I sometimes wonder what it was that kept us going. Perhaps it was the exuberance of youth or the excitement of the life we lived.

SOE was a family. But it was an enclosed, watertight family. We couldn't talk to anyone outside 'the racket', as we were called in-house, about our activities. But it was also enclosed on the inside. Although I soon learned that members of every occupied country were working in the building doing the same thing as we did, there was no contact between us. The secret was absolute.

Being part of Churchill's Secret Army was fascinating. It was a stimulating, thrilling life, full of action – and emotion. I was recruited as a bilingual secretary, but that was only a minor part of my job. As far as I remember I didn't really have a job title. I was a general dogsbody to begin with: preparing and delivering *messages personnels*, which were broadcast to France every evening by the BBC, and typing up agents' reports after they returned from the field. Later, at Beaulieu, I was involved in training new agents, wishing them luck when they left and being present at their debriefing sessions on their return.

We lived very intensely. We knew many agents. There were those who had just returned from 'the field', by various means. Sometimes they had to escape quickly because their identity had become known to the Gestapo or they had been badly wounded, in which case a Lysander, a small light plane able to land steeply in a restricted space, was sent to fetch them. These operations were very dangerous, and many pilots were killed.

Other escaping agents made their way across the Pyrenees on foot at night, following a guide. Occasionally the guide was bribed to betray them to the Spanish border police. Even if they made it safely across the frontier, often they were arrested by these same Spanish police before they could reach the farmhouse which was supposed to shelter them until they could continue their journey. They would then end up in Miranda or Lerida, euphemistically called prisons, but in reality little more than concentration camps. Mercifully, during their training they had been taught several crucial escape tactics, the first being how to rid themselves of handcuffs. Those that succeeded in escaping – and they usually did – made their way to Lisbon or Gibraltar, from where they were flown back to London. Others got to the Spanish coast and smuggled themselves onto ships leaving for North Africa and, once there, somehow managed to get to the SOE office in Cairo, from where they were also flown back to England. Sometimes it took the agents as much as six months to make their way home, during which time we often had no news, and didn't know whether they were alive or dead.

I remember one young agent, Harry Peulevé, who broke both his legs on landing by parachute in south-west France, not far from the Pyrenees. He was hidden in a farmhouse and treated by the local doctor, who was sympathetic to the Resistance movement. But it was dangerous for the farmer and his family to shelter Harry for long, so, temporarily patched up and hobbling on two sticks, he crossed the Pyrenees at night, following a guide. And those guides walked fast. They had to in order to cover a great deal of ground under cover of darkness. Harry finally made it back to England and, after a long stay in hospital, went straight back to active duty and was again parachuted into France.

We also met prospective agents who had been selected for training and were preparing to leave for Arisaig, or Group A, in the north of Scotland. At Arisaig, they were subjected to harsh physical exercises, assault courses, crawling under barbed wire, often in the middle of the night and in pouring rain, leaping over high barriers, running fast and walking for long distances over hills and mountains and other rough territory carrying heavy backpacks. Or being dumped in the Highlands in the middle of nowhere, frequently in a howling gale, and left to find their own way back, living off berries or whatever they could salvage from the countryside. This arduous training was intended to get them into tip-top condition. Once 'in the field', they would need to be fit.

At Group A, all trainee agents learned how to live off the land, to poach and to stalk. They also learned to map-read, use a compass, lay mines, set primers and booby traps, handle explosives, including grenades and dynamite, and assemble, dismantle and use Bren and Sten guns, commando knives and arms of all kinds, including German weapons, since the *maquis* (the name given to groups of résistants living together in the woods and forests) often had to rely on captured German material. They were taught to shoot at moving targets, dummy figures which suddenly appeared from nowhere and darted tantalizingly in front of them from behind trees, and to kill, silently, using the double-edged knife with which they were all provided on departure – or with their bare hands. When they left Arisaig, they had to be able to blow up a railway bridge, an aircraft or a telephone exchange, and to jump out of a moving train travelling at forty miles an hour without serious risk to life or limb. And to live off the land for days, even weeks, without buying food.

After Arisaig, the agents went on to the parachute school at Ringway, near Manchester. Here they learned how to jump from a plane and, perhaps more importantly, how to land correctly, bending their knees as they approached the ground to prevent fractures. They began by practising their jumps in a hangar, then progressing to a hot-air balloon before actually jumping from an aircraft. Many trainees said that the balloon jumps were the worst, the most frightening of all – much worse than the real thing. It was the deathly silence which was unnerving: the noise of the plane's engines as the agents prepared to jump was almost comforting in comparison. For reasons which I never understood, the men were obliged to make six practice jumps before parachuting into enemy territory, while women only had to make five.

From Ringway, the agents went on to the different secret training schools dotted about the country, where they were instructed in the various skills necessary in order to become a good spy: radio, sabotage, propaganda, use of arms, escape tactics, how to react under interrogation or torture. They ended their training at Group B in Beaulieu, where all the houses on Lord Montagu's Hampshire estate had been requisitioned for SOE's use. Group B was the most intellectually demanding of all the training schools and is still, even today, known as the 'finishing school for secret agents'. Only once the trainees had perfected all those other skills were they welcomed at Group B. And it was there that they really learned the art of spying – and of disguise!

Training completed, before being parachuted into France or being sent to a holding house to await departure, the agents would rendezvous at Orchard Court, a luxurious flat in Portman Square not far from Baker Street, which had also been requisitioned for the use of SOE. We wished them luck, adding '*merde*', the unusual expression the French use to wish people *bonne chance* or good luck, and waited for their first radio communication.

On leaving, agents were designated to a specific area, but they were rarely infiltrated together, and they did not all arrive by parachute. Those destined for the south of France often went in by submarine, which would surface during the night about three miles from the coast. The agents would be lowered into the sea in a rubber dinghy. It was up to them to row or paddle themselves ashore, then deflate and bury the dinghy. Or, if the dinghy was attached to the submarine by a long, thick rope, to tug hard at the rope, so signalling that it could be hauled back. They then waited on the shore for daylight before venturing into the nearest town.

For obvious reasons infiltrations by submarine had to be carried out on moonless nights, which must have made the agents' journey to land even more hazardous. I never heard of one who didn't make it, although one French group came close. Having celebrated rather too copiously with the submarine crew the end of their journey and the beginning of their 'great adventure', when lowered into the dark waters they happily set off in the wrong direction, rowing briskly towards the coast of North Africa. They had to be rescued by the more sober members of the submarine crew, who were quickly lowered into dinghies and raced after them to turn them back in the direction of the French coast. Other agents, destined for Brittany, were taken by the Royal Navy as near to the coast as possible, where they would be met by fishing boats, often manned by Breton sailors, who would take them ashore.

Feluccas were another matter altogether. According to one agent, the smell on board a felucca was worse than the smell in any stable. There were two of them – twenty-ton vessels used to ferry agents from Corsica or Gibraltar, landing their passengers on the beaches of the south of France at dead of night. Often a very bumpy cruise! They were manned by Polish sailors who rarely spoke any English and had been offered to SOE by General Sikorski because the Polish Navy refused to have them: they were considered too rough and tough to handle. But, as far as I know, they never gave SOE any trouble.

Once in the field, the three agents joined up and formed what was called a *réseau*, or circuit, from which they recruited and trained local résistants into a fighting unit, and then organized sabotage operations, such as setting fire to arms depots and munitions factories and blowing up railway lines and bridges to prevent the German Army from moving or advancing. After D-Day, these sabotage operations seriously hampered German reinforcements being rushed to the Normandy coast. They also gained the support, rather than inciting the anger, of the local population because, being carried out on the ground, they were more accurate and rarely incurred civilian casualties, which unfortunately was not always the case with RAF bombing raids.

During the occupation there were dozens of these *réseaux* dotted all over France, each known to London by a codename, usually a French Christian name followed by an English trade or professional name. The organizer, or *chef de réseau*, was, as his title suggests, the 'boss', and it was usually his codename, the one by which he was known to members of his team, which was given to the *réseau*. For example: Guy/Musician, Gérard/Tinker, Antoine/Ventriloquist, Prosper/Physician, Sylvestre/Farmer, Hercule/Lighterman, Gaspard/Monkeypuzzle, to mention only a few. I always thought this last one amusing, and could never understand how 'Monkeypuzzle' could be either a trade or a profession. Each agent had four names. His real name was kept in the files at HQ while his false name appeared on his false, 'made in England' identity card. Then there was the codename by which he was known to the members of his *réseau*, and the codename by which he was identified at HQ, plus the name of his *réseau*. I wonder that we didn't end up schizophrenic, trying to juggle all this.

Some *réseau* organizers had no fixed address, and, for reasons of security, the members of an organizer's Resistance group were unable to contact him. *He* contacted *them*. Such extra security precautions were probably the reason 'Roger', who was tracked by the Germans for eight or nine months, was able to evade capture for so long, only to be caught at the eleventh hour through a very simple oversight.

Each organizer was assisted by a radio operator and a courier, both SOE-trained. Occasionally, the organizer had a lieutenant, but that was not the norm. A lieutenant was sometimes 'dropped' when heavy arms were parachuted in. A machine-gun, for example, could not drop as it was and had to be sent in kit form, and if there was no one on the ground who knew how to assemble the kit, it was useless. So an instructor, or 'lieutenant', was dropped with the material to teach the members of the local *réseau* how to put the weapons together.

Sometimes, their mission accomplished, lieutenants had to wait for a considerable length of time before they could be picked up and flown back to London. One of them remarked upon his return, after having been obliged to spend several weeks with a *réseau* before he could be repatriated, that he had always admired the courage of those agents who were dropped from the night sky into enemy territory, but until he had actually shared their life he had been unaware of the dangers and the permanent psychological strains to which they were subjected. And a pilot, who had been in the same position after his Lysander had become bogged down in the waterlogged field in which it landed, in spite of the efforts of a local farmer who brought a pair of bullocks in an unsuccessful attempt to free the plane's wheels from the mud, said exactly the same thing. This pilot finally had to abandon his aircraft and remain as a 'guest' of the *réseau* until another plane could be sent in to rescue him.

The second member of the team, the radio operator, or 'pianist', as he was known in house, was really the lynchpin of the *réseau*. He was the focal point of the group, the pivot on which the whole *réseau* turned, its umbilical cord, and as such was treated rather like a prima donna. He was rarely allowed to take part in sabotage operations, or accompany the reception committee receiving drops, although, as always happens, there were exceptions to this rule, because should anything happen to the radio operator the organizer no longer had any means of communicating with HQ in London. Even if there were another *réseau* operating nearby, they could not call on them for help. Security was so strict that each *réseau* was kept in ignorance of the existence of others in the vicinity. Every *réseau* was watertight and self-contained so that should a group be 'blown' (the code we used when a network was infiltrated or captured by the Gestapo), being ignorant of its existence, they could not, even under torture, reveal that there were other *réseaux* in the area. Such information in enemy hands might have a domino effect.

The radio operator, being indispensable, was possibly the most important of the three agents, since it was through him that contact with London was made to request supplies or replacements, instructions and also calls for help. As far as was possible, considering the dangerous conditions under which he worked, the radio operator was kept hidden. But all the same he was the one member of the team the most exposed to risk. An organizer or a courier could 'lie low' if they suspected that they were being watched. A radio operator could not.

Before leaving, every radio operator was given what was called a 'sked', a specific time during the day when he was to contact London, not to ask for news of Grandma or little Willie or the latest cricket scores, but so that the organizer, through the radio operator, could send details to HQ of enemy movements and report sabotage operations which the *réseau* had carried out, or which were scheduled for the days ahead, and also to request a drop of men, munitions, food, money or clothing. During the war, in France alone, as well as agents, SOE dropped arms to equip 425,000 résistants, plus hundreds of radio sets, pairs of combat boots and other items of clothing, all requested during the radio operator's daily transmission.

The time allotted to the pianist was personal. It could be midday, midnight, ten to five, half past eight, or a quarter to three.

If the radio operator missed a 'sked' it wasn't taken too seriously. He could have had a problem finding a 'safe house' from which to transmit, or he might think that the Gestapo had learned of, or suspected, his existence and were watching out for him. So we waited for his sked the following day. But if after six or seven days there was still no news, we knew that there was little chance that we would hear from him again. He was either dead or in hiding, or had been captured and probably would not return.

And many of them did not return.

The loss of life among radio operators was 25 per cent higher than with the other members of the team and it was estimated that they had a one in ten chance of surviving. Their missions were also the most stressful. They needed a cool head and nerves of steel in order to cope, since they were always 'on the run'.

They had orders from London never to transmit for more than fifteen minutes from the same place – because the Germans had a very sophisticated detection system and could tell after twenty minutes where a transmission was coming from anywhere in France, down to the very street and even to a specific house in that street – and never to transmit more than twice from the same safe house. So radio operators were continually seeking a safe house. This was not easy, because it put anyone who sheltered them, even for the short time it took to set up their material and transmit, in a difficult and dangerous situation. If ever the radio operator was discovered by the Gestapo while he was transmitting – and it was usually the Gestapo who did the tracking – it was not only the operator who was arrested, tortured and sent to a concentration camp but every member of the family that had sheltered him.

Sometimes a householder agreed to take in a radio operator for the duration of a transmission, and then denounced him to the Gestapo. So the pianist was constantly on the qui vive, forever moving from place to place, often with the Gestapo on his heels. They had to live on their nerves. And they had to be very disciplined and have a strict routine because they not only had to transmit to London daily, often under great pressure, but had to code the organizer's messages before transmitting, decode incoming messages, then burn any incriminating papers. All this as well as maintaining and carrying out repairs on their radio sets and, if necessary, dismantling and hiding their equipment, often in a barn or outhouse, and then assembling it again once the danger was past. It is not surprising that a radio operator's training was two or three months longer than that for other agents selected for missions as organizers, couriers or saboteurs.

Ideally, the 'radio' had a 'lookout' when transmitting. But if that were not possible, they tried to operate behind a curtain, near a window, where they could watch for any suspicious person loitering in the street below or entering the building. They would never transmit with their backs to the door either.

Although the pianists usually transmitted from a safe house, some preferred to work outside a town or village. One young radio operator, Henri Diacono, had a horror of transmitting inside a house since he was haunted by the idea that the Gestapo might burst through the door and surprise him. So he used to go out into the open country, throw his antennas over the branch of a tree and transmit from there, in what he considered to be relative safety. But he always took two armed résistants with him, who stationed themselves in strategic positions ready to warn him and, if necessary, open fire should the enemy suddenly appear.

These precautions enabled Henri to continue transmitting when the people he was working closely with, a Frenchman and his son, were surrounded, together with other members of the group, taken away and shot, almost before his eyes. Henri, who had just celebrated his twenty-first birthday 'in the field', escaped to the countryside and continued transmitting despite the fact that the Germans were searching for him. At one point he was almost surrounded by a group of German soldiers, all firing in his direction, but he managed to shoot his way out and escape.

I later asked him if he had been afraid when facing, alone, a battery of German guns.

'When I was in training the mere thought of it happening terrified me,' he replied. 'But once I was actually faced with the situation, no, I didn't feel at all afraid. It was more a feeling of exhilaration. It was their life or mine.'

Henri and I met again after the SOE files were opened in 2000, and we discovered that we had been living in adjoining villages outside Paris for the previous forty years without either of us being aware of the other's existence. Henri also told me that the training he had undergone was so intense that symphonies still rang in his head from morning to night: 'We learned Morse code by listening to recordings of such classics as "The Wedding March", da-da-di-da, and Beethoven's Fifth, di-di-di-da. We even dreamt in Morse, and when we woke in the morning the birds outside the bedroom window were singing in Morse. It was in our interest to listen intently and cram as much knowledge into our heads as possible, considering the huge losses amongst radio operators.'

The pianists weren't always denounced by their so-called hosts. Sometimes, they were betrayed unwittingly. Young boys were occasionally used as intermediaries between the courier and the radio operator, because a youth rarely attracted suspicion. But it was through a boy of fifteen that Yvonne Baseden, code-named 'Odette', was betrayed.

She had been parachuted into France with 'Etienne'(Gonzague de Saint-Geniès), organizer of the Scholar *réseau* near Lyons, in March 1944, to act as his pianist. Three months later, on 25 June, two days after receiving the first massive daylight parachutage (codenamed 'Cadillac') from a fleet of US Flying Fortress aircraft, Yvonne and Saint-Geniès went to a safe house they used, La Maison des Orphelins, a cheese factory outside Dole, to celebrate with a slap-up meal the safe receipt and storage of thirty-six consignments of arms. Yvonne had a locally recruited courier, Denise, but for some reason that day a sub-agent, a teenage boy, was entrusted with Yvonne's radio set. He was carrying it to the Maison des Orphelins and had almost arrived at the factory when he was stopped by the local police, questioned and searched. When the gendarmes found the set, he was arrested and taken into custody. He was then interrogated, under torture, by the Gestapo. Terrified for his life, he told them where he was taking it.

Yvonne and Saint-Geniès were in the middle of dinner when a lookout announced that a number of German soldiers were approaching the house. The group of résistants at the table scattered, most of them to the attics, and when the intruders arrived they found only the caretaker. They were about to leave when one of the soldiers noticed the table, set for eight, with the remains of a half-finished meal. An NCO, impressing on the terrified caretaker that he meant business, fired a shot in the air, unfortunately hitting both Saint-Geniès and a member of his *réseau*, who were hiding in a false ceiling, which had been specially constructed for use in an emergency.

The Germans made a cursory search but, discovering no one, were on the point of leaving when one of them noticed blood from Saint Geniès's wound dripping through the ceiling's thin partition. He alerted the others, who then made a thorough search and found the rest of the group hiding in the attics between the large wooden blocks used to separate the cheeses which were stored there. In order not to be taken alive and risk giving information under torture, Saint-Geniès, who had experienced the German treatment of prisoners before he had escaped from a Stalag and arrived in England for training, swallowed his L (suicide) pill and died immediately. The other members of his *réseau* were arrested and taken to the prison in Dole.

Yvonne was later transferred to Dijon, where she was tortured, but did not give away any information, and then to Fresnes, near Paris. Luckily, the Gestapo thought she was just a young French girl romantically attached to the Resistance; they did not connect her with the radio set, and none of the fellow *résistants* arrested with her gave away her true identity. From Fresnes she was transferred to prison in Saarbrücken. Eventually, though, the Gestapo discovered their mistake. Realizing that Yvonne was not the starry-eyed girl they had believed her to be, but an SOE agent and the radio operator they had been searching for, she was transferred to Ravensbrück concentration camp, where she remained from September 1944 until the liberation of the camp in April 1945. In spite of her toes having been broken during torture, she was put to hard labour, probably hewing stones, and kept on a starvation diet. She developed tuberculosis and was not expected to live, which probably saved her life. She was not executed with the other women SOE agents in the camp before the Allies' arrival. The camp commandant probably thought it was not worth wasting a bullet on someone who was about to die anyway. (Both Yvonne and her locally recruited courier, Denise, are still alive, Yvonne living in England and Denise in France.) A few years ago, at a commemoration ceremony at the F Section Memorial in Valençay, they were joyfully reunited for the first time since Yvonne's arrest in 1944. Each had believed the other to be dead.

In 2008 I was asked to lay the wreath on Remembrance Day at the SOE memorial in Westminster Abbey. There was already a crowd gathered in front of the plaque when suddenly Yvonne inched up next to me. 'I heard it was you laying the wreath,' she whispered, 'so I asked my son to bring me to the ceremony.' I was very touched, since she now rarely ventures out alone and never without her walking stick. Sometimes it is difficult to imagine the tremendous acts of bravery these now frail old ladies once performed.

Apart from the *chef de réseau* and the pianist, the third member of the team was the courier. Until the beginning of 1942, women were not allowed 'in the field', nor to train as agents. Then the British authorities realized that a woman walking in a town or village during the day was far less conspicuous and therefore much more useful than a man, especially a young man, who ran the risk of being rounded up in a *rafle*. A *rafle*, or raid, was when the Gestapo would suddenly appear, usually in the middle of the day in a crowded place, arrest all the young men in sight and send them to work in Germany as forced labour, usually in a munitions factory, on the railways or on the land, regardless of the profession shown on their identity papers.

The courier often accompanied escaped British airmen, who had been shot down and managed to evade German capture, and escaped prisoners of war, most of whom didn't speak a word of French, from 'safe house' to 'safe house' until they were able to cross the frontier into relative safety, and hopefully make their way back to England. Her real mission, however, was as a messenger for the *chef de réseau*.

Female couriers were also a great help to the radio operators since a young man, especially a young man carrying a heavy suitcase, risked being stopped and searched, whereas a woman carrying a shopping bag was able to move around more freely. In the beginning the transmitting set, or radio, weighed about twenty pounds and fitted into what could be mistaken for a small weekend case. So it was nearly always the courier who carried the radio from place to place, hiding it in the bottom of a basket and covering it with leeks and carrots and turnips, giving the impression that she was just another housewife on her way home from the market. As such, she was rarely questioned or searched.

Maureen O'Sullivan was a courier who was stopped. One day Maureen had to carry the transmitter further than usual so she strapped it onto the back of her bicycle. But she was held up at a level crossing. While waiting for the train to pass through, a car full of Gestapo officers drew up beside her. One of them wound down his window, pointed and asked her what she had in her suitcase. She knew that if she hesitated or appeared flustered she was lost, so she gave a big smile – like most of the young couriers she was very pretty – and said: 'I've got a radio transmitter and I'm going to contact London and tell them all about you.' The officer's eyes narrowed. The train whistled through and as the barrier was slowly raised she hesitated as to whether to risk making a run for it. But she knew she stood no chance of escaping, so she just continued to smile. Finally the officer smiled back and said: 'You're far too pretty to risk your neck with such stupidities,' saluted and drove off. As she later said, 'He could have asked me to open the case and I'd probably have been shot. But at least I'd have been shot for telling the truth!'

The French called the agents sent from London *les hommes de l'ombre* – the men of the shadows – which was a very apt description. We, however, called them the Crosse and Blackwell Brigade. After being recruited, their uniform badges and buttons were changed. Their insignia was no longer that of their regiment, squadron or ship, but now read 'By appointment to His Majesty the King' – the logo on the Crosse and Blackwell pickle jars. More affectionately they were known as 'Buck's Boys', in honour of F Section's head, Maurice Buckmaster.

Prospective agents were recruited from every branch of the Allied forces stationed in England. They were young, usually between twenty and thirty-five, although a few were approaching forty. But they were the exception rather than the rule. Yeo-Thomas was forty, and Lise de Baissac thirty-seven when they parachuted into France; Yvonne Rudellat, who went in by submarine, was forty-five. The recruits were courageous, motivated, often very idealistic and, glancing through old sepia photographs, mostly devastatingly handsome. And they were all volunteers. There were no special advantages or privileges given to those who joined SOE. They received the same pay as their comrades of the same rank working in a ministry or filing papers in a government office.

SOE recruits were the elite, the cream of whatever country they represented. They became, in effect, lone commandos, often on the run with the Gestapo at their heels. They knew from the start that they had only a 50 per cent chance of survival. Right up to the last minute before they left, they were told that they were free to withdraw, and no one would think any the worse of them. I don't know how many, if any, changed their minds, but I personally never heard of anyone who did.

Of course, if they elected not to go, they would have been sent to the 'cooler'. And perhaps the idea of being sent to that remote castle, a fortress really, in the very northern tip of Scotland, nick-named 'purgatory' by the agents, made the prospect of being hunted by the Gestapo a better option. And it was a straight choice between the two. Once trained, the prospective agent could not be returned to his unit: he knew too much. What happened at the 'cooler' is still shrouded in mystery, although rumour had it that, cut off from the world without a calendar, a watch, clocks or timepieces of any kind, the inmates lost all sense of time and place, becoming almost zombies in their isolation. Or perhaps they were 'brainwashed' to wipe out the memory of their intensive SOE training, so that when they were finally released they had forgotten all the secrets they had learned. Or what they had learned had become so 'out of date' that it would no longer be relevant or useful to the enemy if revealed. I never actually met an agent who had spent time in the cooler. But that is hardly surprising. They would have been kept well away from Baker Street. It might even be that, because of the extremely tight security we all lived under, these prospective agents were not released until the war ended. How true any of these theories are I don't know. But there must be some truth in the stories. And whatever happened in the cooler, if the general public had known about SOE at the time we would probably all have been locked away as either insane or a public danger.

Once an agent was infiltrated behind enemy lines, by whatever means, it was as if an iron curtain had come down between him and London. He could neither send nor receive personal messages. The only news the family in England received, if there was a family, was an official card sent once a month by Vera Atkins, Buck's assistant and a very prominent member of F Section, saying 'We continue to have good news of your son/ your husband/your daughter. He or she is in good health.' That's all, nothing personal. But the agents working behind the lines did not even receive that. They were completely cut off from home, country and family. They arrived in the field in civilian clothes, without the protection of a uniform, so that if they were arrested they could not claim the status of prisoners of war. They were spies. And a spy's fate awaited them. They had false papers giving a false name, false profession, false family, false birthplace, false education, false nationality. Everything about them was false. Before leaving they were obliged to absorb their cover story to the point where, even if they were dragged from bed at three o'clock in the morning, drugged with sleep, when questioned they automatically repeated the details of their false identity. They literally became another person.

Prospective agents were warned that if they were arrested, London could do very little for them. Before leaving, each one was given an 'L tablet', which they jokingly called 'the insurance against torture' and which they hid somewhere on their person. Some asked for it to be sewn behind the collar of their jackets, in the corner of a handkerchief or inside a pocket or the lining of a coat or jacket. The men often carried pipes which were hollow in the middle where they could hide messages written on very thin, flimsy paper, but also hide their L tablet. Some even had a filling in a tooth removed, the L tablet placed in the hole, and a false filling fitted on top, and one woman I knew concealed hers in a tube of lipstick. If arrested by the Gestapo, the agents were advised to crush the tablet between their teeth and swallow it immediately. It was lethal potassium cyanide and would kill them within two minutes. But once crushed, the tablet gave off a very particular and easily recognized odour. If the Gestapo smelt it on an agent's breath they would have their stomach pumped to keep them alive. Speed was essential.

The Vatican even issued special dispensation to Roman Catholic agents who might otherwise have been hesitant about taking or even accepting the L tablet. But in these exceptional circumstances, they were allowed to take their own lives with the blessing of the Church. But even then some Catholic agents were reluctant – Yvonne Baseden ('Odette') refused to carry her L tablet, while my friend Bob Maloubier told me that he accepted his, then immediately flushed it down the loo. Perhaps others did the same.

If for any reason agents were arrested but chose not to use their cyanide capsule, they were under strict orders not to 'talk' for forty-eight hours in order to give the members of their *réseau* and other resistance comrades time to disperse and, hopefully, escape. It was an order that cannot have been easy to obey, especially when a torturer was pulling out your finger- and toe-nails one by one, submitting you to electric shocks or the 'water treatment' or suspending you from the ceiling by your ankles or wrists and beating you till you become unconscious. You would then be revived, only for your captors to start tormenting you all over again.

Yeo-Thomas, who before the war had been the director of the famous Parisian fashion house Molyneux, was brutally tortured, possibly more so than any other SOE agent. Known to the Germans as 'Le Lapin Blanc', or 'The White Rabbit', he was finally captured on his third mission into occupied France and sent to Buchenwald, from where he made what can only be described as a miraculous escape. With the connivance of a doctor in the camp infirmary, he exchanged places with a corpse. The doctor had no doubt realized that an Allied victory was imminent and was anxious to save his skin. Three others escaped with him, but once outside the camp, they became separated, and Yeo-Thomas wandered through the German forests for days, living off whatever he could salvage from the land. Exhausted, he was on the point of giving up when he realized that the American lines were only a few miles away, so, tearing off a strip from his camp uniform to make what he hoped would look like a white flag of surrender, he managed to stagger towards them. The guards were about to fire upon him when he put up his hands and shouted, 'Don't shoot. Escaped British prisoner of war.' They didn't shoot. But neither did they believe him. The story of his escape was so incredible that they thought he was a German plant. He was arrested, and taken to a cell to await further interrogation. But on the way there, someone recognized him and exclaimed, 'Why, it's the White Rabbit!', whereupon his handcuffs were removed and he was given a huge meal. After months on a starvation diet and five days living off berries and grass, it proved too much, and he was violently sick. All he could manage to stomach was an orange.

When he was repatriated, shortly before the end of the war, Buck was waiting to greet him, together with Barbara, the young WAAF (Women's Auxiliary Air Force) officer he had met just before his first mission and with whom he was to spend the rest of his life. When Barbara saw him descend from the plane it was lucky that Buck was there to steady her, because she staggered and almost fainted. He was so haggard and ravaged that the shock at his changed appearance was almost too much for her. Shortly afterwards, his father was heard to say: 'My son has returned. But he looks like an old man of seventy.' He was forty. I'll always remember Yeo-Thomas. I admired him not only for his amazing, dogged courage but also because one evening he taught me to make ratatouille – without the ingredients! After all, how on earth could one get hold of courgettes, much less aubergines or tomatoes, in wartime? And onions were so scarce one almost had to go down on bended knee to persuade the greengrocer to part with a couple. Always supposing he had any. Instead, Yeo-Thomas explained the procedures with gestures, a pantomime using phantom ingredients and a non-existent *cocotte*. I tried his 'recipe' after the war when goods began to creep back into the shops, and it was remarkably good! I wouldn't say he was a brilliant conversationalist, but he certainly had a sense of humour and fun. Perhaps it was this that kept him going during his captivity. He spent a great deal of time in F Section's corridors, being great friends with SOE's brilliant cryptologist, Leo Marks. When they were together, if one passed Leo's half-open door, great gusts of laughter always seemed to be billowing out.

During his debriefing, Yeo-Thomas said that the first fifteen minutes of torture were the worst. But he also said that if an agent could manage to get through the first five minutes, he had it made. The most terrible torture always happened at the beginning, but after three days even that became easier to bear: the body seemed to become accustomed to it. I'm not sure every agent would have agreed with him. But it seemed to have worked for him, at least. Others told me that they recited poems to themselves, lines they had learned years before in school, Shakespeare's sonnets or verses from the Bible, or counted up to one hundred and then started again. Anything that might take their minds off what was happening to their bodies.

Prospective agents were aware of all this before they left. They were warned. And they were afraid. Brave men are always afraid, otherwise they tend to do foolish things, taking unnecessary risks which endanger not only their own lives, but also the lives of others. Courage is not the absence of fear: it is the willingness to do the thing one fears. And they all did, leaving for their missions regardless. They were frightened, of course they were. But they faced their fear. *And left.*

Chapter 3

I was sent first to Montague Mansions, a block of flats in the street behind Norgeby House, to work with the Crazy Gang, the secret agents I had met that first afternoon when I was interviewed by Harry Miller. Once I was part of their team, I discovered they were in fact delightful, and very friendly. But all the same the place made me think of a windmill operated by the Marx Brothers. The doors were always wide open and men and women in shirt-sleeves, mostly men, seemed to be perpetually roaring up and down the corridors, shrieking to each other. The entire block might have been teeming with members of the Secret Army, but if it was I never found out. We were such a closed group, even among ourselves.

Montague Mansions was never designed to be an office complex. It was a sedate, rather luxurious block of flats which had been taken over by SOE. And it could not have been a more inconvenient place in which to work. We used to trip endlessly backwards and forwards between Norgeby House and Montague Mansions: the crucial thing we needed or the person we were looking for was always in the other building. The house had three floors plus a basement. I was working on the top floor. And there was no lift. I cannot think how many times I raced up and down those flights of stairs, and I do mean raced. I'd caught the bug from all the other hyperactive inhabitants tearing about the place.

On my way down I flew past Leo Marks's office on the ground floor. Marks was probably the greatest cryptologist of the war. He was very young – only about twenty-two at the time – short and stocky with a bulbous nose but a captivating smile. He had a great personality. His door was always wide open, and there always seemed to be a party going on inside. Apart from the fact that he was very popular, there was the added attraction that his mum always sent him to work laden with cakes and sandwiches, which he shared around – commodities that were not to be found on every table during the war. Leo had been recruited to cope with the coded messages that came in from the different *réseaux* and was in charge of a roomful of decoders, all girls I believe, who worked in Michael House, a neighbouring building belonging to Marks and Spencer.

Before Leo's arrival, messages that the decoders found difficult, even impossible, to transcribe – they called them 'in-decipherables' – were often returned to the pianist with a request for retransmission. But given how much pressure the radio operators were under, it was inevitable that they made mistakes. Sometimes the organizer dictated messages to the pianist while he was actually transmitting, which meant he had to encode them as he transmitted – an almost impossible task. And the result was often a jumble of letters which the girls couldn't decipher. But when Leo arrived he decided that there was no such thing as an 'indecipherable'. If the pianist had risked his life to send the message, then the least people at the receiving end could do was work at it until a solution was found rather than ask the radio operator to risk his life again. He inspired the girls with his enthusiasm, but sometimes they still had to admit defeat. Then Leo took over, going through endless permutations until he finally deciphered the message – I believe the greatest number was over 900, and it took him three days to work it out. Leo found perfectly encoded messages suspicious. He concluded that they came either from a German operator who had somehow managed to secure the code or a pianist who had been arrested and was being forced to continue transmitting under German control, thereby enabling the enemy to discover plans for drops as well as other useful information. But this unfortunate situation was not as dramatic as it might appear, because it also worked the other way round, to our advantage. If the Section head knew that the code, and possibly the radio operator, were in enemy hands, he was able to feign ignorance of the fact and reply to the 'false' message with 'false' information – which might explain how the rumour was spread that the D-Day landings were to take place near Calais, sending German troops scurrying to the front in the wrong direction. Leo could always recognize an operator's 'fist', or the way he transmitted. And he could also tell whether the message actually came from our pianist or from a German operator who had either captured the code or was working his set.

One of my first tasks on arrival at Montague Mansions was to make sure that the *messages personnels*, which went out on the BBC every evening, were delivered to the basement by five o'clock. These were always prepared at the very last minute. I don't know why. To my mind, they could easily have been handed to me earlier, enabling me to make a regal descent of the staircase, instead of having to breathlessly hurtle down it like an unexploded bomb and slither into the basement at the last minute, where an elderly sergeant, a hardened veteran from the First World War, was in charge. Well, in a sense. He had a staff of one: a young corporal, who sat at a table in the far corner of the room, wearing headphones and tapping out something on a machine. I don't know what. I had quickly taken to heart the order I had received on my first day not to ask questions. The sergeant appeared to have been born with an unlit home-made cigarette screwed permanently to his upper lip. What he did I don't know. He didn't appear to do anything. But I imagine he must have had some kind of function. He was a pleasant chappie, but then I suppose he had no reason to be otherwise, since his sole raison d'être appeared to be to stand and glower at the poor corporal. I felt sorry for the young man. But, since he never looked up from his tapping, I couldn't smile and convey my sympathy.

These *messages personnels*, which were not coded but were broadcast *en clair*, were the brainchild of Georges Bégué, the first F Section agent to be parachuted into occupied France, in May 1941. He dropped 'blind', that is with no reception committee waiting to receive him, and had to find his own 'safe house', from where he transmitted the first radio message back to London. The person who received him, Max Hymans, lived in Valençay and later became a prominent member of the local Resistance movement, which, with his help, Georges Bégué recruited. But once the *réseau* was up and running, Bégué realized that in order to receive the necessary supplies of agents, money, arms, food, ammunition, clothing and combat boots, and also to inform HQ of enemy movements and sabotage operations, a system had to be devised whereby an agent in the field could safely communicate with London without fear of a message being intercepted by the enemy. Not only had the organizer to send a message via the radio operator during one of his daily 'skeds', but there had to be some means by which London could safely reply, announcing when the requested drop would take place. And that reply had also to be rapid and watertight, with no chance of the enemy intercepting it and using it to their own advantage, which would have been a hazard had it been sent to the pianist. So the *messages personnels* were born.

I've no idea what happened to the *messages personnels* once I'd handed them over, nor do I know how they arrived at the BBC. I imagine someone must have collected and delivered them. I remember one afternoon crashing into the basement at the last minute and bumping into a young Free French sergeant I had often swayed with on the crowded tube in the early morning. While clinging desperately to the overhanging straps, in an attempt to remain upright, we always greeted each other with nods and smiles, since we were both attempting to read a newspaper sent out by the Free French. He got in after me and, oddly enough, left at Baker Street, my stop. Now I knew why. He must work somewhere in the building. We gaped at each other in surprise. I said, 'You!' He smiled and nodded. I never saw him again. Perhaps he'd decided to travel by bus. Or perhaps he'd been locked up in a dungeon somewhere because he had been 'recognized'. We worked in a very funny set-up.

The BBC played a very important role during the war. For France alone there were eight or nine programmes broadcast daily. And the French listened to them, risking arrest if they were discovered. The Germans also tuned into to the BBC's programmes and jammed the lines, making listening almost impossible. Sabine, a friend of mine who was a young girl during the war, told me that before tuning in to the BBC every evening to listen to the news from London, her father used to put a blanket over their wireless set to cushion the sound. He then disappeared beneath it, followed by as many members of the family as could squeeze in. As she was only eight years old at the time, her presence wasn't considered essential. But she apparently pushed herself between a collection of knees to hear the ominous boom of Big Ben followed by the opening bars of Beethoven's Fifth Symphony – da, da, da, dah – before the threat of suffocation forced her to abandon her post. But one evening her father peered round the blanket and called her back, making room for her close to the set. She was puzzled, but when she began to question him he put his finger to his lips and said, 'Shush . . . listen.' 'I could hardly believe it,' she told me all those years later, her eyes shining at the recollection. 'The voice of the young Princess Elizabeth, the heir to the British throne, came over the crackling airwaves. I was so excited, I held my breath. She spoke for about five minutes sending a message of hope and encourage-ment to the children and young people of France. At the end she said, "My sister, Margaret Rose, is here beside me waiting to greet you." And the two young princesses sent their final good wishes before they said goodnight. For me it was the most wonderful moment,' Sabine continued. 'The princesses' tinkling voices had given us hope in the midst of a dark and dreary war.' She cannot have been the only young person in France who was helped and encouraged by our future Queen that evening.

The BBC was listened to by millions of French people, and the opening bars of Beethoven's Fifth were whistled loudly in the streets, the whistler often putting up two fingers, the defiant victory signal used by Churchill, to accompany the tune. Sud-denly a voice had pierced the darkness, bringing hope and encouragement, boosting their morale and giving them the strength to resist throughout the years of occupation.

The main programme of the day went out at seven-fifteen every evening. Big Ben chimed the hour. The introductions were made, followed by the latest news. The correct news was always reported, good or bad. And there wasn't much good news to report in the beginning. Perhaps that's why the French went to such great pains to listen, knowing that the news they heard from London was the truth, because all they were fed by Radio Paris were lies and German propaganda.

I asked Jacques, my husband, who was in France during

the greater part of the war, before he joined General (later Maréchal) de Lattre de Tassigny's First French Army, to tell me what the reactions were to the BBC broadcasts. This is what he said.

'When I was a student, I believed that Paris was the hub of the world, that the sun never set on the French colonial empire and that the French Army, victorious in World War I, was invincible, the best army in the world. So when, in June 1940, France collapsed, the German Army paraded down the Champs-Elysées, Hitler was photographed at the Eiffel Tower and German domination and rule penetrated every fibre of my country's life, disillusionment and humiliation dealt me a devastating blow. A dark cloud had descended on France. In the occupied zone it hovered overhead. In the so-called "free zone" under the control of the Vichy Government it threatened on the horizon. We were now part of Nazi-dominated Europe, cut off from the remaining, but dwindling, free world. And our former ally Great Britain had become, so we were told, our enemy.

'The media – newspaper and radio – was in German hands. The French prime minister, Pierre Laval, loudly declared that he wished for a German victory, while with eloquent violence Philippe Henriot, the French propaganda minister, known as the French Goebbels, poured out his bitter hatred of the Allies, the Jews, the résistants and, among others, General de Gaulle.* Every day, Radio Paris broadcast a talk by a well-known journalist, Jean Hérold-Paquis, who always ended his commentary with the stirring words: "England, like Carthage, shall be destroyed." Into

---

* In June 1944 a group of French résistants disguised as Milice marched into the Propaganda Ministry in the rue Solferino in Paris – now the HQ of the French Socialist Party – and shot Philippe Henriot dead as he reached the bottom of the stairs. Rumour has it that this murder was orchestrated by SOE and carried out by an SOE agent. But the rumour has never been confirmed.

this despair, the voice of the BBC sounding daily during eight or nine French news bulletins was the only weapon, the only ray of hope we had left during those dark times. It was strictly forbidden by the Germans to listen to these broadcasts and, if we were caught, the risk was great: arrest, prison, often ending in a concentration camp. In an attempt to stifle this voice of hope and freedom the Germans jammed the BBC French broadcasts, making listening almost impossible. But since these programmes were available on several wavelengths, we managed to tune in and, with luck, hear them.

'Big Ben would chime, followed by toc toc toc toc, toc toc toc, the V for Victory signal tapped out in Morse, then, as the signature tune, Handel's – an anglicized German, what irony! – *Water Music*, faded a confident voice would announce: "Ici Londres. Les Français parlent aux Français." ("This is London. The French speaking to the French.")

'These programmes in French were produced by a brilliant team of journalists, writers, university professors, politicians. Every evening the news of the day was commented on by Pierre Bourdan, a trusted, well-known French journalist. He did not hesitate to say: "I will not hide the truth from you. Tonight the news is bad." Every evening, too, General de Gaulle's spokesman, Maurice Schumann, in his warm, passionate voice, launched an impassioned patriotic call. He had a gift for strong slogans, such as "Pétain, le vainqueur de Verdun et le vaincu de Vichy" ("Pétain, victorious at Verdun, vanquished at Vichy"). And once a week "les trois amis" met in the studio to discuss the latest developments in the war: the stage and film producer Jacques Duchesne, who, after the war, under his real name, Michel Saint-Denis, was responsible for many brilliant productions at the Old Vic; Jean Oberlé, the journalist who had arrived in London as the correspondent for AFP in 1939; and the naval officer Jean Marin; all broadcasting under assumed names so as not to incriminate their families still in occupied territory. Their lively discussions were one of the highlights of the BBC broadcasts.

'At the end of the primetime evening bulletin, the famous *messages personnels* were broadcast. Listening clandestinely in occupied France to these seemingly nonsensical, meaningless phrases, we realized that they conveyed important messages for Resistance fighters and *maquis* groups. And we rejoiced that the fight was being carried on. The voice of the BBC was listened to by millions of French people, bringing hope, encouragement and the strength to resist, boosting their morale throughout the years of occupation.'

The *messages personnels* were devoid of any sense. Indeed, in most cases, they were a complete nonsense. After the war I met a man who had been a newsreader in the BBC French Section. 'I often felt a right Charlie reading those *messages personnels*,' he confided. 'Some were serious, others amusing, but many of them were completely idiotic. I couldn't make head or tail of them. But I knew they were important, and had a hidden meaning for those listening on the other side.'

They were important, but occasionally there were *messages personnels* that were neither requests nor instructions. One agent had left for the field a couple of months before his wife was due to deliver their baby. Naturally he was concerned, so the Section arranged for a message to be sent out for five nights running when the baby came, in the hope that he would hear it. Should it be a girl, the message was to read, in French of course: 'Clémentine looks like her grandmother', and if a boy, 'Clément looks like his grandfather'. But in this case, there was not one but two babies – twins – and they arrived early. No one knew what to do. 'Ask Buck,' piped up one bright spark. So we did. It might have been one of his bad days – he did have a lot on his plate. But, for whatever reason, he didn't seem very interested. 'Oh, do what you think for the best,' he said, and turned away. So the message went out: 'The two Cléments look like their grandfather.' The message reached their father. But I'm not sure that it wouldn't have been kinder to let the poor man wait until he was safely home to discover the outcome of the happy event. He might not have been all that pleased; he already had two boys!

Another agent left for the field without either he or his wife even suspecting that she was pregnant. Nowadays, with all these new-fangled devices, women seem to know after about five minutes, but in that far-off, less 'technical' age it was unusual to know for certain for at least two months. When the agent returned from his mission, I saw him racing down the corridor waving what appeared to be a piece of paper. I didn't take much notice, thinking he was yet another member of the Crazy Gang exhibiting their usual exuberance. But when he skidded to a stop and paused for breath, he thrust a photograph of an adorable little girl in my face. She was sitting upright on a cushion, wearing only a vest and a pink ribbon in her hair, looking accusingly at the camera. She must have been eight or nine months old. I can understand her angry expression. I don't think I'd have been very happy to have a photograph taken of me wearing only a vest waved in the air for every passer-by to see. 'Look what I found waiting for me when I got back,' he exclaimed proudly, before dashing off to dangle his precious trophy at someone else.

The messages certainly sounded odd, and I can easily believe that the enemy was puzzled and could make neither head nor tail of such phrases as: 'The little white rabbit sends greetings to his friends and also to Daddy Rabbit' or 'The next door's goat has eaten grandpa's vest'. Through SOE's intelligence grapevine we heard that the Germans knew the messages were important and were desperate to work out what they meant. We also heard that they thought the 'personal messages' were broadcast using a very sophisticated code and they spent hours trying to decode them. But since they were broadcast 'in clear', the Germans never succeeded. It's impossible to decode something which hasn't been coded in the first place! They had a meaning only for those who were expecting them.

On the night on which a drop was to take place the same message was repeated on the nine-fifteen news bulletin to confirm that nothing untoward had happened since the earlier bulletin to prevent the operation taking place, and that the drop was actually going ahead. Anything could have cropped up in between the two bulletins: weather conditions might have suddenly deteriorated, or HQ might have received news that the reception committee feared that they were under suspicion and that the drop would fall into enemy hands, or the members of the *réseau* expecting the drop had been arrested or were in hiding. Should the 'confirmation' not be broadcast, the operation was automatically cancelled.

These drops didn't happen overnight. It took time to organize them, especially since they were taking place every night during the 'moon period' – the ten to twelve nights each month when the moon was bright enough for the pilots to navigate by – to the numerous *réseaux* not only in France, but in every other German-occupied country. And this is where the cooperation between the RAF and SOE was invaluable.

It's all very well to train agents and prepare them for infiltration behind enemy lines, but if you can't get them to where they need to be, and once there they cannot receive supplies, the whole system collapses. There were always submarines, fishing boats and feluccas which discharged agents into enemy-occupied territories, but by far the most popular and most tested method was by parachute. And for that SOE needed the cooperation of the RAF, which was not readily available at the beginning of the war, when 'gentlemanly warfare' was still the order of the day among the 'top brass'. Lord Portal, the Chief of the Air Staff, even declared that he was not prepared to use the

RAF to drop civilians into enemy-occupied territory to act like bandits and kill regular soldiers, even if they were the enemy. It wasn't cricket! But eventually the strategic importance of SOE's operations overcame the hierarchy's opposition, and in August 1941, 138 Squadron was formed as a 'Special Duties' squadron, with 161 Squadron being added in late 1942.

All the same, this obstacle overcome, dropping thousands of tons of stores and equipment to the Resistance didn't happen without planning. They were not dropped randomly into a field 'somewhere near Paris, or Lyons or Marseilles'. A complex, detailed, but sadly not always foolproof plan had to be carefully worked out beforehand: the precise 'dropping ground' sought out, measured and prepared by the *chef de réseau* before any drop could take place, and résistants made ready on the ground before the plane arrived to collect and dispose of the supplies dropped. 161 Squadron flew 6,000 sorties between 1943 and 1945 and 138 Squadron, which began dropping supplies a year earlier, flew considerably more. The history of the Special Duties Squadrons is intimately linked with the history of SOE, since supplies, and often agents, were carried by Hudson, Stirling and Halifax aircraft, the mainstay of both supply- and agent-dropping activities for most of the war.

The two squadrons flew solely on SOE missions and were soon known as the 'Moonlight Squadrons'. The pilots were all very young, mostly between nineteen and twenty-three. One, who was actually twenty-seven, was called 'uncle' by the others in deference to his great age! The members of the squadrons were among the most experienced pilots in the RAF. They had to have at least 250 hours' night flying time behind them before even being considered. They flew at night without lights, navigating only by the moon, following the course of rivers, church steeples, cathedral spires, chateaux, towns and villages; it was rare that they missed their target. These pilots all signed the

Official Secrets Act and lived apart from other RAF squadrons at Tempsford, near Bedford, and Tangmere, near Chichester. Only these two airfields were used by agents departing on missions. They were never used by any commercial traffic during the war and were completely unknown to the general public.

When the supplies were ready for despatch, the BBC broadcast the *message personnel* the organizer had sent, to warn him that the drop would be parachuted to him within the next few days. As soon as the organizer heard his own message broadcast at the end of the BBC French Services' evening programme, he would inform the courier, who would then cycle into the nearest town and stop at the *bar-tabac*, where the owners were usually very cooperative. Over a drink she would slip in the news that the first message had been broadcast. And when the local résistants dropped in on their way home from work for their *coup de rouge*, the barman would pass on the message. The courier would then cycle to the outskirts of the town or village, often with the message hidden in the rubber band on the handlebars of her bicycle, and leave it in a prearranged 'dead letter box', which could be under a certain stone or hidden in a wall behind a loose brick for résistants living or working outside the town to collect. But on the night when the drop was to take place, there would be a subtle change in the message: a colour would be introduced. For example, 'The goat next door has eaten grandpa's vest', or 'There's a cow asleep on the duchess's sofa' would become 'The goat next door has eaten grandpa's blue vest' or 'There's a brown cow asleep on the duchess's sofa'. No wonder the Germans were puzzled. Then the courier would send out the warnings. The résistants would gather for the rendezvous before nightfall in an isolated building or farmhouse outside the village or town: not all leaving together, and taking different routes, in order not to alert the Germans as to what was going on.

When it was dark, after the curfew, taking lorries, farm carts, bicycles, anything with which to transport the material to be dropped, they would head for the landing site, where, hiding in the shelter of the surrounding trees and bushes, they would wait for the sound of the approaching plane's engine. Sometimes they waited all night in vain because the plane had been shot down en route. But more than half the planes managed to get through the German flak and ward off the fighter planes sent up to intercept them. They would usually arrive at around one o'clock in the morning, depending on the season and the distance they had to cover. Since the pilot flew without lights, and as soon as he crossed the Channel was subject to enemy gunfire, he could not take off before dark.

Once he heard the drone of the approaching aircraft, the organizer would leave the shelter of the trees and flash a pre-arranged signal with his torch pointing upwards. The code was always a letter of the alphabet which changed every night and was known only to the pilot and the organizer. The pilot would reply giving the same signal, then make a U-turn, while two résis-tants would leave the shelter of the trees to join the organizer. The three of them would form an L with their torches flashing to indicate a corridor into which the pilot, now returning after his U-turn, would drop his cargo. The planes used for these drops were massive Whitleys, Halifaxes or Hudsons, with a pilot and co-pilot, an observer, a navigator and one or two rear gunners. There must have been a crew of seven or eight.

At the plane's approach, should the person on the ground give the wrong signal – flashing 'P' or 'H', or any other letter of the alphabet instead of the prearranged letter for that night – the pilot would turn around and fly home immediately. He didn't hesitate. If it was a trap, he and his crew, as well as his pre-cious cargo, would have fallen into German hands. It was in the organizer's interest to get the letter right!

Ideally, the *messages personnels* announcing these drops were broadcast for three nights in succession, five if possible, in order to give the *chef de réseau* time to organize his reception committee and be at the chosen landing ground, waiting to receive the drop. Not all the résistants lived in the mountains and forests. That was only the *maquis*, which was composed for the most part of former soldiers or Army officers who were disillusioned by France's capitulation and wanted to continue the fight against the invader. There were also young men who had taken refuge with a *maquis* group in order to escape being sent to Germany as forced labour. They lived together in camps in the forests or mountains, away from their families, far from towns and villages, often supplied with food sent up to them by the local villagers. But there were many other résistants who remained at home, living their normal lives, yet at the same time were part of the local *réseau*.

A lengthy pre-warning to announce a drop was not always possible. For instance, when a severely wounded agent or one who was in hiding with the Gestapo closing in on him had to be got out of the country in a hurry, it was imperative to send in a plane, often with only a few hours' notice. Then the *chef de réseau* would despatch an urgent message requesting that a Lysander, or 'Lizzie', as the pilots affectionately nicknamed them, be sent in as soon as night fell.

Besides being much more dangerous, a Lysander pick-up was a completely different operation from a drop by Hudson, Whitley or Halifax. The plane, having to land to pick up its passengers, needed a much larger area as a landing ground, without too many holes, and preferably on a height. The 'Lizzie' flew unarmed, with only a pilot and a despatcher, usually an RAF sergeant, and with the observer's place left empty for the passengers. From the rear it was completely unprotected, its only safeguard from the Messerschmitts sent up to intercept it the grey and grey-green paint with which it was camouflaged! The Lysander was also slower than the larger planes, with a maximum speed of 212 mph and a cruising speed of 165 mph, and was therefore much more vulnerable.

A Lizzie could only take three passengers. Being so light, it was frequently tossed about in violent air currents when the pilot, in order to avoid flak from anti-aircraft guns on the ground and German fighter planes in the sky, had to twist and turn to such an extent that not only the passengers but also he and the despatcher were horribly sick! A Lysander was also used to pick up an organizer whom London needed to see for a 'briefing' session, or a dignitary HQ wanted to interview.

When the sound of the plane's engine was heard, and after the prearranged signal had been exchanged, four résistants each lit a bonfire, prepared in advance – this was later changed to four flashing torches, or flashing bicycle lamps – forming a flare path along which the plane would rumble almost to a standstill. The pilot would make a U-turn, bank the plane steeply then descend almost vertically and cruise along the flare path. He did not cut off his engine: he hardly stopped. The despatcher threw open the door, the replacement, if they were collecting a wounded agent, leapt out, those departing leapt – or were thrown – in, and they were off. It was a rapid and very dangerous operation, which had to be carried out in less than three minutes.

The return journey by Lysander was always perilous, because the Germans had been alerted by the engine noise, but also by the bonfires. Consequently, the plane was almost always subject to very heavy flak all the way to the coast, and many pilots lost their lives.

Hugh Verity, one of the best-known of 138 Squadron's young pilots, picked up the famous résistant Jean Moulin from a landing ground in France and flew him to England for consultations with General de Gaulle. They had such an horrendous return journey he said on landing that he was ashamed to face his 'Joe', the nickname pilots gave to all their passengers, after the bumpy ride to which he had subjected him. Climbing down from the cockpit, Hugh Verity turned to leave. But 'Joe' came up to him, held out his hand and thanked him for a safe landing. Jean Moulin returned to France but was later captured and died under the most cruel torture. We heard that every bone in his body was broken by his torturers and that he was unrecognizable, no longer a human being, when death mercifully released him.

The journalist Pierre Brossolette re-entered France by submarine, landing on the Mediterranean coast, not far from Narbonne. Like Jean Moulin, he was later captured, and, after suffering excruciating torture in the infamous Gestapo HQ at 84 avenue Foch in Paris, he was left alone in a cell on the fourth floor of the building, with his hands tied behind his back. He somehow managed to climb up to a window high in the wall and hurl himself to his death. Neither of these brave men ever revealed anything.

More than half the planes making night sorties over occupied France arrived safely back at Tempsford or Tangmere between four and six in the morning, depending on what part of France they were coming from, and also the time of year. Ideally, they had to have crossed the Channel, away from German flak, before dawn. But they often arrived in a dreadful state, the plane's undercarriage riddled with bullets, the wings torn half off, having suffered terrible damage on the return journey. Sometimes the pilot managed to land but the plane burst into flames as soon as it touched down, imprisoning him in the cockpit. The passengers sat at the back of the plane and were able to leap to safety. There was always an ambulance and a rescue team at the airfield, but if the rescue team did not manage to pull the pilot to safety, he was burnt alive. Even if the team did manage to haul him out of the cockpit, he was often horribly burnt and so terribly disfigured he was barely recognizable, since it was usually his hands and face which were exposed to the flames. Plastic surgery was in its very early stages during the war. Although Dr Archibald McIndoe, one of its pioneers, did his best and often worked wonders with terribly mutilated flesh, I've seen young pilots with hands which were nothing more than claws, and faces which no longer existed: merely a piece of skin dragged between the ears, with two holes for the nose and a slit for the mouth and eyes – without the protection of eyelashes – peering out. The goggles the pilots wore usually protected their eyes to some extent, but even so some pilots were blinded. Yet when they had taken off from that very airfield only a few hours before they had been healthy, handsome young men with their whole lives before them. Now their 'normal' lives were virtually over, and many were so disfigured they were no longer able to live in society and spent the rest of their lives making poppies for Remembrance Day in one of the Star and Garter or Cheshire Homes.

Out of the 329 high-risk landings and pick-up operations by plane organized by SOE, 105 failed. 161 Squadron made 13,500 sorties into occupied Europe, and in France alone landed 324 agents and picked up 593. There were in total 600 casualties among their air crews, whose effective strength was 200. So between 1943 and 1945 the force was literally wiped out three times. And 138 Squadron had considerably more sorties to their credit – with corresponding losses. It is almost impossible to imagine the scale of the SOE's clandestine operations, let alone the huge losses inflicted upon the Special Duties Squadrons.

Chapter 4

After working in Montague Mansions for a while, I was transferred to Norgeby House. The main building was teeming with people, representing every occupied country. It was by no means a quiet life, but at least it wasn't as hectic as my days with the Crazy Gang. On the surface, there appeared to be some kind of order. We had a much closer contact with the agents, whether they were departing or returning from the field or setting off to begin their long training. And I soon became very well acquainted with the whole process.

Every returning agent was given a huge breakfast at the airfield on arrival and then immediately taken to Orchard Court, a luxurious block of flats in central London, for a Y9, the code-name for a debriefing. They were usually able to give very valuable information about what the conditions were really like behind enemy lines.

SOE also had another flat along the Bayswater Road, less well known in the Section than Orchard Court. We used to take the bus to go there, a tuppenny-ha'penny fare, which dropped us right outside the door. I have heard that agents who were under suspicion were kept under lock and key there, as well as Germans who said they wished to defect to the Allies and join SOE. Escaped prisoners were supposedly interrogated there, too. I never attended any such interrogations, but I was told that there was one foolproof question the interrogating officers posed to any prisoners they suspected of being German spies: what was meant by the phrase 'a maiden over'. It was deemed that such arcane cricketing terms would only ever be identified by a true Brit. Another was to enquire whether they knew the name of Buck's dog. Every agent had met Buck's faithful companion, which accompanied him to the office every day, and would certainly have remembered its name. Unfortunately, after so many years, that is a detail I cannot remember!

SOE occupied the whole of the first floor of Orchard Court, and the people living in the other apartments going about their everyday business hadn't the remotest idea – I doubt they even suspected – what was going on under their very noses. The French agents jokingly nicknamed Orchard Court *la maison de passe* (the brothel)! It was anything but! More like Clapham Junction, with people coming and going non-stop in every direction. Arthur Park, a lovely man, was the major-domo or butler – I don't think he had an official title. He was in charge of the flat and, for security reasons, had the difficult task of keeping agents of different nationalities apart. Not always easy since often there were agents leaving for various countries, all clustered there together, while waiting to be collected by their conducting officers. But Arthur held a trump card! Orchard Court had a black marble bathroom – with a bidet, which was an unheard-of appliance in England at the time. Today no one would bat an eyelid at the bathroom's exotic design, but in those far-off wartime days a black marble bathroom was the height of eroticism. And everyone wanted to view it for themselves. So should he have a collection of agents leaving for different countries all at the flat at the same time, Arthur would shut them in separate rooms, after promising to personally give them a tour of the famous bathroom – if they behaved. But that if ever they escaped to take a peep for themselves they would not be allowed even a glimpse, and would have to leave with their curiosity unsatisfied. I became very popular in the Section because I had actually seen the black marble bathroom, so my company was often sought by those eager to learn the details.

Arthur was a middle-aged Brit who had lived most of his life in France but who, after Dunkirk and the fall of France, had had to leave his French wife and hurriedly make his way to England to serve King and Country – only to discover on arrival that he was too old for active service. He was perfect for his job at Orchard Court, however: very firm, but very gentle. I remember telling him so and asking him why he had been chosen. 'The General [Colin Gubbins, the head of SOE] told me it was because I knew how to keep my mouth shut,' he replied, smiling. He had a lovely smile. And it was that smile which departing agents carried with them, since Arthur was one of the last people they saw before leaving. And one of the first persons they saw upon their return.

One afternoon in the early 1960s I was in Paris helping with a Toc H tea party for elderly British residents when the organizer came over to where I was busily buttering scones: 'There's a gentleman here who says he knew you during the war,' she announced. 'He's sitting at that table over there. Would you like me to bring him to meet you?' It was Arthur. To the astonishment of the other helpers and, I imagine, most of the other people in the room, we fell into each other's arms, delighted to meet up again. After the war, when he was demobbed, Arthur had returned to his French wife, whom he had left in Paris in 1940. But sadly, not long after they were reunited, she was diagnosed with cancer and died. They had married late in life and there were no children, so Arthur was now alone. We 'adopted' him, and our children became his 'grandchildren'. Before he died he spent many happy Christmases with us. We used to collect him on Christmas Eve and take him back to his little flat on Boxing Day. I think that after the noise, the excitement and the hustle and bustle of our family festivities he was happy to collapse into his old armchair by the window looking down into the courtyard . . . and sleep.

Sitting in on the debriefings and witnessing the different reactions of the returning agents was a revelation. Some came back with their nerves shattered, their hands trembling uncontrollably as they lit cigarette after cigarette. Yet others who appeared, to me at least, to have lived through much more harrowing experiences returned completely relaxed, behaving as if they had just spent a fortnight lying on a sea-lapped tropical beach soaking up the sun.

One agent had been the organizer of a *réseau* in Normandy. His radio operator had been killed, and he had sent an urgent message to London requesting an immediate replacement. Although every agent learned something about wireless communications, it was only the basics, and without the pianist he was cut off from any substantial contact with HQ. I don't know whether trained radio operators were in short supply at the time, or whether there was some other explanation, but London sent in a man who didn't speak French. It was a disaster. He was a danger not only to himself, but to the whole *réseau*. The organizer, furious, sent a signal to London saying 'Send me a Chinese next time', to which London replied: 'Looking for a suitable Chinese.' Perhaps understandably, the organizer returned with his nerves in shreds.

But there was another *chef de réseau* who, although he had been very cleverly evading the Germans for months, had finally been captured. He was arrested, imprisoned and sentenced to death. He was to be executed at dawn the following morning. We were all in despair. He was only twenty-nine, and the father of two young children. The next morning the whole of F Section was silent, without its usual frantic activity. Suddenly there was a loud commotion. A signal had arrived. 'He's escaped and is in hiding, but the Germans are searching for him everywhere and are closing in. The situation is desperate. They won't be able to keep him hidden much longer. Must send in a Lysander tonight.'

All hell broke loose. 'Get on to the Air Ministry immediately and tell them we must have a Lysander tonight,' Buck shouted. The rest of us scattered in different directions to try to find an available plane. I still don't know why one of the 'Lizzies' from our own squadrons wasn't used. Perhaps they were all already booked for other operations that night. But our crisis coincided with the period during which the RAF was heavily engaged in intensive bombing raids over Germany's principal towns and cities, organized by Air Marshal Arthur 'Bomber' Harris. 'Bomber' Harris has often been severely criticized for what some considered his ruthless bombing of German cities. His critics seemed to have forgotten that enemy bombers reduced London, Coventry, Hull, Liverpool and other important British towns to a heap of rubble. But the Air Marshal held firm, replying to them: 'They have sown the wind, so they shall reap the whirlwind.' But no one dared tell Buck that there was not one plane available for the next two or three nights. Finally his assistant approached him with the news.

'I don't want a bomber,' Buck exploded. 'I want a Lysander.' As I mentioned, Buck could be very choleric and often blew a fuse, and when he did, it was best to keep out of his way. Yet as quickly as he boiled over he simmered down. 'Oh, get hold of the Yanks,' he said at last. 'They won't let us down.' They didn't. That night at ten o'clock there was a Dakota on the airfield waiting to take off, manned by an experienced pilot, all set to pick up his 'Joe'.

The following morning the rescued agent arrived at Orchard Court to be debriefed. He was as cool as a cucumber. It was impossible to even imagine the nightmare he must have lived through, yet he seemed to have taken it all in his stride and showed no immediate signs of stress or 'nerves' after his terrifying experience.

In 1944, another agent found himself in the same situation. His return was less dramatic, but his arrest and escape were remarkable. Francis Cammaerts, codenamed 'Roger', had been a schoolmaster and a pacifist. As a conscientious objector at the outbreak of war he was sent to work as a farm labourer. When his younger brother, an RAF fighter pilot, was killed during the Battle of Britain he was so incensed at his brother's untimely death that he laid down his pitchfork and joined the Army. Cammaerts's father was a famous Belgian poet, and he was bilingual, so he was approached by SOE, trained and parachuted into France.

The Gestapo had also been searching for 'Roger' for several months. He remained one step ahead of them until, through a stupid mistake, they finally tracked him down. They arrested not only 'Roger', but also two other agents who were with him at the time, a considerable coup for the enemy and a massive blow for SOE. All three were imprisoned in an impregnable fortress and sentenced to death, with the executions set for the following morning. Once again the whole of F Section was in despair. We knew them all and, apart from the personal anguish, the loss of three important agents at once was devastating. The following morning the Section was again like a morgue. You could have heard a pin drop when once again there was a loud commotion. There had been another last-minute miracle, and a signal arrived announcing their escape.

It had been orchestrated by their amazingly courageous and

audacious courier, Christine Granville, with the help of a large sum of (fake) money parachuted in by SOE from North Africa, combined with a great deal of persuasion and many threats from Christine. She also managed to persuade one of the senior prison officers to help her. He had realized that the war was almost over, that the Allies were advancing and taking village after village and that it was to his advantage to be on the Allies' side now that Germany was doomed to defeat. The three agents, together with Christine, who had been waiting for them a short distance from the prison, were driven to a point just outside the Allied zone. From there they drove themselves to a neighbouring town in time to join in the festivities celebrating its liberation after the German retreat. They did not immediately return to London, but when after a few months they arrived in the office they too appeared, on the surface, to have suffered no ill effects from their terrifying experience.

Once the war ended, Francis Cammaerts settled down with his wife and young family and resumed his teaching career without, on the surface, having any dire repercussions from his close brush with death. He said afterwards that, during the night before his scheduled execution, he didn't remember feeling any particular fear, merely a sense of regret. He thought, 'What a pity', and left it at that. But who knows what after-effects he may have suffered without showing any outward sign of stress or pain? We only see the outside: the face people wish to show us. The mistake is to think that an outer calm represents what is going on inside. Many agents carried with them inner scars for a very long time, some for ever.

Recently I met 'Roger's' eldest daughter, Joanna, and asked her about her father. 'Roger' had died at ninety, and, after his wife's death a few years earlier, Joanna had cared for him. 'I heard that he was very restless,' I ventured. She looked surprised but assured me that his restlessness was due to the fact that, as he gradually rose to the top of his profession, it had involved the family moving a great deal, at one point spending several years in Africa. But that as far as she could see he hadn't appeared to have had any serious after-effects as a result of his wartime experiences. 'He drank a lot,' she smiled. 'But then they all did. And,' she added with a twinkle in her eye, 'he was a great womanizer.' 'Roger' was extremely attractive: I was not surprised that women fell for him like ninepins. 'My mother was a wonderful woman,' Joanna ended. 'She understood him, and they had a very happy marriage. When she died a few years before he did, my father seemed to go to pieces and lose interest in life. He adored her right till the end.' 'Roger' has now almost become a legend, and his story is very ably told in Clare Mulley's recent book *The Spy Who Loved* on the incredible life and adventures of his Polish courier, Countess Krystyna Skarbek, alias Christine Granville.

Attending those Y9 debriefing sessions, I grew up . . . fast. When I was recruited I had been a happy-go-lucky, starry-eyed teenager with, so I thought, the world at my feet. But, listening to the often harrowing stories of these returning agents, some of whom had lived closely with death, torture and betrayal and yet were not very much older than I, and some of whom were shattered by their experiences, brought me down to earth with a bump. Witnessing their courage and devotion to the task in hand, one could not help but be affected. It changed me almost overnight from a starry-eyed girl into a woman: and perhaps prepared me for the suffering which later I myself was to encounter. I slowly came to understand and to accept that life is made of hills and valleys, highs and lows and that suffering is part of it. Everyone suffers at some point in life. No one escapes. Some suffer more than others and there doesn't appear to be any reason why. I also learned that torturing oneself in an attempt to find an answer or a reason for this seeming injustice is the road that leads to madness. There is no answer. I wonder if this questioning of why some suffered while others escaped was not the beginning of my search for a meaning to life, and the road which led me to faith.

Until the war I had been sheltered, protected from the blows and buffetings which daily life inflicts. I hadn't questioned the whys of suffering because I had not experienced it: my questions about life began during the Y9s, where I was face to face with men and women who had suffered both mentally and physically and survived. So when my turn came, remembering their different reactions, I realized that it is the way a person reacts to suffering which shapes them and forms their character. I could either let the pain dominate me and make me bitter, or I could use the pain to my advantage, learn from the experience, albeit a painful lesson, but through it grow and become a more rounded, more mature person. Watching these returning agents' reactions and hearing their stories I realized that people are not jellies; they cannot be poured into a mould, left to set then turned out – all equal. We are individuals with our individual characters, and sensitivities. And some are more resilient than others. I learned not to judge, certainly not by outward appearances, and not to criticize, but to accept people as they are.

Those Y9s gave me a mental picture of what it was like to live in an occupied country, showed me what many were enduring under the Nazi jackboot: and I realized how very near we had come to being an occupied nation. Their often down-to-earth recounting of their experiences gave me a great insight into the terrible psychological strains and pressures the agents were subjected to. Their life in the field was a journey through fear and darkness, often treachery, and they lived with great loneliness. Even before their departure, and certainly once back in England, they were isolated. They could tell no one outside the small F Section circle what they were doing, share with no one but us their doubts, their anxieties, their fears. I also realized that, in order to carry out their difficult missions, courage was not enough. They needed more than the quick burst of adrenaline required for a 'hit and run' mission; they had to possess a special kind of courage: a cold-blooded nerve which endured for days, weeks, sometimes months, even when doubt and exhaustion almost overwhelmed and drowned their spirit. They needed endurance and, usually, a passionate belief in a cause. Living so near the edge of death, they were more aware of life than the rest of us are. Many of us tend to take life for granted. They didn't.

The agents I met during interrogations at Orchard Court were nearly all people of unusual sensitivity, able to make quick decisions and accurate assessments of a person's character, but possessing the inner strength to kill or order the execution of a comrade who had betrayed them. SOE seemed to draw officers of exceptional quality who would have been considered outstanding in any form of warfare. They were not military geniuses, who fitted neatly into the British forces' organization charts. They were individualists, self-reliant people who preferred to operate singly rather than in large groups, happy to be their own master and make their own decisions, rather than being obliged to obey orders made by others, which they often considered futile.

In those sessions I also learned that we each have a different pain threshold, that point at which, in spite of oneself, the body succumbs and gives in. Listening to the agents' often harrowing stories, I came to understand that it is easy to think, even to boast when in the relative safety of a free country, that one will never crack, never give in, never talk, never betray one's comrades. But no one can know their breaking point in advance. That moment, perhaps transitory but often devastating in its consequences, when, faced with terror, threats and insinuations that one has been betrayed or that the enemy knows all the secrets anyway, a person reaches the end of his tether. His body and his spirit can no longer endure the torture, the pain, both mental and physical, and he will crack and thereby betray not only himself, but his comrades, his fellow résistants and the cause for which he is fighting. Perhaps that is why SOE advised departing agents to swallow the L pill if ever they were arrested, so that they would never have to discover what their breaking point might be. In Gestapo hands an agent who cracked was as good as dead. I never met one who did. But perhaps they were the ones who didn't return!

Orchard Court was not only the place agents returned to after a mission. It was also the last place they saw before departing for the field. Arthur Park's firm handshake, his warm smile of encouragement and his friendly pat on the back as they left Orchard Court were precious memories for many agents long after the war was over.

Departing agents were driven to Orchard Court in the afternoon prior to leaving to change into their 'made in France' clothes. These outfits were specially designed for them by a Jewish refugee tailor from Vienna who had a workshop in Whitechapel. The cut of a jacket or the way a shirt collar is set or the buttons and zip fasteners are placed differs from country to country. Had they been infiltrated into France wearing British tailored clothes, even with the original labels removed, and 'Galeries Lafayette' or 'Printemps' sewn in their place, it could have betrayed them. When they got to the flat, their new outfits would be waiting for them. After changing, their uniform and their personal effects were packed into a suitcase and placed in a locker to await their return – or, should they not return, to be sent to their next of kin. In 1943, when things began to 'hot up' for SOE, and more and more agents were being trained and sent into the field, the facilities at Orchard Court, though considerable, became rather strained, and the overflow of agents was taken to another SOE flat, at 32 Wimpole Street.

Towards the end of the afternoon, Buck or Vera Atkins would arrive at Orchard Court to accompany the departing agents, now togged out in their new clothes, to Tempsford or Tangmere. If they were flying from Tangmere, on arrival they would be taken to Tangmere Cottage just across the lane from the airfield (there were similar facilities at Tempsford, a converted farm named 'Gibraltar') and given a slap-up dinner with wine flowing freely – but not too freely – after which they would be taken to a small hut on the airfield. Here they were searched to make sure they had not left something compromising in a pocket. Every possible precaution was taken before the agent climbed into his flying gear to make absolutely sure that during the journey down from London he had not inadvertently slipped into one of his pockets a box of Swan Vesta matches, a cigarette end with 'Player's Please' written on it or a London bus ticket. It seems unbelievable but even the turn-ups on men's trousers were unfolded and carefully brushed in case they had collected some British dust between Orchard Court and the airfield!

This procedure completed, they were given their new identity papers, ration cards, work permits and a sum of false 'French' (made in England) money. A small suitcase was crammed with temporary rations, tins of food, cigarettes and chocolate, which could also be used for bargaining, since such luxuries were almost unobtainable in France. Their ankles were bandaged to cushion the shock on landing, and they were helped into their cumbersome flying suits. They were like an enormous eiderdown, because inside the planes it was not only dreadfully noisy, but also terribly cold. The suit was very heavy since there were about twenty pockets containing a trowel with which to bury their parachute and flying suit on arrival, a small compass, maps of the area for which they were destined, a first aid kit, emergency rations and, for the men, a hand gun and a dagger. Women agents rarely carried guns, though, like the men, they were given a sharp double-edged knife – for silent killing, in case their grip on an enemy throat was not strong enough. The parachute was then fixed in position, the helmet adjusted, and they were finally ready to leave – looking like the Michelin man!

When the departing agents arrived at the plane, a Whitley, Halifax or Hudson, often walking the few yards which separated them from the plane with great difficulty because of their cumbersome outfit, the pilot would be standing beside the cockpit, waiting for them. Introductions were made, but no names were exchanged, except perhaps the codename which each agent had been given. As he climbed into the plane, an agent left his 'real self' behind him. The pilot was the only member of the crew, except the despatcher, whom they met or with whom they had any contact. Nor was their departure the glamorous take-off sometimes depicted in films or on the television There was a large hole in the fuselage of the plane into which the agents put their head and shoulders: they were then pushed from behind until they disappeared inside, and crawled on all fours to the front of the plane, where sleeping bags were waiting for them. They were advised to try to sleep, since the journey could be long. Sometimes there was only one agent leaving, sometimes three, but there were generally two of them. Rarely did more than three agents leave on one flight.

Before they left, Buck always gave each agent a present: a gold pen, cigarette case or cuff-links for a man and a gold pen or powder compact for the women. 'Just to let you know we shall be thinking of you,' he used to say, adding with a smile, 'you can always hock it if you get yourself into a tight hole and need money in a hurry.'

The despatcher, the only member of the crew actually in the cabin with the agents, was on board to attend to their needs. During the flight, the despatcher liaised constantly with the pilot and the navigator, discussing their position and the distance left to fly, so as to know when to rouse the agents. The men often slept soundly: the women usually only dozed. The despatcher was kept busy arranging the containers full of supplies which would be dropped to the reception committee waiting on the ground, after the agents had left the plane. These containers were very heavy cylinders, sometimes requiring three or four men to carry them to the waiting lorries or farm carts. The supplies they held included grenades, Sten guns, revolvers, machine-guns, batteries, wire so thin it was invisible to the naked eye, which was used for tripwires – and sometimes as a weapon – and bicycle tyres. People did an awful lot of cycling during the occupation, and tyres were not only in short supply in France but virtually unobtainable. Unless they were lucky enough to get new ones from SOE, when tyres wore out, people just cycled on the uppers! There were also drops of tea, coffee, cigarettes, chocolate, clothing, boots, money and whatever other supplies the organizer might have requested.

When the plane approached the appointed landing ground, the pilot pressed a button and a red light would appear in the cabin. The despatcher would then wake the agents with a cup of coffee and sandwiches, help them out of their sleeping bags, hook their parachutes to a static line and open the trapdoor in the floor of the plane. The agents would sit opposite each other on either side of the trapdoor, their legs dangling in mid-air. They were told not to look down at the ground rushing by beneath them, but to fix their eyes on the despatcher's raised arm. The despatcher's eyes would be glued to the red light and the second it turned to green his arm would come down and he would shout 'Go', although the noise of the plane invariably drowned him out, and, one after the other in rapid succession, the agents jumped from the plane, each one destined, after landing, for a different *réseau*. If they hesitated, the despatcher would give them a kick, because otherwise they might arrive kilometres away from their scheduled landing zone. Unfortunately, even those who jumped to command sometimes landed some distance from the reception committee and were obliged to find their own way back to the dropping zone. Others dropped into a stream or a bog or were left suspended in a tree and had to be rescued. It was almost impossible to gauge the exact moment at which to jump in order to land at the feet of the waiting reception committee. Mind you, most of them did. The moment they jumped was probably the worst moment of all for the agents because in order to avoid being sucked back into the plane's slipstream they had to do a freefall, counting to twenty or twenty-five before opening their parachutes.

The agents soon started circulating silly stories about the drops, some of them rather macabre. In one an agent who had supposedly counted up to the required twenty-five pulled the cord to release his parachute, but the parachute failed to open. 'Blast,' he said. 'The problems are already starting. I bet when I land the bicycle they promised would be hidden in the bushes won't be there either!' The agents also joked that the inside of every parachute carried a number and a note from the person who had packed it, stating: 'Should this parachute fail to open, contact the authorities giving this number, and you will be refunded!'

The people in charge of the factories packing parachutes today would be horrified by what went on in the war. The parachutes were all hand-packed, usually by exhausted women who had had no sleep because of the air raids and who were also worn out not only by the heavy burden of having to shoulder the responsibilities of their family alone, but by the war itself. And sadly, but perhaps not surprisingly, mistakes did occur: some parachutes failed to open – and some agents became just another casualty of war.

As soon as the agents had left the plane, the despatcher

would quickly heave out the containers, each one attached to a parachute, the number depending on what stores the organizer had requested. His mission accomplished, the pilot would dip his wings in salute to the reception committee waiting on the ground to receive the drop and head for home, on a wing and a prayer.

In the event that the returning plane was bringing dignitaries or agents back to England, Buck remained at the airfield. He was always on the tarmac, waiting to greet the new arrivals when they landed in the early hours of the morning. I don't know when he slept. He worked eighteen hours a day, often leaving the office around seven in the evening to go home to Chelsea for dinner with his wife, returning a couple of hours later and working until three or four in the morning. And he was always back at his desk again next morning at the usual time.

There has never been a full biography of Buck, although he wrote two memoirs, both published in the 1950s. But memoirs tend to be subjective, not objective. A biography can tell the real story, especially when the biographer has the personal papers and diaries at his disposal. And when Buck wrote his memoirs it is entirely possible that there was information he felt he could not reveal at the time. But he might have confided it to his diary and his son, Tim, who has all his father's papers and diaries, intends to see that his father's biography is written. Any information that might have been restricted in the 1950s would not present a problem now. Sadly, many stories, some scurrilous, incorporated in books about SOE or agents have referred to him, describing him as careless, vain, uncaring, indifferent to the fate of the agents he sent into the field. This has greatly distressed his family, especially his two children, Sybil and Tim, who were teenagers at the time and witness to their father's hard work and dedication to the job in hand. After the war, when visiting or dining with their father, they met many agents, and none of them ever expressed anything but friendliness and admiration for Buck.

There is one book especially, recently published, which saddened and caused eyebrows to be raised by the few people left who actually worked with Buck and Vera Atkins. None of us could believe that Vera would ever have said the things she is reported to have said about Buck unless she was losing her reason and her memory at the time, which was not the case. She remained lucid until the end. Like all of us, she had her faults, but disloyalty was not one of them. She and Buck had worked together as a close team during the war. They were very different in their approach, but each respected and admired the other. At one point I had thought that their close relationship went beyond the professional, but realized afterwards that I was mistaken. Buck was very much in love with Anna, the woman for whom he had divorced and had married in 1943. Between him and Vera there was merely a deep understanding and mutual respect for the other's capabilities. They were both very hard-working and conscientious. They were 'on the same wavelength' and made a wonderful team, remaining firm friends, visiting each other frequently, and doubtless reviving old wartime memories, until he died.

I can only add that, working with Buck – we were a very closely knit group in F Section, only thirty people, so we got to know one another very well – and after the war keeping in touch with him until his death, my memory of him is of a very compassionate, caring man. He was always deeply concerned about his agents and far from careless and uncaring about their fate. Admittedly, he made mistakes: he was a human being, not a robot, and we all make mistakes.

What critics fail to understand is that SOE was a fledgling organization; it was unconventional and improvisational, since there were no precedents, no previous experience or strategy to help and guide its leaders, no charts, reports or manuals to instruct those in charge. They were obliged to make the rules up as they struggled along and therefore needed not only flexibility but also imagination in order to adapt to situations and crises which arose. So it was inevitable that some decisions proved wrong, even disastrous, and mistakes – sometimes fatal mistakes – were made, especially in times of stress and extreme tiredness, and Buck experienced both. He has been accused of knowingly sending agents to their deaths. What those who make these accusations forget, or don't take into account, is that in the early 1940s we did not have all the means of instant communication that we possess today. There was very little radar, and transistors, computers and mobile phones did not exist. Had we possessed the modern inventions of the second millennium at the time, many mistakes made by all who had the responsibility of making life-and-death decisions would certainly have been avoided. Once the plane had left the ground and crossed the Channel, carrying across the dark skies agents to be parachuted behind the lines, should a signal arrive saying that the *réseau* they were destined for had been infiltrated, the members had been arrested or were in hiding and the reception committee waiting to receive them would be the Gestapo, there was no means of contacting the pilot to tell him to turn back. Buck and everyone else knew that the agents were being dropped to their deaths. But there was absolutely nothing he could do to prevent it.

As for being vain and, after the liberation of Paris, going to France and strutting around preening, which was a comment I read in another recently published book, this is, to my mind, a monstrous accusation, although in all fairness I can see how that mistake might have been made. Buck was a very approachable person with a ready smile, and he liked people. During the mission to France soon after D-Day, which included many other British officials, there were apparently flattering speeches

Chapter 5

Sadly, some missions ended in tragedy due to treachery. Henri Déricourt, who before the war had been an experienced French pilot, was the man responsible for choosing the landing sites and dropping zones, known as DZs, in France. But he turned out to be a 'double agent', working ostensibly for SOE, but also for the Gestapo and the Abwehr (German military intelligence).

I never met Déricourt, though I have heard a great deal about him from Bob Maloubier, who knew him before the war when Déricourt was a stunt pilot working in a circus. Bob is convinced he was not a double agent, as some believe, but a triple agent in the pay not only of SOE and the Gestapo and the Abwehr, but very possibly MI6 as well. He was an astute, one might say devious, man, who had great personal charm and managed to play his cards very successfully, juggling between his three masters. He was responsible for grouping together letters, both personal letters from agents to their families and official mail containing sensitive information which could not be trusted to the 'radio' since it risked interception by the enemy. This mail was sent with any plane which landed for delivery to London on arrival. But before Déricourt handed them to the pilot of the plane he gave them to his Abwehr contact, who opened and copied them before handing them back, which may explain why the Prosper/Physician *réseau* was 'blown'.

Déricourt used to be at the DZ to meet the agents when they landed and would take them to the isolated farmhouse, from which the members of the reception committee had left a few hours earlier. Here they would be given a substantial meal and a bed for the rest of the night. I remember one returning agent saying that they had had a very bumpy journey on the way over, being tossed about all over the place as the pilot attempted to evade the German flak and the fighter pilots sent up to shoot them down. He was feeling sick and groggy when he landed and the wonderfully rich meal awaiting him proved to be too much. On the pretext of getting a breath of fresh air, he walked out to the bottom of the garden and was violently sick!

Should they not be destined for a local resistance group, they would grab a few hours' sleep, and at dawn a member of the reception committee would accompany the agents to the local railway station. Before arriving, the agents would separate and take the first train to Paris or the nearest large city: each one travelling in a different compartment without any sign of recognition passing between them, either on the platform while waiting for the train or on the train itself. When they left the train, they would then head off separately in different directions.

Déricourt often not only accompanied the newly arrived agents to the station, but also travelled on the same train. He would have informed the Gestapo in advance of the drop and told them at which mainline station the agents would arrive the following morning. The French police would be waiting at the barrier to do a 'spot check', which was not unusual. Déricourt would give a prearranged signal, often an almost imperceptible nod or inclination of his head as he passed or walked behind the agent approaching the barrier. The agent would then be picked out by the police for a 'snap' inspection of his or her papers. And although the papers were in order – London saw to that before they left – it was always possible for the police to pretend that there was an anomaly and take the agent into custody for further investigation, from where he was inevitably handed over to the Gestapo. Some were never seen alive again.

The largest and most important *réseau* in France in 1943, the Prosper *réseau*, based in the Paris area, had tentacles stretching out all over the country from Belgium to the Poitou. It was decimated by the treachery of Henri Déricourt, with the near-fatal result that, after Prosper's collapse, F Section's resistance in France threatened to come to an end. One thousand five hundred people were arrested, and hundreds of agents and locally recruited résistants belonging to the group were seized, tortured, deported to concentration camps and sent to their deaths.

Among them was Prosper's organizer, Francis Suttill, who was brutally tortured before being sent to Sachsenhausen concentration camp and hanged. His courier, Andrée Borrel, was one of the four women F Section agents who were burnt alive at Natzweiler. And the radio operator, Noor Inayat-Khan, having survived many months of solitary confinement in various prisons, terrible torture and, for the last four months of her life, being shackled wrists to ankles, was finally shot in the back of the head, too weak from starvation and torture to be able to crawl across the floor. It was said that when she died she no longer resembled a human being; she was just a mass of raw meat, the skin hanging off her back from her many beatings. But, like Suttill and Andrée Borrel, she never once talked or gave the enemy any information.

One of the first members of the Prosper *réseau* to be arrested was Suttill's lieutenant, Gilbert Norman, codename

'Archambaud'. Norman was later accused of being a traitor and betraying his comrades. He did, but unwittingly. He was tortured and brainwashed to such an extent that the Gestapo convinced him that it was pointless to withhold information, since the other members of his *réseau* had all been arrested and interrogated and had revealed the names of his colleagues, as well as the place where their considerable supply of arms was hidden, none of which was true. In actual fact Francis Suttill and Norman's other resistance colleagues were arrested after a confession was dragged out of Norman. To add to his agony, when they were all brought in for interrogation, the Gestapo seated him at a desk in the entrance to the building in the avenue Foch, giving the members of his *réseau* the impression that he had defected to the German camp. When they arrived he became the recipient of their incredulous and often contemptuous stares and realized that he had been tricked into betraying them. His colleagues believed he was responsible for their arrest, which in a way I suppose he was. But had he intentionally betrayed them? To all outward appearances it looked very much like it, and the word 'traitor' clung to him. However, many people who were later questioned did not think so. His father apparently spent the rest of his life trying to clear his son's name. But even if he had collaborated with the Gestapo, it did not save him. He later suffered the same fate as his organizer, Francis Suttill, and was hanged at Sachsenhausen concentration camp.

Buck had had his doubts about Déricourt's loyalty for some time. But he was never able to actually pin any accusation on him. The disaster of the collapse of the Prosper circuit confirmed Buck's suspicions, and he decided to recall Déricourt to London for a debriefing. When the plane landed, Gerry Morel, who had been sent by Buck to bring Déricourt back, was standing in the doorway. Although a major in the British Army, as a precaution in case of capture Morel was wearing a squadron leader's uniform, which would enable him to claim prisoner of war status as a member of the aircrew. He ordered Déricourt to climb in, but Déricourt, taken by surprise, refused to leave without his wife. There was a terrible scene, and a heated argument broke out between the two men, during which in the wind Morel's cap blew off and had to be chased across the airstrip by one of the reception team. The whole landing and take-off operation was supposed to be effected in less than three minutes. After fifteen minutes the pilot shot his head out of the cockpit and began banging on the fuselage, yelling: 'What the hell's going on?' He threatened to leave without Morel.

When they landed back in England Buck was on the airstrip, waiting to receive Déricourt. He was not amused when Morel confessed to returning without him. However, Déricourt had promised to leave on the next flight provided his wife could accompany him and, for once, he kept his word. The following week, when the plane bringing radio operator Noor Inayat-Khan and courier Cecily Lefort to work for the Prosper and Jockey *réseaux* respectively landed, Déricourt's rather vulgar wife was waiting with him on the airstrip, covered in jewels and wearing a floor-length fur coat. On arrival in England they were given a suite at the Savoy, where they were seen dancing, he wearing a squadron leader's uniform, to which he was not entitled, his rank being flying officer, and sporting DFC and DSO ribbons on his chest, to which he was not entitled either.

In spite of Déricourt's protestations, Buck refused to allow him to return to France. He was given a splendid flat in a fashionable part of London – I believe it was Kensington – where he and his wife entertained lavishly. I can understand Déricourt's anger and frustration at being kept in London. Being a double agent was extremely dangerous, but it was also a very lucrative business. Déricourt, although from humble origins – his mother was a seamstress and his father a postman – had amassed a fortune through his treachery, ending the war a very rich man. He not only owned a royal hunting lodge in the countryside outside the capital but also a luxury flat in the sixteenth *arrondissement*, the most expensive district in Paris, with a live-in Spanish maid for the rare occasions when he wished to use it. After the war he became a pilot for the company which later became Air France. One evening, he was passing through British customs on the way to his plane and said he had nothing to declare. The customs officer asked him all the same to open his overnight case. Underneath his pyjamas was a layer of gold bars. He was arrested, but at his trial he managed to charm the judge and convince him that he was a 'war hero'. The judge did not give him a prison sentence but let him off with a £500 fine – peanuts to Déricourt – though his gold bars were confiscated.

Buck was not the only one to be suspicious of Déricourt. Vera Atkins, Buck's close assistant, had never trusted him. She was convinced, right from the start, that he was playing a double game, and it may well have been at her insistence that Buck had him recalled.

But the French authorities might also have been keeping their eyes upon Déricourt. In 1946, when he returned to France, he was arrested and imprisoned, and in 1948 he was tried for treason. At his trial Déricourt managed, as usual, to be very convincing. He had fooled many people, who spoke in his favour, though Buck refused to testify for him or even to attend the trial. But Nick Bodington, Buck's one-time assistant and former 'right-hand man', went to Paris, claiming to have been sent by SOE to testify in Déricourt's favour. Although untrue, this so-called 'authentic' testimony from a former very influential member of F Section helped swing the balance. Déricourt was acquitted and saved from the firing squad.

Vera Atkins and Nick Bodington had always disliked each other intensely, which can't have made life easy for Buck. Vera did not hide her feelings about Bodington, whom she always suspected was in league with Déricourt, playing a double game. Since Buck had absolute confidence in Vera and trusted her completely, especially her judgement, which he relied upon, it may well have been Vera who persuaded Buck to have Bodington rusticated for six months during the war. She was in Paris at the time of Déricourt's trial and bumped into Bodington in the street. 'Nick, if you attend Déricourt's trial,' she apparently threatened him, 'I'll never speak to you again.' Bodington calmed her down, assuring her that there was no question of his doing so, and she took him at his word. He then went to the Palais de Justice and testified in Déricourt's favour. Vera kept her word, and never spoke to him again.

Déricourt's insatiable greed finally got the better of him. He went to Laos and, together with a pilot friend and two small planes, formed a company, Air Laos – known colloquially as 'Air Confiture' (Air Jam), since it was common knowledge that they were trafficking opium. With these two planes they evacuated rich refugees from Laos to Saigon – at a price! Déricourt's plane could carry six passengers, but he regularly crammed in eight. One afternoon in November 1962 he returned to base and decided that he could do one more flight while it was still light. There were ten passengers waiting. He took eight, refusing the last two. They pleaded with him, upping the exorbitant fare he charged by so much that he finally accepted. The seriously overloaded plane was unable to rise above the trees. It crashed soon after take-off, with no survivors. Déricourt's body was never found – there were only limbs and torn flesh scattered over the jungle floor. However, a funeral was held with great pomp and ceremony for the well-known 'war hero', with many attachés from neighbouring embassies and other dignitaries present. Déricourt deceived everyone right to the end!

After the war there was also suspicion in the hierarchy

surrounding Bodington's loyalties. There were questions about whether or not he was a double agent working closely with Déricourt, so perhaps Vera's mistrust was not unfounded. It has also been said that he was a 'mole' planted into F Section by MI6, who disliked SOE intensely. His pre-war connections with the Germans, when he was a Reuters correspondent in Paris, seemed to give weight to the theory that he was a double agent in touch with, and passing secret information to, former friends he had known at the German embassy. These friends were now high-ranking officers in the Gestapo and the Abwehr. But no definite evidence has yet come to light.

Nick Bodington was not liked by his colleagues. They complained that he was mean, never having his wallet on him when it was his turn pay for a round of drinks in the pub. In appearance, he was not an attractive man, though he married three times. He seemed to be a loner, intelligent, but without a great deal of charm. Henri Déricourt, on the other hand, was a handsome man who had great charm and was very intelligent. What a pity he did not put his talents to better use.

Chapter 6

There were also bona fide agents who played the double game in order to obtain important and useful information, which they then passed on to London. But, in doing so, they were taking an enormous risk.

I heard of one F Section agent, though I never met him, who almost lost his life pretending to be a double agent. He was the organizer of a resistance group who, in order to glean information which he then passed on to London, was 'friendly' with the German soldiers stationed in the area. He naturally kept his double game a secret even from the members of his *réseau*. It would have been too dangerous if the Germans had discovered his deceit. But the members of his *réseau* became suspicious and began to doubt his loyalties when they saw him being 'hail fellow well met' with the enemy. And especially when they saw him spending evenings in bars with these soldiers, laughing and joking and encouraging them to have another drink. When their tongues were loosened by too many glasses of red wine, the agent often obtained vital information which he then transmitted to

London. Oblivious to their organizer's ingenuity, the members of his own *réseau* wanted to execute him for treason, convinced he was a traitor. But he persuaded them to wait twenty-four hours and send a *message personnel* to London, requesting urgently that it be broadcast the following evening. 'If you hear this message on the BBC's French Service programme tomorrow evening, you'll know I am genuine,' he told them. 'But if you don't, then go ahead and do what you have to do.' They agreed to keep him under close arrest for twenty-four hours. The following evening the message came over loud and clear, convincing the members of his group of his innocence. He was untied, handshakes were exchanged all round, and that evening the red wine flowed freely.

Another F Section agent who risked his life playing the double game stands out in my mind, probably because he was the 'coolest' man I ever met. Stocky, strong, nearer forty than thirty, Benny Cowburn was a dour, tough, down-to-earth Yorkshire-man with an accent you could cut with a knife, even though he had been brought up and had spent most of his life in France.

A member of F Section, he was parachuted into France four times and would probably have gone for a fifth try had the German surrender not put an end to his activities. On one of his missions Benny was dropped as organizer of the Tinker circuit in the Aube. Here, like his F Section colleague, he also played a very dangerous game, pretending to be friendly with the local Germans, greeting them on the streets and spending evenings drinking with them in cafes. But he also was taking an enormous risk. On the surface it looked as if he was working for the enemy, and the members of his *réseau* could easily have believed that he was a German plant, in other words a traitor, and summarily executed him. They never did. So I imagine he must have inspired absolute confidence.

Ben trusted nobody, not even the members of his *réseau*. He did everything himself because, as he put it, his résistants 'blabbed in cafés'. One accepted such a remark from Ben simply because he loved France, had chosen to live in France and in some ways was more French than English. Whether his accusation was true or not, I don't know. But he wasn't taking any risks. So he made his own ammunition from the raw material parachuted in, working alone in a little hut in the mountains. At about three o'clock one morning, when he was busy at his work bench, there was a knock on the door of the hut, and a voice shouted: 'Open up! German patrol.' Quickly shovelling what he could out of sight, he went to open the door. To his immense relief it was his 'friends', a local group of German soldiers. 'Whatever are you doing here in the middle of the night?' they asked, open-mouthed.

'I'm making bombs,' Ben replied. 'I'm going to blow up yon railway line to stop you chaps advancing.' The soldiers looked at him aghast, then burst out laughing, saying the French equivalent of 'You are a one!' One of them actually winked and nudged him joking: 'Real British humour, eh!' never realizing that he had in fact spoken the truth in jest, since they all believed he was a local-born Frenchman.

'Got any beer?' asked their leader.

'Sure chaps,' Ben replied. 'Come on in and help yourselves.' He backed away and sat at his bench with his arms spread out in an attempt to hide his material. They helped themselves to beer, but he declined. 'No, you go ahead. I never drink when I'm working. Need to keep a clear head otherwise I might blow myself up. Dynamite's tricky stuff to handle.' They apparently roared with laughter again and thought he was even more amusing.

After chatting for a while they rose, saying: 'Better go, we're on patrol. We'll leave you to carry on making your bombs.' And, laughing heartily, delighted with their own sense of humour, they gave him a friendly slap on the back and left. Like the woman courier at the level crossing, he'd taken the risk and got away with it.

I met Benny again after the war, quite by chance, when we were invited to dinner by a delightful elderly couple, Marthe and Henri Brun, friends of my husband. To my surprise Benny was there. It really is a small world. We learned that Henri Brun had sheltered many escaping Allied airmen during the war and that he had saved Benny's life by hiding him behind the shutters on the balcony of their third-floor flat in the rue de la Pompe and helping him to escape across the roof when the Gestapo came looking for him. And I realized that evening that there must be dozens of other people, unsung heroes and heroines in France, who had done the same thing: served their country and the Allied cause in the same way and, when the war was over, disappeared unrecognized into the shadows.

Benny came alone that evening, but shortly afterwards Jacques and I had dinner with him and his delightful French wife. I was surprised when I met her. They seemed at first sight to be a very ill-matched couple. I had expected to meet a sturdy, jolly-hockey-sticks, no-nonsense woman, but she was exactly the opposite. She was in fact what everyone imagines a typical *parisienne* to be: tiny, elegant, vivacious. When they stood side by side his burly frame seemed to completely blot out her delicate body. After dinner, which was excellent – she was a very good cook – she chatted animatedly with Gallic flutterings of her hands while he sat smiling, contentedly puffing at his pipe, his eyes resting affectionately on her, happy to let her take centre stage. Occasionally their eyes met, and a smile would flit between them. It was obvious that they adored each other and, contrary to appearances, were a very happy couple. Once again I was taken by surprise, as I had often been during the debriefings at Orchard Court all those years before, when I thought I had understood once and for all that one cannot judge from appearances.

Pearl Witherington stands out in my memory because her story is a very romantic one. Were it to be made into a film, or written as a novel, people would say it was too far-fetched to be true. And yet it was true. Although British, Pearl had been brought up in France and in 1939 was engaged to a Frenchman, Henri Cornioley. At the outbreak of war Henri was drafted into the French Army and taken prisoner at Dunkirk. When France fell, now being enemy aliens, Pearl and her family fled across Spain and into Portugal, finally arriving in England, where, angry at France's defeat and having no news of her fiancé, she joined the WAAF. But she was anxious to return to France to 'get her revenge' on the Germans who had taken her fiancé prisoner and were now occupying what she considered to be 'her country', since she had never before actually lived in England. It was only a place she visited during the holidays.

Pearl was an ideal recruit for F Section and was soon spotted and sent for training. But although she spoke French like a native, she looked unmistakably English, which presented a problem. However, she solved it by piling her plaits on top of her head in the hope that she would be mistaken for a German. Thus disguised, she was parachuted into the Indre-et-Loire to join Maurice Southgate's Stationer *réseau*, not knowing that Henri, her fiancé, had escaped from his prisoner-of-war camp and joined the Resistance. After her arrival back in France, she found him again. He was a member of the *réseau* which had received her! They both returned to England after the liberation of Paris in August 1944 and were married quietly in London the following October. As the French would say, 'incroyable . . . mais vrai!' ('unbelievable . . . but true!'). Pearl and I became good friends and remained so right up until her death only a few years ago. On her return from the field I asked her whether she had been afraid when, waiting to jump, she had sat on the edge of the open trapdoor in the floor of the plane, her legs dangling in mid-air, while the plane circled over its target.

'Afraid?' she expostulated. 'The only sensation I felt was a terrible urge to pee. As soon as I landed I did my "rouly-bouly", tore off my parachute and leapt over a hedge. A few seconds later, I saw pinpoints of light from a torch seeping through the hedge and heard a man's voice whisper hoarsely: "Where the devil has she gone? I saw her come down. There's her parachute. But where is she?" I couldn't immediately reply,' Pearl giggled. 'Because if he'd looked over the hedge, all he'd have seen was my bare bum!'

Pearl was parachuted into France to act as a courier, and her cover story was that she was a travelling saleswoman for cosmetics, the job her fiancé had done before the war. I found this cover very odd, because Pearl was what one might call a 'no-nonsense' woman. I don't think I ever saw her wearing even a trace of make-up. But she was also an amazing woman. When Maurice Southgate, her organizer, was arrested and sent to Buchenwald concentration camp, she and Amédée Mainguard, a Mauritian F Section agent, promptly divided their large Stationer *réseau* area into two. Pearl took over the northern side of the Indre, which became known as Wrestler – a very appropriate name – and Dédé, as he was called, turned the south side into the Shipwright circuit. The Germans had put a million francs price on Pearl's head, but no one denounced her.

After D-Day, together with Henri, her fiancé, Pearl headed an army of 3,000 résistants and held up the German advance, taking 1,800 prisoners. When the war ended she was awarded the MBE, but in a civilian capacity. She sent it back, saying she had never done anything civil in her life. She later accepted it . . . when the category was changed to 'military'.

In 2008 I went to Pearl's funeral, together with the three remaining F Section male agents in France, one of whom had trained and been dropped with Pearl. It was held in the small French town where, during the war, she had operated and to which she and her husband had retired. There were about 300 people present on that cold February day, standing in the wind

96

and the intermittent rain. It was held at the entrance to the chateau, since demolished, which had been Pearl's headquarters and where a monument had been raised to the memory of those who fought there. Her husband's ashes had been buried under the monument a few years before, and that afternoon Pearl's urn was placed beside his. It was an amazing ceremony. Forty-eight standard-bearers and two surviving members of her Resistance group were present, as well as many local dignitaries, a high-ranking French officer and the military attaché from the British embassy. Pearl was ninety-three when she died, and her two remaining comrades-in-arms can't have been much younger, but they insisted on standing to attention throughout the whole ceremony. 'Pauline [her codename] is a legend around here,' one said afterwards, wiping his eyes.

Only a few years before she died, when she was well into her eighties, Pearl was finally awarded her wings. Yvonne Baseden, who is in her early nineties, was given her wings about ten years ago. To mark the occasion, a splendid champagne lunch was organized in her honour at the Maison des Orphelins, where she and other members of her *réseau* had been arrested, to which former locally recruited members of the *réseau* were invited. Yvonne had not seen most of them for almost sixty years. But they came – a group of old men in their best suits, which many of them hadn't worn since their weddings forty or more years earlier – and clustered around to congratulate her. With the celebratory champagne before lunch they presented her with her parachute, and with the armagnac after lunch, her pistol. She had refused to carry it at the time – it had been buried – since, if she had been caught, it would have been too much of a giveaway. Yvonne remained very calm and composed, although it must have been a very moving moment for her, and naturally her organizer, Gonzague de Saint-Geniès, who did not survive, was remembered with affection in their conversations. Her thoughts must have gone out to 'Lucien', with whom she had worked so closely, whose memory seems still to be very vivid, and his death so painful for her to recall. She was obviously very fond of him and even after sixty years could hardly bear to talk about him. Was there some romantic attachment there? I don't know. Yvonne is a very private person: it would not be kind to pry.

The reason given as to why, unlike the men, these women agents had not received their wings years before was that a parachutist had to have made six jumps before being awarded wings: and, before they jumped into enemy-occupied territory, women agents in training did only five. The men did six! Also that they had to have made night jumps, which apparently the women never did – except the night they jumped into enemy territory. But that doesn't seem to have counted! How many former women agents died without ever having received this recognition?

Another of my friends, Lise de Baissac, received her wings just before her ninety-ninth birthday. She died shortly afterwards. But many women agents died without ever having received this recognition of their bravery. Lise came from Mauritius, a compatriot of Dédé. She was dropped 'blind' near Poitiers under cover of being a widow living quietly. On landing she had to find accommodation for herself and then link up with Mary Lindell's Marie-Claire escape route, based in Ruffec. There were many of these escape lines all over France, known at HQ as Section D/F, which were often run by F Section women agents. The main one, the Pat line, stretched from the Belgian border to the Pyrenees, and was operated by a Belgian national, Henri Guise, codename Pat O'Leary: hence the 'Pat' line. These lines transferred airmen who had been shot down and had managed to avoid being arrested by the Germans and escaping prisoners of war from safe house to safe house, until they were able to cross the Spanish frontier.

From Ruffec, Mary Lindell organized the Marie-Claire line, linking up with Lise de Baissac's safe house near Poitiers at the edge of the occupied zone. When a transfer was to be made, Mary would send a message to Lise, announcing the arrival of one, two or three 'parcels' around a certain date, according to the number of escapees she was to expect.

Mary was an incredible character: an aristocratic English woman with an almost grown-up family, married to a French count. She was very much the 'countess', especially when dealing with obstreperous Germans, whom she treated with haughty disdain. She lived up to her theory that if you share confidences in a bar or bistro in a very loud voice, nobody takes a blind bit of notice; but lean confidentially towards another person and whisper and there is a sudden silence, with every ear tuned in to hear what is being said. Putting this theory into practice, Mary totally disregarded the fact that she was an 'enemy alien' likely to be arrested and interned if discovered, and even worse if her activities as an SOE agent were revealed, and treated the occupying forces with contempt. When travelling on public transport she frequently spoke English, calling from one end of a crowded bus to her passengers – often 'downed' airmen cowering at the other end hoping to escape notice – that this was their 'stop'. She appeared to be indifferent to the possibility that she could be arrested and taken into custody.

Mary took enormous risks and finally paid the price for her complete disregard for security. Although the Gestapo were not actively searching for her at the time, her luck ran out when with her son Maurice, who helped her in her mission, she was about to cross the frontier into Spain. At Pau station the border police must have been suspicious, because she was arrested, through a simple, careless oversight. She had neglected to renew her visa, which was a few days out of date. There is no record of Maurice's arrest, so perhaps she managed in her high-handed manner to convince the police that he was in no way connected with her.

On her way to Paris for interrogation Mary attempted to

escape, jumping from a moving train as it approached a bend. But as she fell to the ground her guard shot her three times in the head and picked her up for dead. How she didn't die from her wounds is a mystery, but she survived and was imprisoned in Dijon. It was there that she met a fellow SOE agent, the radio operator Yvonne Baseden, who, from a nearby cell in the prison, was astonished to hear Mary singing loudly in English. The two women finally shared a cell before they were both transferred to Ravensbrück, where Mary, her spirit still undaunted after her imprisonment and the torture she had endured, continuing in her usual high-handed manner, declared that she was a Red Cross nurse and took over the running of the infirmary, bullying the Germans into giving her the medicines and supplies she needed. Her captors named her 'the Arrogant English Lady'. It's incredible that she managed to get away with such behaviour. I imagine that with Mary it was a question of 'nothing ventured, nothing gained'. She was certainly an example of, I believe it was Yeo-Thomas's theory, 'age is a most unreliable means of assessing capabilities', since she must have been over forty at the time.

Mary was a formidable woman! I did not meet her until after the war, here in Paris, where she returned to live once peace was declared. By that time she had mellowed into a gentle, dignified 'old lady', but was still very much the 'countess'. Looking at her sitting peacefully in an armchair, drinking tea, it was almost impossible to believe or even imagine the amazing feats she had performed during those traumatic years.

In September 1944 Mary's young compatriot and former cellmate Yvonne Baseden was sent to Ravensbrück concentration camp, where she remained until 1945. She became very ill, suffering from torture, malnutrition and advanced tuberculosis. The camp doctor said that there was no hope of her recovering: she was dying. However, in her position in the infirmary Mary saved Yvonne's life by engineering a place for her on one of the last convoys of Swedish Red Cross buses to leave the camp. These humanitarian convoys to a neutral country had been negotiated by Count Bernadotte, the head of the Swedish Red Cross. When she arrived in Stockholm Yvonne spent some time in a sanatorium before being repatriated to England, where she was nursed at the military hospital in Midhurst for another year until she finally regained her health. She later married and had a son.

Upon her return to England, I asked Lise de Baissac, Mary Lindell's co-worker, what it was like to parachute alone to no reception committee, and whether she had been afraid. She had, after all, been obliged to make her own way and find accommodation in a strange town in an occupied country with the Gestapo or the Milice on every street corner; enough to make anyone afraid. Lise was a very quiet, reserved, undemonstrative person. 'Afraid?' she queried. 'No. If anything, it was boring. Living quietly, being unable to make friends with anybody, was awfully lonely.'

Lise later went back to France, parachuted this time on a more 'active' mission: to organize a *réseau* of her own in Normandy. But on arrival she decided, with Buck's permission, that she would rather work as a courier for her brother Claude, then organizer of the Scientist *réseau* in Brittany. Buck must have had tremendous confidence in Lise's competence and cool-headedness when he gave her permission, once in the field, to transfer to her brother's *réseau*. As far as I know, it was the only time that such a partnership was allowed. The risk was too great since, under interrogation, an agent might 'crack' if confronted with a close member of his family being tortured. It was one of the Gestapo's charming ploys with hostages or others they suspected of working for the enemy. This partnership was also most unusual since not only relatives, but even people who had been friends, or had known each other before the war, were never allowed to work together. Pearl had been at school in Paris with her organizer, Maurice Southgate, but, knowing only his code-name before her departure, she discovered only on landing in France that her organizer was her former school friend.

Not long before she left for the field, one of F Section's most efficient and prolific radio operators, Yvonne Cormeau, was shown a photograph of 'Hilaire', the organizer of the Wheelwright *réseau* in south-west France, which she was to join, and realized that she knew him. George Starr ('Hilaire') and her late husband had been members of the same cricket team when both families were living in Brussels before the war. But Yvonne never mentioned their earlier friendship to anyone, in case it would prevent her from leaving.

I have since wondered about the effect that their mother suddenly disappearing for what could be a year, without any news or any knowledge of her whereabouts being passed on, must have had on the young children these women agents often left behind. Odette Sansom left three little girls, the youngest only three years old, in a convent when she was parachuted as a courier to Peter Churchill's *réseau*. Their father was in the British Army, nothing to do with SOE. He and Odette were not divorced but they were certainly estranged. However, they did get divorced after the war, and Odette married her wartime lover and organizer, Peter Churchill. But that marriage also ended in divorce, and she later married Geoffrey Hallowes, another former agent, who was several years younger than her.

I recently met her middle daughter, Marianne, and asked her how she felt about being left in a convent.

'That convent was dreadful,' she answered, casting her eyes dramatically towards the ceiling as her mother would have done. 'But what were your feelings towards your mother?' I probed. 'Did you feel bitter and resentful at being abandoned?' She paused and bit her lip, frowning.

'I was only six at the time and the little girl in me cried: "Mummy, Mummy, how could you do it? How could you leave us?"' Then she smiled. 'But the adult in me says: "I'm so proud of my mother and what she did." And,' she added, 'she gave us two wonderful stepfathers.'

Violette Szabo left Tania, aged two, with her parents. Violette's husband, a sergeant in the French Foreign Legion, had been killed in North Africa, so when her mother was executed at Ravensbrück, Tania was left an orphan. Yvonne Cormeau also left her six-year-old daughter in a convent. Her husband had been killed in Chelsea during the Blitz, so had she not returned I don't know what would have happened to the little girl. Yvonne's family would most probably have been in France and strangers to the child. Did she have English grandparents or family to turn to? Did any of them? What happened to these children during the school holidays, at half-term or on visiting days? Were they left isolated? I don't know the answer to that either.

Yvonne Rudellat, who also perished in a concentration camp, was the oldest F Section woman agent. She was forty-five and a grandmother when she was infiltrated into France by felucca, with two male agents, Henri Frager and Harry Despaigne, landing between Cannes and Juan-les-Pins, very close to the villa where the Duke of Windsor used to stay. Yvonne was divorced from her English husband, and her daughter was a twenty-one-year-old mother at the time and in the ATS (Auxiliary Territorial Service). But even at twenty-one, it is good to have family to turn to, a mother to give a listening ear or to welcome one home on leave. A grandmother to coo over and babysit her child. In their circumstances I don't think I could have volunteered to train as a secret agent and be infiltrated behind the lines into enemy-occupied territory. I wonder what motivated them? I know that in Violette's case anger at her husband's death and desire for revenge on the people whom she considered responsible were the driving force. But in the end I wonder whether she thought it had been worth it. As for the others, I have no idea.

There were several couples who met while in training and married. But they were never allowed to work together or to be sent to a *réseau* anywhere near where the other was operating, resulting in some very heartrending goodbyes. Guy and Sonia d'Artois parted almost immediately after their honeymoon. Sonia was dropped into France first and Guy parachuted soon afterwards, but to a different *réseau* in another part of the country. Their story had a happy ending. They were reunited at the end of the war, and Guy took his wife back home with him, to Canada.

Yolande Beekman was in the same position. Sadly, her honeymoon was the only glimpse she had of married life. After saying goodbye to Jan when it ended, she was dropped into France as a radio operator to work for 'Guy', Gustave Bieler, organizer of the Musician *réseau* near St-Quentin. 'Guy' was a Canadian who had left a wife and two young children behind when he sailed for England to enlist in the British Army. He wasn't obliged to enlist. The war was being waged in a country he hardly knew, many miles away across an enormous ocean. What motivated him? Four months later both he and Yolande were arrested and brutally tortured: but neither spoke. In September 1944 'Guy' was shot at Flossenbürg, and Yolande (codename 'Yvonne') shot at Dachau. Other agents never had a chance, or the time, to get married before leaving.

Eliane Plewman was one of these. She was already married to a British Army officer not connected to SOE but, while in training, she met and fell desperately in love with a Corsican student, Eric Cauchi. They became lovers and were inseparable. During the weeks while they were waiting to leave, their love became even more intense and passionate as they realized that time was running out and they would soon be parted. For how long? Neither of them knew. After two abortive attempts to leap into the dark sky over occupied France, she to join the Monk *réseau* in Marseilles, and he the Stockbroker *réseau* in the Jura, having faced heart-rending goodbyes on the airstrip, they found themselves sitting opposite each other at the breakfast table the following morning: the flight had been cancelled at the last moment. But in August 1943, at the third attempt, they finally left. Once again, Eliane and Eric, the man who would have become her husband had she not been executed at Dachau the following March, just one month after he had been shot and killed in a brawl in a bar in the Doubs, clung to each other, unable to say goodbye, while two planes hummed on the airstrip waiting to take each one to France – but to different destinations.

Chapter 7

There were nine women agents belonging to RF Section operating in France during the war. Out of the thirty F Section women agents infiltrated into France, fifteen never returned, twelve having been brutally executed in various concentration camps, many in Ravensbrück. Four women agents were cremated alive at Natzweiler, also known as Struthof, camp, in Alsace. They were given an injection of phenol, which they were told was an anti-tetanus jab. Being suspicious, they resisted, but to no avail. The injection paralysed them. They were then heaved, helpless into the furnace. The last one to be incinerated was coming round from the injection when her executioner tilted the stretcher before tipping her into the flames. She sat up and, in an attempt to save herself from such a terrible fate, viciously scratched his face. Sadly, her attempt was unsuccessful. She was burnt alive like her three companions before her. Their four scorched and blackened corpses were removed from the incinerator the fol-lowing morning.

There is some confusion as to which one of them it actually

was who fought so savagely to save her life. Some reports say Vera Leigh, others Andrée Borrel. But does it really matter? Knowing it doesn't lessen the horror of this horrendous massacre. And perhaps for the families left behind – three of them had mothers alive at the time – it was better not to know. The knowledge of their daughter's fate must already have been a terrible enough memory to carry with them for the rest of their lives, a wound which I am sure would never heal. One can only hope that they imagined that besides being paralysed by the injection, their daughters were also unconscious, and that the flames consumed them before they revived and realized what was happening.

I knew Vera Leigh's mother and her younger sister, Frances, very well. They were personal friends, living very near me. Her mother never forgot her daughter's excruciating death. How could she? And she never forgave. She had a plaque put on the wall of Holy Trinity Anglican church in Maisons-Laffitte, which the family had always attended. It read: 'In memory of Ensign Vera Leigh, brutally murdered by the Germans.'

Vera's mother was a formidable old lady. She died at over ninety and, as the years passed and wartime memories faded, she was asked more than once to remove the plaque, which had become offensive to some people in that multi-national congregation. Regular attenders included a German lady married to a Japanese, and in the summer there were often German tourists visiting the church. But she always refused, stating categorically, leaving no room for argument or discussion: 'My daughter was brutally murdered by the Germans. Full stop.' But after her death Vera's sister, Frances, had it modified. It now reads: 'To the memory of Ensign Vera Leigh killed by the Nazis in 1944.' The message is the same, but the executioners are now limited to a specific group, and not to the German people as a whole.

The soldier responsible for heaving these four woman into the incinerator was brought to trial after the war, where he told the story of their final moments, his face still bearing the scars of the last agent's fingernails; scars which he carried with him for the rest of his life. He pleaded that he was merely a soldier carrying out orders. But what orders! He was a private or corporal, I believe, so perhaps he was terrified of disobeying, and of the subsequent dire punishment disobedience of the Reich would incur. But apart from the scar on his face, what a 'scar' to have to carry on his conscience till the end of his days.

Every June there is a ceremony at Natzweiler, attended by dignitaries from many countries, and also the descendants of those who perished: now only ageing cousins, nephews and nieces, or great-nephews and -nieces of those prisoners who died in that infamous camp. How many of them in the same way? That also is something we shall never know.

Very recently I received a telephone call from an elderly lady, a relative of Diana Rowden, one of the four women incinerated at Natzweiler. She wanted to know whether I could tell her where Diana was buried. I thought at first it was Diana's mother; mercifully I remembered that she had died some years ago. But I was left with the painful task of telling this lady that there was no grave and in the end, at her insistence, revealing how she had died. I imagine the circumstances of her daughter's execution had been so painful that Diana's mother had not been able to share even with her relatives exactly what had happened.

The fate of these four women agents might never have been known had it not been for another F Section agent, Brian Stonehouse, who was himself a prisoner at the Natzweiler camp when the four arrived. They had been transferred from another camp, Ravensbrück I believe, where they had been condemned to death by hanging. But at the last minute, for reasons unknown, the decision was overturned, and they were hastily transferred to Natzweiler. Natzweiler was a men's camp, so the arrival one afternoon of four young women did not go unnoticed. The men were intrigued because, before the four girls arrived, they were ordered to stop working and return to their huts, where the windows and shutters were all tightly fastened and the curtains closed. But Brian, and I imagine others also, managed to peep through a crack in the shutters and saw the four women cross the campus and enter the crematorium block, never to be seen again. After the war Stonehouse, a well-known artist and portrait painter in civilian life, drew and painted from memory a picture of their arrival. It hangs today on the wall of the staircase at the Special Forces Club in London, an incredible likeness of each one of them.

It was only his artistic talents which had saved him, a radio operator, the most vulnerable and most hated by the Gestapo of all SOE agents, from execution. Brian was incarcerated in four different concentration camps. After his initial arrest and imprisonment, he happened to have a pencil and a pad in his pocket and sketched an extremely good likeness of his guard. The delighted guard spread the news of this new prisoner's talents, which information reached the ears of the commandant of the camp he had been sent to. He summoned Brian and ordered him to draw his likeness, which Stonehouse did. The commandant was equally delighted with the finished sketch and did not issue the order for his execution, or even obey such an order, had it been issued. When Stonehouse arrived at Natzweiler, his fourth and last concentration camp, as in the previous ones, his talent saved him. He returned unscathed after the war.

Without his artistic talent, we might never have known the fate of these four women, which, I imagine, is what the Germans intended to happen. They would have been just four more agents who had disappeared without trace. Would it have been a fate easier to bear for their grieving families? That is something else we shall never know.

Quite by chance, I recently heard the story of one such family.

I had arranged to meet a friend at the Special Forces Club for lunch. When I arrived my friend was waiting in the bar, together with an elderly lady. The moment this lady turned round and smiled, I recognized her. It was Helen Oliver. I had known her for years without actually knowing a great deal about her except that her twin sister, Liliane Rolfe, had been an agent who had not returned. We went into lunch and were chatting amicably, when suddenly she began to talk about her sister, something she had never done before, certainly not with either of us.

'Liliane and I were twins,' she mused. 'Mirror twins.'

I raised my eyebrows in surprise. I had never heard of mirror twins.

'There was no "telepathy" between us as there often is with twins, but we mirrored each other. I am right-handed and my sister was left-handed. We were the opposite sides of the same coin.' She paused and seemed to be looking into the distance at something far away that we could not see. 'During the war, I didn't know what Liliane was doing,' she went on. 'No one in the family did. But I guessed it was something clandestine, since we had no news from her, not personally, although we had an official notification every so often telling us that she was alive and well.'

She paused again, as if not sure she wanted to go on. 'It was strange,' she continued quietly. 'I remember it so clearly, even after all these years. One night, not long before the war in Europe ended, I was fast asleep when, just before dawn, I was suddenly awakened by an overwhelming foreboding. A dread . . . an awful fear that something terrible was about to happen. I didn't know what it was, but I was trembling, and very frightened. I couldn't shake it off.' She paused again. 'It was so vivid, that impression of disaster, that I was unable to go back to sleep. I told myself it was a nightmare, although I hadn't been dreaming. I knew, I felt, that something evil had crept all over me.'

She folded her napkin and pushed her plate away. 'They always give one too much here,' she smiled, as if wanting to change the subject, dismiss the terrifying thoughts from her mind. But she went on all the same. 'That sensation was so vivid,' she continued, as if impelled by some force outside herself to share her fears, 'that I wrote about it in my diary the next day.' She looked out of the window and down into the square below. 'I learned later that it was at that precise moment that Liliane had been executed and then thrown into – was it the gas chamber or the incinerator? I don't remember, it was so long ago.'

I don't know whether Helen ever learned the details of her sister's mission, or of her last months – and her death; but I hope not. Liliane, codenamed 'Nadine', was parachuted as a radio operator to organizer George Wilkinson's ('Etienne') Historian *réseau* near Orleans in April 1944. A few months later she was arrested, tortured, imprisoned and sent to various concentration camps, enduring hard labour, starvation and degradation. She ended up at Ravensbrück, where, in a murderous spate of killings, she was executed together with Violette Szabo and Denise Bloch.

We have heard that Liliane was so weak from torture, beatings, malnutrition and probably rape, since, in the prisons run by the Nazis, after being tortured the women prisoners were routinely gang-raped, she could hardly stand: she had to be helped to her execution by Violette Szabo, who died with her. They were most probably shot in the back of the head, but there was a rumour that they were hung. We shall never know the truth. Whatever it was, it was grim and doesn't bear thinking about.

Violette could hardly drag herself along since she was pregnant as a result of one of the rapes, and her legs were covered with ulcers, making it difficult for her to walk. Denise Bloch, the third F Section woman agent to die that dawn, was not in a better state. The three of them supported each other as they staggered to their deaths.

Mercifully at the time Liliane's family was unaware of her activities.

I don't know why Liliane's twin sister chose to share these memories with us that day. And I wonder if the agony they revived had not been too much for her. She rose to her feet, a small, fragile old woman, but still beautiful. I could imagine what the two of them must have been like when they were young, before Liliane was murdered. They had been brought up in Paris by an English father and an emigrée White Russian mother, and Helen, at ninety-seven, still had the beautiful high Slavic cheekbones and delicate bone structure. She looked like an ageing ballerina, with her slim figure, her grey hair swept back into a chignon. She smiled and excused herself, saying she had an appointment, and left the room, a slight, upright old lady who carried with her such tragic memories. And I couldn't help wondering how many others carried the weight of a loved one's sacrifice and would continue to carry it right to the grave. Such memories cannot be erased.

It was terrible that many agents' families were left in ignorance of their fate. It is true that in many cases no one knew what had happened to them. News had ceased to arrive, and the authorities could only surmise that they had perished in a concentration camp, since Hitler had ordered that all arrested or imprisoned SOE agents had to disappear, leaving no trace. Would it not have been kinder to inform the family or next of kin that HQ feared the agent might not return? Looking back, it seems almost unforgiveable that many families were given hope and went on hoping long after their husband or son or daughter had ceased to exist. And even long after the war had ended.

What was particularly distressing was that the official monthly cards sent out by Buck's assistant, Vera Atkins, announcing that she had received good news from their husband, son or daughter and that they were alive and well, were still being sent to their families months after the agents had perished. Did Vera do this deliberately, thinking to ease the blow once they finally learned that their son or daughter, husband or wife had not survived? Or did she honestly believe that these missing agents would return? Vera was no fool. I cannot think she would have been ignorant of the fact that, having disappeared, the agents were probably no longer alive.

Vera was the perfect example of an aristocratic English-woman. She spoke with an upper-class accent and arrived for work every morning at Baker Street in a taxi, always stylishly, but simply, and expensively dressed. And the same taxi collected her to take her back to her Chelsea flat at whatever time she finished in the evening.

But Vera concealed her true identity almost until her death in 2000.

There was in fact nothing English, or even British, about Vera. She was born in Bucharest, the daughter of a wealthy Romanian Jewish businessman, and had only arrived in England with her Jewish mother after her father's death in 1933. Throughout the war she still had family, including two brothers and their wives, living in Romania. In enemy territory! Vera had many friends in high places. She had apparently been recruited as a spy in the early 1930s by the German ambassador to Romania, Count Friedrich Werner von der Schulenburg, a family friend, who became one of her lovers – another surprising revelation, since she gave the impression of being cold and very strait-laced. No doubt all part of her cover-up. Vera was in secret contact with Count von der Schulenburg during the war – with or without Churchill's knowledge? She knew the prime minister well, and he apparently trusted her judgement. Although high up in German diplomatic circles, the count was secretly anti-Nazi. After the abortive attempt on Hitler's life in July 1944, along with hundreds of others suspected of being involved in the plot, he was executed in the same gruesome manner as the prisoners at Flossenbürg: hung with piano wire attached to a meat hook, suspended on a wall. The news of his execution apparently affected Vera deeply. But, true to character, outwardly she showed no emotion.

I don't know whether Buck knew of her origins. Certainly no one in F Section did. But I don't think Buck could have known either, since, had they come to light, she would never have been recruited or, if discovered, allowed to remain in SOE, and certainly not in such a key position of authority. For a top-secret organization it would have been not only unthinkable, but highly dangerous to employ someone whose origins lay in a country which was now collaborating with the enemy. However did she manage to slip through the tight security net? The intrigues within SOE were almost as tangled as those on the outside!

Vera terrified me. I suppose it was because I was young, twenty years her junior. She was so icy, so poised, so very . . . sophisticated! She smoked Balkan Sobranie cigarettes attached to a long cigarette holder, her bright blue eyes piercing who-ever she was interviewing through a haze of smoke. Some of the agents nicknamed her 'Madonna', others 'Marlene Dietrich'. She was certainly no madonna: there was nothing gentle, meek and mild about Vera; a rod of steel would have described her more accurately. I imagine that she could be a wonderful friend, but a formidable enemy. Perhaps the beautiful, aloof Marlene Dietrich was the better nickname. Or perhaps she was a strange mixture of the two.

Her elegance and her 'English' reserve combined meant that I was very much in awe of her and avoided her as much as possible. If I needed anything I always crawled round the corner to her assistant, who was much more approachable. In fact, I was seventy years of age before I dared address her as anything other than 'Miss Atkins'; and then it was only when she insisted that I stop this nonsense and call her Vera. Her real name was Rosenberg, but she had adopted Atkins, an anglicized version of her mother's maiden name, Aitken or Etkin, when they arrived in England. I don't think she was ashamed of her origins, but she knew that if they were revealed, she would immediately be removed from the job she loved and sent to the Isle of Man, where countless other 'enemy aliens' were kicking their heels in exile.

Vera was devoted to the agents, especially the women. It was thanks to her efforts that after the war the fate of many of those women agents who had disappeared was discovered. In 1946 she persuaded, or bullied, the British government into allowing her to go to Germany to trace the fate of the missing women agents. They reluctantly agreed, gave her a car and a driver and granted her a temporary commission in the WAAF. As a squadron leader, she had access to accommodation in the officers' quarters of the numerous British military bases in Germany, and doors which would have been closed to a civilian were opened to her.

Vera did a titanic job. She travelled tirelessly the length and breadth of Europe, but she especially scoured Germany, visiting prisons and concentration camps and interviewing former prison warders and camp guards, both male and female, in fact any person who could possibly have had contact with the missing women agents, winkling them out if they were no longer in active service, and no doubt bullying and threatening them if they were unwilling to talk. She apparently reduced Kieffer, the former number one at 84 avenue Foch, to tears, though his emotion aroused no sympathy in her. He was later hung by the French. She even managed, in her high-handed manner, to gain access to cells where convicted war criminals were awaiting execution.

She also entered the cell of one notorious German war criminal whose name I unfortunately cannot remember. He is reported to have said that on entering his cell she sat down, lit a cigarette, but didn't offer him one, then sat back on the hard wooden chair and looked him up and down. 'I am not leaving this cell,' she announced, 'until you tell me what happened to . . .' and read out the list of names of the women whose fate she was trying to trace. Since he was doomed, condemned to be hung a few days later, he saw no reason not to give her the information she demanded, which is how she came to piece together the fate of many of the women whose disappearance she was seeking to unravel. He said afterwards that her interrogation of him was far worse than the interrogations he had endured at his Nuremburg trial!

She also interviewed Rudolf Hoess, the infamous command-ant of Auschwitz concentration camp. When he was led into the room where she was waiting to interrogate him Vera said he was 'a miserable little heap of humanity, his knees literally knocking together with fear'. But when the Army officer who had accompanied her accused him of murdering one and a half million people in the camp his terrified, subservient attitude abruptly changed. He leapt to his feet, an angry, defiant light in his eyes, banged his fist on the table and shouted: 'I didn't murder one and a half million people. I murdered two million, three hundred and forty-five thousand!' This statement was put in writing, which Hoess signed. (Some accounts say two million people murdered by him, and he rectified it to four million. But I think the first account is the more accurate.) Shortly afterwards he was taken back to Auschwitz and hanged on one of the line of gallows which he had had erected.

Vera was also greatly helped by the fact that the Germans

kept very strict records of prisoners, the concentration camps and prisons they were sent to, and their fate. And many of these records still existed at the time. But she had to find them. And she did find them. Did Vera perhaps remember how she had, knowingly or unknowingly, deceived the families by with-holding news of their relatives' disappearance and allowed them to believe and hope that they would see them again, when their dear ones had long since been reduced to a pile of ashes outside a crematorium? Was it her conscience which forced her to work so tirelessly on their behalf once the war was over?

How can one illustrate or even try to explain what actually happened in these terrible concentration camps – whether it be Dachau, Belsen, Mauthausen, Gross-Rosen, Buchen-wald, Auschwitz, Sachsenhausen or the even more appalling, if that is possible, extermination camps, like Mittelbau-Dora or Flossenbürg? Only, I imagine, by actually talking to those who lived and survived such unbelievable experiences. Only they can lift the veil and show us what life was really like in those camps. Sometimes their stories are so horrendous one can scarcely believe that human beings could behave in such a way, inflicting such cold-blooded torture on other human beings. The officers and guards at Flossenbürg lived in pleasant houses adjoining the camp, some even inside the camp. They committed atrocities during the day then went home in the evening to read bedtime stories to their children, have a cosy dinner with their wives and often end the evening weeping sentimentally as they listened to a Beethoven symphony. Yet only a few hours before they had mercilessly beaten starving prisoners who were try-ing to scavenge a few potato peelings from the kitchen dustbins, or programmed a flogging and execution ceremony for these same starving prisoners for dawn the following morning. This schizophrenic attitude, this dichotomy in their minds, is almost unbelievable.

117

I think the present generation of Germans, many of whom were born after the war, are carrying a heavy load of guilt for the crimes of their fathers and grandfathers, in some cases great-grandfathers, crimes for which they were in no way responsible.

I witnessed this in 2008 when a plaque was unveiled in memory of fifteen F Section agents executed at Flossenbürg, only one of Hitler's terrible extermination camps. Hitler's *Nacht und Nebel* ('Night and Fog') directive gave instructions that certain inmates and every SOE agent held in the camp, many having been transferred there from neighbouring Dachau with express orders to annihilate them, were to disappear without trace, which most of them did. Hitler wanted all evidence of his barbarity to be crushed, annihilated, the destiny of those agents never to be revealed. He added in his orders to Himmler that no SOE agent was to survive. But that none was to be allowed to die before he had been tortured till every 'secret' had been squeezed out of him.

I was asked to lay the wreath at the unveiling. There were very few direct family members of those who perished present to mourn. Jacqueline, the daughter of 'Guy', Major Gustave Bieler, the Canadian who was shot, together with two other F Section agents, at Flossenbürg in September 1944, had travelled from Montreal to lay a wreath in memory of her father. The Canadian military attaché came from the embassy in Berlin to accompany her. Although Jacqueline was too young when her father left for England to remember him, it was nevertheless a very emotional moment for her. Other relatives, now mainly only nieces and nephews or grandchildren of the victims, were also present. They knew that one afternoon in March 1945, a few days before the Americans liberated the camp, in order to wipe out all trace of them, the remaining twelve F Section agents were viciously flogged then hung, side by side, three at a time, with piano wire attached to a meat hook and suspended from the wall where the plaque was unveiled.

This was a favourite form of execution practised at Flossen-bürg, and in other concentration camps. It was particularly barbaric, since it took the victims twenty minutes to die by slow strangulation. The youngest of the F Section agents to be executed that afternoon was nineteen; the oldest thirty-six. These executions usually took place very early in the morning, and all the prisoners in the camp were assembled to watch before they dragged themselves off to work in the nearby granite mines. Often the guards chose members of the same nationality to flog their compatriots before they mounted the scaffold, and should the selected prisoner not flog hard enough – the condemned man could have been his best friend – he was replaced. He then joined the line of those awaiting flogging and execution.

Jack Agazarian, one of the last of the twelve agents to be led to the slaughter that afternoon, managed to smuggle out a note for his wife. He told her what was happening and wrote; 'I am in the last cell so they will be coming for me very soon. I just want to thank you for everything and tell you that I love you.' I don't know how the note got to Francine Agazarian, but she did finally receive it. Although only in her twenties when she was widowed, Francine never remarried. I don't think she ever recovered from her husband's death. She used to go every year to Flossenbürg to commemorate the massacre there, but sadly she died shortly before the unveiling of the plaque honouring her husband and his comrades. There has since been some speculation, and in-deed controversy, especially since suspicion about Bodington's loyalty has been voiced, about why Jack Agazarian was sent to France on that second mission at all. Both he and Francine were agents. Like most of the women agents Francine was very pretty, but she was not only pretty, she also had a very sweet face. She had returned from her mission shortly before her husband arrived back in London from his. He was exhausted, and they left on leave for a well-deserved rest. But before their leave had really started he was recalled to accompany Bodington on a short mission into France to contact a high-up Abwehr officer Bodington had known in Paris before the war. No one knew why Bodington had insisted that he must have Agazarian as his radio operator. Any other available radio operator could easily have gone in his place. When Agazarian protested that he was on leave Bodington assured him that it was only for a few days, and then he could rejoin his wife. Jack never returned. Although he had gone officially as Bodington's radio operator and contact with London, when they arrived Bodington sent Agazarian to the rendezvous. But as soon as he arrived in the café where he was to meet his contact, he was arrested by the Gestapo. Bodington said afterwards that they had tossed for it and Agazarian had lost. But why? Agazarian didn't know the Abwehr officer he was to meet. It was Bodington, as a former friend, who had been sent to contact him. It has also been rumoured that Bodington knowingly sent Jack to his death because he believed that Jack had discovered the truth about Déricourt and intended to reveal his treachery to the authorities. On the face of it there doesn't appear to be any other explanation.

I was conducted to a reserved seat in the front row, and before the ceremony started the organizer came to me, accompanied by two German teenagers, a boy and a girl. 'Your wreath is the middle one against the wall opposite the plaque,' he explained. 'When it is time for you to place it, these two young people will collect the wreath, come over to you, walk one on each side of you to the plaque and hand you the wreath. Then they will accompany you back to your seat.' We smiled at each other and at those two young people. It was all we could do. They spoke no English, and I hadn't spoken German for over fifty years so, apart from a few basic phrases, it was non-existent. But smiles are universal and can convey a wealth of meaning. That beautiful gesture by people for whom the war and its horrors were merely a page of history was, I felt, a living illustration of how the present generation of Germans was attempting to make amends, to say sorry for what their forebears did.

That day, at the ceremony at Flossenbürg, there were still a few former prisoners who had survived. I spoke to some of them, and the stories they told were horrendous. But what struck me as incredible was their complete lack of bitterness. None of the guards at the camp had been brought to trial after the war. There was one woman guard at the camp, Gertrud something or other, who apparently was even more brutal than the men, if that was possible. She died peacefully in Berlin in the late 1980s. Yet not one of the survivors expressed anger or voiced recriminations. It seemed that their terrible experiences had lifted them onto another plane, one which we other human beings who have never descended to such depths of deprivation and despair have not achieved, and hopefully never will. They did not criticize their inhuman guards or seek revenge. It was almost as if they were living outside themselves, viewing what had happened to them dispassionately.

I'll never forget one old Jewish former prisoner who had been taken to Flossenbürg at the age of eleven and had lost his entire family in the camp. He had only been saved from execution – they were hanging boys of his age – because the other prisoners had hidden him in a tunnel and fed him what scraps of food they could scrounge, even though they themselves were starving. They subsisted on one bowl of watery soup a day plus any scraps of potato peel they managed to scrounge from the dustbins out-side the kitchens – even though they were severely beaten if they were caught going through the dustbins. This young boy was in a very emaciated condition when the liberating army res-cued him and took him to an American military hospital, where he was nursed back to health. He was later adopted by one of the soldiers who had found him, and taken back to the United

States to be brought up as a typical North American boy. Being a very talented musician, he later became first violinist in the Pittsburgh Symphony Orchestra. That afternoon, in front of the plaque at Flossenbürg, he asked if he might play a Jewish lament for his lost family. When he put down his bow there was a deathly silence. And not a dry eye in the assembled crowd. 'We must turn the page and forgive,' he said slowly. Then he paused and ended quietly. 'But we must never, never, never, never forget.'

He was a lovely old man. I will never forget him. But then all the survivors were unforgettable. When the ceremony was over we were taken behind the wall where the wreaths were gathered before the unveiling to the cell block. It was eerie to walk along that narrow passageway bordered by the high stone wall and see the row of now-empty cells. One could imagine what they had once been like: teeming with starving, frightened human beings, most of them knowing that they faced a gruesome death.

Walking behind me was a tall man leaning on a stick. He tapped me on the shoulder. 'That was my cell,' he said simply. I turned to look at him, then back at the now empty cell, devoid of furniture except for one single iron bed. No covers. No mattress. Just the rusting springs.

'It's very small,' I murmured.

'There were three of us in it,' he went on. 'I'm a Dane. SOE Danish Section. There was another Dane and a Canadian in the cell with me.' I looked up in surprise.

'Wherever did they put three beds?' I enquired naively. 'There's no room.'

'There weren't three beds,' he explained. 'That cell is just as it was in 1945. No furniture except the iron bed. We took it in turn to sleep on it. Otherwise we slept on the floor.'

'You must have been cold,' I sympathized, looking at the dirty cement floor, 'especially in winter.'

'Freezing,' he agreed, 'and damned hungry.'

I glanced at the number above the door: 20. I knew that those in the first nineteen cells had been executed. He understood my glance without my having to voice any further questions.

'When those in number 19 were taken out we began to be very worried. They were all Brits. I know because we used to tap messages through the walls of the cells and whisper into the air vents. That's how we knew the Allies weren't far away. Luckily the Americans arrived and liberated the camp before the guards had time to liberate us.' He sighed. 'But too late for the poor Brits.'

He turned round to where a heavy book was open on a ledge.

'Look,' he said flipping through the pages. "This is the list of prisoners. There's my name.' He pointed to the page and then to the badge on his lapel.

I meant to ask whether it wasn't difficult to return to a place which held such painful memories, but we were being moved on to the crematorium and the large mound containing the remains of 500 prisoners, all shot at random in one afternoon, and the moving memorial huts each dedicated to the different groups represented in the camp. I found the Jewish hut the most affecting.

I returned home from that trip a changed woman. So many things we think important and get into a fuss about now seemed so futile. When I arrived in Paris there was a woman waiting with me at the airport for the bus to take us into town. It was late arriving. Although the officials on duty apologized, she fussed and fumed and threatened every official in sight with dire consequences because she had been kept waiting. I thought perhaps she had a train or a plane from another airport to catch, but no, when I asked her she said she lived in Paris. But she wanted to get home! We all did. 'It's the principle of the thing,' she fumed. 'It's unpardonable. That bus should be here, waiting for us.' She took a deep breath and cast a venomous glance at the poor official who had been the recipient of her anger. 'The company will be hearing from my husband first thing in the morning,' she threatened. 'Then some heads will roll.' The bus came to a standstill beside us at that minute. I let her get in first and took a seat as far away from her as possible. Perhaps a week earlier, I thought to myself, I would have agreed with her 'principles'. But that evening, as we waited in the sunshine, I felt sorry for her. After what I had seen, I couldn't understand how anyone could be so petty.

Chapter 8

A drop could be cancelled at the last minute, sometimes even when the agent was about to board the plane. This need not have been for any dramatic reason but simply because fog had suddenly risen over the Channel, and since the pilot flew without lights he obviously couldn't fly in a fog! And for the same reason drops could only take place during what was called 'the moon period' – nine or ten nights a month. If the warning came at the beginning of the moon period, the agent was hidden in a nearby manor house and a second attempt to leave would be scheduled for the following night. But if it were the last night of the moon, there was nothing he could do but return to London . . . and wait three weeks.

Henri Diacono was scheduled to drop as a radio operator on 17 December 1943. He finally got away, after three abortive attempts, at the beginning of March 1944. Desperate to be in the field doing the work he had spent almost nine months training for, like Lise de Baissac on her first mission, Henri agreed to 'drop blind' on a moonlit night and make his own way to his *réseau*, rather than hang around London any longer waiting, perhaps again in vain, for the next 'moon'. On landing he therefore was obliged to bury his parachute and flying suit, find his way to the nearest railway station and link up with his Resistance group.

One woman agent had seven abortive attempts to leave on seven successive nights before finally having to return to London.

This return to base after a failed attempt for whatever reason – unfavourable weather conditions or the infiltration of the receiving *réseau* – was very difficult for the agents. They were hyped-up, adrenaline flowing freely, and suddenly they were back in London, obliged to hang around for three weeks until the next moon. When this happened the agents were usually put up at 32 Wigmore Street, a house that had been taken over by SOE for use as a hostel. There was a lounge and a bar which served bar snacks, but no hot meals, so the agents often went to Casa Pepe in Soho. Another popular restaurant was Chez Rose. But the favourite was Chez Céleste. Céleste was a Frenchwoman who served steak without requiring the client to hand over food coupons. It was horse! Even in the lean wartime years no bona fide, dyed-in-the-wool Brit would touch it. But the French had no such scruples! Not only was Céleste very popular with F Section agents, BCRA staff also patronized her. I'm not sure the general would have approved!

The only trouble with Céleste was that her restaurant was not licensed to sell wines and spirits. But the problem was solved by Monsieur Berlemont, who ran the York Minster, the 'French' pub opposite Céleste's restaurant. So, having ordered their steak, the agents would take a jug, provided by Céleste, and nip across the road to the York Minster for a 'fill-up' of red wine, which they then carried back to their table, where their steak would be waiting. Monsieur Berlemont was famous for his pub but also because of his magnificent moustache. It was reputed to be the longest moustache in London and measured twenty inches across from end to end. I imagine he must have been obliged to go through a door sideways.

Perhaps these touches of home and the combined ministrations of Céleste and Monsieur Berlemont helped soothe the agents' feelings of frustration after a failed drop. They were frustrated, many of them very uptight and often angry. They knew it was nobody's fault, but some expressed anger all the same. I like to think it was at this time that we women at HQ were able to help them. They had no one else they could talk to, no one else on whom they could vent their frustration and their anger, no one with whom they could share their apprehensions. They were instructed not even to tell their wives about their mission, but I'm sure many of them did. I would have been furious. Perhaps furious is not the right word. I would have been disappointed and hurt if my husband had not confided in me. It would have shown such a lack of trust. After all, what woman who loves her husband would gossip about his clandestine activities, even to her best friend, knowing that in doing so she put his life at risk?

So, if they had to return to London and wait for the next moon, we tried to help them cope with their disappointment and frustration at this setback, to take their minds off the future, to think about other things – pretend, in fact, that it wasn't happening. We went to cinemas, theatres, dined in good restaurants, danced in nightclubs. But, looking back, I cannot help wondering whether that was what they really needed – or wanted.

Like all children born in the 1920s, when I was six weeks old I was christened with great pomp (so I'm told: I don't remember a great deal about it!) in Valetta, the capital of Malta, where I was born, taken to church every Sunday morning afterwards, taught to say my prayers by my bedside every night and was confirmed at fifteen. My confirmation was a low-key ceremony, not at all like my children's *communion solennelle* in the Catholic church in France, where the girls are decked out like brides and the boys like novice monks and there is a great family celebration lunch afterwards, during which the communicants are showered with splendid gifts, most of which bear no relation at all to the event. I was confirmed in Wales, where I was at school at the time, and I remember taking the instruction beforehand very seriously. I even considered becoming a nun, but quickly gave up that idea when I discovered the charms of the opposite sex.

My confirmation ceremony was held in the evening, the bishop was there, and my mother came for the church service. I did receive a few presents. An ivory-backed prayer book and a beautiful soft black-leather bible with gilt-edged pages. It lay on a shelf for years, gathering dust, though I did proudly carry the prayer book to church every Sunday morning. But there was no sumptuous post-confirmation meal. No one had sumptuous meals. It was wartime! After I married, I continued the church and bedtime prayer habit with my children. But it was only a habit, like cleaning my teeth. I never believed that my prayers went any farther than the ceiling and then bounced back off the top of my head.

I have since become a committed Christian, and it has changed my life. And I cannot help wondering whether, if during the war I had had the strong faith I now possess, I would have been able to help those frustrated, sometimes apprehensive departing agents more. I shared many confidences with departing agents. Many of them were married with young children and they told me of their worries, their fears for the future of their families. Their own fear of torture and of death. But all I could offer them were the bright lights . . . and platitudes.

I remember one agent in particular. He was a Jew, a radio operator, and he was leaving on a second mission. Two missions were not unusual. I think the record was seven. But for a Jew to go at all was dangerous, yet many of them did, though a second mission, especially as a radio operator, was almost suicidal. I was with him on the evening before he left. There was no romantic association, I was merely keeping him company. After all, he was an 'old man': he was thirty-five!

During the evening he drew out of his pocket a small velvet case and opened it. Inside was a slim gold chain holding a star of David above a dove of peace. He held the box out to me. 'I would like you to have this,' he said simply. I was taken unawares, confused at being offered what, after all, was an expensive piece of jewellery.

'I'm very touched,' I stammered, 'but I couldn't possibly accept it.' He looked so disappointed.

'Please do accept it,' he pleaded. 'Please do. My entire family in Paris has perished in a concentration camp. I have no one left in the world, and I would like to think that someone remembers me, and perhaps thinks of me while I am over there.' I was young at the time, embarrassed by his tragic revelation, and at a loss as to what to reply.

'In that case,' I said at last, 'I will take it and keep it safely for you until you return.'

I have often wondered since whether he was trying to tell me something. He may well have been a messianic Jew. Was he asking me, without putting it into so many words, whether I also was a believer? Asking me perhaps to pray for him? To pray with him now before he left? I'll never know . . . because he didn't return.

Chapter 9

Late one Saturday evening in early February 1944, Buck told me that I was being transferred to Beaulieu, to Group B, where, after all the strenuous exercises they had endured, future agents finally learned the art of spying.

'Pack your bags,' Buck smiled, 'and catch the two-thirty train from Waterloo tomorrow afternoon, and get off at Brocken-hurst.'

It was rather short notice, but one's worldly possessions in wartime didn't amount to much, so my packing didn't take long.

'A soldier in a car will be waiting for you outside the station,' Buck ended.

We never left the train at Beaulieu Halt, a small station which would have been much nearer our destination, because, since it was so small, our movements would have been more conspicuous.

The Wrens, whose seductive hat I had once coveted, were stationed not far away, so naval uniforms were everywhere. But there were no Army units in the area. Beaulieu was a small, delightful village where everyone knew everyone else, so a group of khaki-clad figures to-ing and fro-ing from the local station might have caused raised eyebrows, leading to awkward questions being asked.

When I stepped out of the train at Brockenhurst station, where the promised car with a soldier at the wheel was waiting, I walked into a winter wonderland. It had been snowing for several days, and after the slush and grime and the devastation and rubble of bomb-shattered London, I almost believed I had stepped into fairyland. It was like a scene from a glorious technicolor film. The snow was crisp and clean, and as the car whisked me through the small country town and on to Lord Montagu's estate, the trees were sparkling, tinkling with diamond pendants of frost.

The soldier decanted me in front of a small cottage deep in the forest. And it was there that I was to spend the rest of the war together with Jean, a South African, and Dorothy, a charming, elegant, distinguished woman in her mid-thirties. We were looked after by a marvellous housekeeper who clucked over us like a mother hen and concocted wonderful meals out of absolutely nothing.

Jean was a FANY, the official title First Aid Nursing Yeomanry, an elite unit of upper-class girls who didn't appear to have anything to do with nursing. The corps had been very active during the First World War, when they drove ambulances and staff cars. They may have lived up to their title during the Boer War, when the unit was created, but during the Second World War nursing was not part of their curriculum. They were almost exclusively attached to SOE as 'drivers and secretaries'. But in reality, they performed many other duties. The FANYs wore khaki uniforms with maroon buttons and insignia and, like Army officers, shining Sam Browne belts. Their uniforms, which were beautifully tailored, were made of barathea, like the officers' dress uniform, not the rough serge worn by recruits to the ATS and the WAAF.

Most of the future women agents, if civilians and not already members of one of the armed forces when recruited, were given honorary commissions in the FANYs. But, for reasons of which I am still unaware, FANYs were not considered to be part of the Army. They were a unit on their own, with the result that many women agents who had been commissioned into the FANYs were ignored by the War Office upon their return, receiving neither a pension nor benefits, in some cases resulting in great hardship.

Jean, the FANY with whom I was to share the former gardener's cottage, was a little older than I. She had left South Africa, her home country, and followed her fiancé, who, when war was declared, had immediately embarked for England to enlist. Unfortunately for Jean, by the time she had managed to secure a passage from Durban and disembarked at Southampton, her fiancé had already left with his regiment for the Western Desert. So Jean was very much a 'lady-in-waiting'.

Dorothy, the third member of our little group, was a very pleasant woman, very easy to live with, but she was also something of a mystery. However, we didn't ask questions: it had become a way of life. It was only after the war that I learned something of what Dorothy's real role had been.

Although we three women at Group B were euphemistically known as 'secretaries' for want of a better word, most of the secretarial work was done by a splendid little cockney corporal called Frank. Frank was a treasure. He had a wonderful sense of humour, was endlessly cheerful, endlessly helpful, was never flustered or impatient, did 99 per cent of the work with a huge smile and got us out of all kinds of scrapes. He was engaged to a girl called Doris, who worked in Woolworth's.

On the eve of VE Day, we had a splendid celebration party at the House in the Woods, where the officers lived, to which, there being no longer any need for security, the Montagu family and other local guests were invited. I had danced till dawn and beyond and was staggering across to the office in the early morning, rather the worse for wear, when Frank suddenly popped up out of a rhododendron bush. The rhododendrons on the estate were magnificent and all in full bloom at that time of year. 'Since it's victory day,' he said, 'may I kiss you?'

'Frank,' I gasped, taken by surprise and not quite myself after my splendid night on the tiles, 'what about Doris?'

He smiled and winked at me, then whispered. 'I'll tell her it's my last sacrifice for the war effort.' Not very flattering for me!

Soon after the files were opened in 2000, my husband heard this story and he wanted to know the outcome. Had I allowed him to kiss me or not? I told him it was one of the most closely guarded secrets of the war, locked in a secure safe, which would not be opened for 100 years. He's noted in his diary to ask me the question again in 2040!

There were twenty-five officer instructors on the estate. I think all but two were former agents who were 'blown', the code word for agents whose identity had become known to the Germans and who had had to hurriedly return home. One of the two was handsome, charming, efficient – everybody liked him. He had in fact with his brilliant mind organized the training programme for Beaulieu. He was recalled to HQ in London early on in the war and rapidly climbed the hierarchical ladder of 'the Firm', as the Intelligence Service was called, to become head of the highly sensitive Russian Section at the Foreign Office. From there he kept Moscow informed of all Foreign Office secrets. His name was Kim Philby. In 1963 he had to hastily flee his native land and seek asylum in Moscow when the British government discovered that he had been spying for the Russians since his days at Cambridge in 1933. He was, in fact, one of the 'Cambridge five'.

The other officer, Jock, was a rather rough diamond, not at all like his colleagues, who were all very public-school and every evening changed into service dress for dinner. Jock was a tough Glaswegian who knocked around in battle-dress and hob-nailed boots and never appeared to change into anything. He was not a permanent fixture at Group B, but turned up periodically. These officers lived in the House in the Woods, about ten minutes' walk away from our cottage. It was a lovely house which Edward VIII and Mrs Simpson had apparently used for secret weekend rendezvous before his abdication.

Our HQ was a rather ugly stockbroker-Tudor house called the Rings. It was situated between the cottage and the House in the Woods, and here the commandant, Colonel Woolrych, a stern man who didn't suffer fools gladly, was in charge. We called him Woolybags behind his back. He was a regular army officer who had been in intelligence during the First World War – and probably ever since. I was rather in awe of him in the beginning and kept out of his way as much as possible. But I was later to discover that beneath that austere exterior was buried a wealth of compassion. An accomplished classical pianist, he used to play the beautiful grand piano in the draw-ing room at the House in the Woods for an hour every morning before breakfast.

We worked every day of the week, finishing at one o'clock on Sundays, and had one weekend off a month, when we usually raced up to the 'bright lights' of London. Often on a Sunday after-noon Jock would bang on the cottage door and shout: 'Anyone want to come for a walk?' In winter, Sunday afternoon was the only time during the week when we could get a breath of fresh air in the forest, since the days were short and by the time we finished working it was already dark. So, when he called, I often tripped off with him. The New Forest was beautiful at any time of the year, and on the estate we had miles of it all to ourselves.

He sometimes became a bit sentimental, but one only had to say, 'Oh, stuff it, Jock,' and he never insisted. However, after the war I saw a film which had been made for the archives in 1943, and I'm sure I recognized Jock. He was a specialist in 'silent killing'. They had filmed a demonstration. It was both horrifying and fascinating at the same time. And I couldn't help wondering whether, had I known about his 'speciality' at the time, I would have tripped off so happily with him for a walk in the deserted forest. Or even whether, had I done so, I would have had the courage to resist his amorous advances!

When in training, the prospective agents were referred to as 'students': they became 'bods' once behind enemy lines, only reverting to human being status when they returned. They lived in about a dozen houses dotted in the woods on the Beaulieu estate, out of sight of our HQ, which had all been requisitioned in 1940 for the exclusive use of SOE. There were the French, Polish Norwegian, Czech, Belgian, Dutch, Danish, Greek, etc. houses. Those destined for work in France were often billeted at 'Boarmans', the 'Orchard' or the 'Vineyard'. The women usually stayed at the 'House on the Shore'.

At Beaulieu there were no 'unisex' houses. As at HQ, segregation was strictly enforced, not only between men and women, but also between the different countries. The maxim 'the less you know, the less you can reveal' was rigidly adhered to, even at Group B. Students destined for different countries in Europe never mixed in houses or classes, or even came across one another. That way, if captured and questioned, they could not disclose under torture that prospective agents from other countries, being prepared for infiltration into occupied Europe, had followed the same training course. Such information would have alerted the Germans to the fact that training was not limited to one or two countries, and could have led to a total collapse of the entire European network. As with the *réseaux*, and the different

135

country sections at HQ, students from different nations were kept strictly apart.

The prospective agents arrived in batches, accompanied by a conducting officer who was not a member of the Beaulieu staff. For the women students, the conducting officer was almost invariably a FANY officer. The conducting officer lived in the various houses with the students they had brought down and often attended the classes: but they were primarily there as counsellors, 'mother hens' really, to look after the students and help them if they had problems. Those students who were to work in the field stayed at Group B for three weeks to a month. But there were other people who came as 'observers' and often took part in exercises and attended classes: the 'observer' stayed a maximum of ten days.

Vera Atkins once visited Beaulieu as an observer and took part in a night exercise, though it is difficult to imagine the elegant Vera doing anything as undignified as prowling around the forest in the early hours of the morning with a group of disguised Beaulieu officers. The officers at Beaulieu taught the finer points of being a secret agent. In a bar or restaurant, never sit with your back to the door. When travelling on public transport, if possible, don't take a seat, stand on the platform or near the exit. Never take a direct route to a rendezvous or hold large meetings, and never, ever hold meetings with several agents gathered together. Punctuality was stressed, and agents told that if the person they were to meet did not show up on time, they were not to wait, but to leave immediately.

There is an amusing story of a Beaulieu student who, during an exercise, was given a rendezvous with an unknown woman at three o'clock outside the post office in Bournemouth. But he arrived early. Thinking that he recognized his 'contact', he approached an innocent young woman who was startled to be accosted. Apologizing profusely, he walked around the block and on his return accosted another supposed 'contact', but with the same result. Taking a third trip around the block, he went to speak to the person who finally turned out to be his real contact. But, when he approached her, an elderly lady hit him viciously over the head with her umbrella and threatened to call the police, accusing him of trying to 'molest nice young ladies'!

The officers usually walked through the forest every morning to the different houses where the classes were held: every officer except Johnny, who needed a truck, because he carried with him an enormous door on which was every conceivable lock one could imagine. He had to teach the students to pick these locks, because once in the field they wouldn't have keys to all the places they wanted to enter. Johnny had learned this technique from a burglar. He must have been a very experienced, highly qualified burglar, because the British government had released him from a long sentence in a London prison on condition that he taught his tricks to SOE. There was also the safe-blower, Johnny Ramensky, who was reputed to have blown open both Goebbels' and Goering's safes. How true that information is I don't know. He was apparently part of SOE, though I never met him.

We certainly were an unusual group of people. It's hardly surprising that MI6, the official intelligence agency, disapproved of us.

It was at Group B that the students were taught how to signal to a contact who was scheduled to call on them, or a radio operator approaching a house before transmitting, that it was dangerous to enter, or even to loiter in front of the house or flat. This was done by arranging in advance to have the curtains or shutters wide open or half closed: closed could mean danger, don't approach; open, it's safe for the moment, come in. A flowerpot or an ornament placed in the middle of the window could mean all clear, but at the side, danger. One agent organized a lookout living at the entrance to her courtyard to loudly play a series of chords from an arranged symphony to warn her that the Gestapo or the police had entered the building. These tactics were also used when meeting a contact. If an agent had a newspaper rolled under his arm, don't recognize him, keep walking. If the newspaper was folded and put in a jacket or coat pocket, coast clear. It was in the agent's interest to remember to get the signals right!

Propaganda warfare was also one of the weapons agents were taught to use, to great effect. This included spreading false rumours: whispering that brothels for the exclusive use of German soldiers were serviced by prostitutes with venereal diseases, that rat droppings, powdered glass and undetectable poisons had been found in German rations. They also learned how to surreptitiously put itching powder into German underwear, I imagine by instructing the women laundering soldiers' clothes, or cleaning their barracks. Another ploy was to paint large 'V for Victory' signs on walls all over France. Some even encased the cross of Lorraine – the Gaullist symbol of the Free French – inside the 'V'. Propaganda leaflets and newspapers were also dropped into France by plane, and it was up to the agents to ensure that as many people as possible read these papers.

There was a very handsome young major at Group B, Peter Follis, a former actor, who taught the trainees disguises. 'Forget about false beards,' he apparently told them. 'That's too obvious. Go for the more subtle disguises: part your hair a different way, dye it, wear glasses, put pebbles in one shoe to give you an authentic permanent limp.' Shrieks of laughter could be heard coming from his classes as agents became hunchbacks or cripples, or gave the impression that they were on their last legs. They used each other as mannequins and, under Peter Follis's direction, were transformed from their mid-twenties or early thirties into sixty- or seventy-year-olds with the clever use of ashes rubbed round the contours of their eyes and to accentuate or create lines on their faces, white shoe cleaner to turn the hair on their temples grey, balls of cotton wool or chewing gum stuffed into their mouths to fill out their cheeks and completely transform the shape of their faces, ageing them by as much as thirty years. And, of course, glasses, usually large horn-rimmed pairs with window panes for lenses.

At Beaulieu future agents or 'trainees' were taught how to use ciphers and to make secret ink out of egg white, lemons and even urine. I imagine the idea was that the writing would be invisible to the naked eye and would only be revealed when held up to a light, a torch bulb or the flame of a candle – after which, should the paper not be destroyed, the writing would disappear. They also learned how to open letters and reseal them without leaving any trace, and how to place objects in such a way on a desk or in a drawer that an agent could immediately detect whether someone had entered and searched the room during his absence.

More insidiously, they learned how to make different concoctions to slip into a drink or a dish which would slowly poison whoever ate or drank it. Or, less drastically, to immobilize a whole barracks for several days with a substance which would give the soldiers severe, but not fatal, abdominal pains. Any trick was worth a try!

Every morning the officers instructed the students in these and other techniques. In the classrooms there were photos of high-ranking German officers, Admiral Canaris – later executed at Flossenbürg – Heydrich, Himmler, etc. There were also photographs of German uniforms which the students had to study closely, and be able to recognize and identify so as to be familiar with the different members of the occupying forces: the Gestapo, the SS, the Wehrmacht, the Abwehr, the Sicherheitsdienst or SD, the Luftwaffe, etc. which, once in the field, they would meet on the streets every day.

At the end of their time at Beaulieu students would be

dumped at night in the middle of the New Forest and, without a torch, map or compass, told to find their way back to HQ and break into the commandant's office without being caught by one of the Beaulieu officers prowling about the forest, hiding behind trees or lurking in the bushes waiting to pounce and 'arrest' them before they reached their target. One student – I won't mention names – managed to evade the lurking officers, break into a room and stumble across the bed of a pretty young girl wearing a lavender satin nightie. He said it was a mistake. But his theory is open to doubt. He was a Frenchman, after all . . . and quite a lad!

Often after an exhausting night of exercises in the forest, an agent would be rudely awakened from a deep sleep at about 3 a.m. by loud hammering on his bedroom door accompanied by strident voices shouting: 'Open up, Gestapo.' And a black mark would be placed against his name if he answered, 'Come in,' instead of the language of the country for which he was destined. The prospective agent would then be hauled out of bed, still drugged with sleep. If he didn't wear pyjamas, he was also in the nude, not an attire which lent itself to a dignified approach when facing a brutal interrogation. After he had been dragged downstairs to a dark room full of Beaulieu instructors, dressed as Gestapo officers, bright lights were shone in his eyes, almost blinding him, and harsh, staccato questions shot at him. Threats, accusations, insinuations, mingled with wheedling promises of release and rewards, if he would cooperate, defect and work for the enemy, were hurled at him from every side: sneers that resistance was useless, the Gestapo already knew everything about him and his activities since his comrades had all been arrested and had betrayed him, rained down on him in rapid succession. In the midst of this turmoil, the poor, unfortunate student was expected to keep his wits about him, answer coolly and correctly in the right language, repeating his 'cover story' inside out, endlessly giving details of his movements and activities – false, of course – down to the minutest detail. Sometimes, after having been thrown back into bed, exhausted, not only by the night exercise but also by the interrogation, he was pulled roughly out of bed half an hour later, and the whole process would begin again. Brutal, but it was a foretaste of what could happen to him if, once behind the lines, he should fall into the hands of the Gestapo.

At Beaulieu the training was very thorough. It was here, at this last school, that the agent's fate was decided, because even after their long, arduous schooling, it was never a certainty that they would be allowed to leave.

Beaulieu, the 'School for Secret Agents', the last training school for these 'Baker Street Irregulars', as they were also known, was also called the 'Gangster School'. I don't know who gave Beaulieu that nickname but I suspect it was MI6, the official government intelligence agency. We were a bizarre group of people, so it's hardly surprising that MI6, the 'real' spies and spycatchers, hated us. We weren't behaving according to the rules . . . or the Geneva convention. They patronizingly called us 'amateur bandits', which of course was what we were!

SOE certainly collected some odd characters – the entire service was made up of unusual, colourful and often eccentric people. Perhaps one of the most colourful, certainly the most flamboyant, was Denis Rake, a law unto himself. Denis was the only known F Section homosexual agent. Before the war he had been an actor and also a circus turn, beginning his career at the age of three as a tumbler, when his mother, an opera singer, happily handed him into the care of a manager at the Sarazini circus and disappeared. As far as I know, his father's profession, if he had one, was not recorded. The young Denis travelled widely with the circus all over Europe and was at one time kept in luxury by a prince in Athens. When the liaison came to an end he turned to musical comedy in London, understudying many famous actors, and after the war became butler to the film idol Douglas Fairbanks. One morning an official letter, addressed to Major Denis Rake MC, arrived at the Fairbanks London house in the Little Boltons. The astonished and mystified screen idol, who had believed Rake to be a charming but harmless 'queer' who was good with the children, confronted his butler with this surprising revelation. Denis apparently smiled and shrugged off his wartime achievements as 'unimportant', saying that he only became an undercover agent in order to prove that homosexuals could be as brave as their heterosexual counterparts!

Rake had heard about SOE by chance, in a pub in Portsmouth, when eavesdropping on the conversation of some airmen who were disobeying orders and talking indiscreetly about dropping agents into occupied France. Intrigued by the idea, he managed to get an interview with a member of Buckmaster's staff, who happened to be the brother of a well-known actor Rake had once understudied. He was accepted for training, but declared 'hopeless' by his conducting officer. At Arisaig, he announced he was scared of 'bangs' and refused to handle firearms or explosives, but worked non-stop at his Morse lessons. Denis had the impression that he was doing F Section a favour by offering to drop as an agent, and declared he would only go on his own terms. But in spite of Rake's independence and his adverse reports, Buck realized that he had the makings of a very fine radio operator and allowed him to continue his training. Since the parachute course had not been a success either, Buck decided to send him in by the sea route. Denis was flown to Gibraltar, where he boarded a trawler, then a submarine and finally a felucca, from which he was transferred to a dinghy a few miles from the coast of south-west France and left to row himself ashore. He later said that when he left the felucca and rowed alone in the dinghy on a moonless night on the dark sea he felt fear such as he had never known in his life.

While working in the unoccupied zone of France he was arrested and badly knocked about, but managed to escape. Learning that a radio operator was needed in John Farmer's Freelance *réseau* in the Auvergne, the occupied zone, Denis volunteered to go. But while making his way from the unoccupied to the occupied zone, he was again arrested and imprisoned in Dijon, where he was tortured and lost several teeth. With the help of a priest, who hid him in a swill bin, he escaped from that prison. He never gave away any information during either of his arrests or brutal interrogations. After making his way across the demarcation line to the occupied zone, he stopped off in Paris, where he dropped into the bar Le Boeuf sur le Toit, which had been one of his haunts in the 1930s. The barman recognized him and introduced him to a German, Max Halder, who, the barman whispered, was a member of an ancient German family and was violently anti-Nazi. Could Max have been a relative of General Franz Halder, an anti-Nazi Wehrmacht officer who escaped execution but was sent to a concentration camp after he was suspected of being involved in the July 1944 plot against Hitler's life? I have not been able to find out, but it seems very likely, since General Halder's father, also a general, was called Max.

The two men discovered that they had much in common, apart from their sexual orientation. They were both lonely and they both hated war. They spent several weeks together, and Denis said afterwards that, had it not been for the war, he and Max Halder would probably have stayed together for many years, perhaps even for ever. But finally Denis regretfully decided it was time he made his way to Freelance, the *réseau* he had volunteered to join, where the now famous Nancy Wake was the courier. John Farmer, the organizer of Freelance, although admitting that Denis was a first-class radio operator, couldn't stand him, though whether it was because of his homosexuality or not I don't know. But Nancy was rather fond of him.

When Buck heard about Denis's antics he blew sky-high and threatened to have him court-martialled on his return, especially since John Farmer, who had been expecting Denis to arrive, had no idea what had happened to him and may well have believed him to be in the hands of the Gestapo.

But Denis's escapade was not as dramatic – or catastrophic, as far as F Section was concerned – as the disappearance of an agent who arrived in the South of France carrying a huge sum of money (counterfeit, of course, 'made in England'), which he was to hand over to the organizer of the *réseau* he was sent to join. For reasons of his own, he never joined the *réseau*. He disappeared – with the money – and was never heard of again. Perhaps a search party should have been sent to the casino in Monte Carlo. And perhaps that is why most drops were made to a reception committee, so that suddenly wealthy agents would not be tempted to defect.

Denis was not the only agent Buck, in one of his sudden outbursts of anger, threatened to have court-martialled. Terry Kilmartin, who later became literary editor of the *Observer*, was a member of F Section staff at Norgeby House during the war years. He had wanted to go into the field, but Buck had always refused. 'I need you here,' he had said calmly, leaving poor Terry very frustrated. I don't know whether he had ever trained as an agent, but he must have learned how to parachute, because one evening Terry took the matter into his own hands and left with a 'Jed team', who were dropped into France that night. 'Jedburghs' were a group of three men, one British, one French and one American, who after D-Day dropped in uniform into occupied France to help Resistance fighters who were 'clearing up' after the retreating German Army. Some of them had horrendous adventures.

I don't know how Terry managed it, but he went. The next morning Buck looked into the office, frowned and asked: 'Where's Captain Kilmartin? He's not usually late.'

There was a heavy silence, then a voice piped up: 'In France, sir.' Buck frowned, obviously not immediately understanding the implication.

'In France?' he queried.

'Yes sir,' the same voice replied: 'He left with the Jed team last night.' Then it was a case of: everyone scatter, he's about to explode. Buck went puce in the face and did explode.

'I'll have him court-martialled when he gets back,' he bellowed, and, furiously slamming the door, stamped off. But, being Buck, he never did. Perhaps he was too kind-hearted, or he may have been so pleased that both Terry and Denis returned that he preferred to forget his threats.

On the night of 5 June 1944 two other agents, Bob Maloubier and Violette Szabo, were scheduled to be parachuted into France for the second time, Violette never to return.

Like Denis Rake, they were both very colourful characters. At seventeen, when France fell, Bob, urged by his father, who had fought with the Allies during the First World War, left his home in Brittany and cycled to the Pyrenees and crossed into Spain. From there he managed to get to North Africa, where, after multiple adventures, he was recruited by SOE and flown to England for training. Bob was probably F Section's greatest sabo-teur. After D-Day, in order to prevent the German Army from sending reinforcements to the Normandy front, by himself he blew up eight bridges. And when the war in Europe ended, not content with having parachuted twice into occupied France, he volunteered for Force 136 in the Far East, where the war against the Japanese was still raging, and was dropped into Laos.

Violette's young husband had been killed fighting with the French Foreign Legion in North Africa. Anger at his death led Violette to join SOE. Violette, who was perhaps the most beau-tiful amongst a bevy of F Section's beautiful women agents, was arrested shortly after arriving on her second mission into France, following a gun battle during which she manned a machine-gun from the back seat of a car until she ran out of ammunition. She then leapt out of the car, and with the Germans in hot pursuit, firing at her from all angles, she attempted to escape across a field and into the shelter of a wood and had almost reached her target when she tripped and twisted her ankle. Her male companion attempted to carry her to safety, but she insisted that there was no point in both of them being caught, and told him to save himself. He reached the wood, but she was captured, tortured and, aged just twenty-three, finally executed in Ravensbrück.

Bob and Violette had first met when Bob walked down the steps of the Studio Club in Knightsbridge and saw Violette, wearing a simple, unadorned black dress, leaning against the piano. He said she was so breathtakingly beautiful that he just stood rooted to the spot, staring at her. They were introduced, and she reached up on tiptoe – she was petite – and kissed him on both cheeks, overwhelming him still further with a whiff of expensive French perfume. Violette had worked on the beauty counter at Bon Marché in Brixton, where she was brought up – she never lost the local accent! – before joining SOE. Whilst in training Violette met and fell in love with Harry Peulevé, like her a 'half and half', and they became lovers. Harry had already left on his second mission into France when she and Bob met. Harry was also arrested during this second mission, but survived the concentration camp to which he was sent. He returned to London at the end of the war, eager to find Violette again and marry her. The shock of discovering that she had not survived hit him badly, and he never got over it. He did eventually marry a Danish woman and fathered two children, but the marriage didn't last. Harry left his wife and young family and wandered the world, taking job after job, endlessly restless, and finally dying in his early fifties.

Bob and Violette became friends while waiting to leave on

their separate missions. I had thought at one time that their relationship went beyond mere friendship, but apparently not, it was just a firm friendship, not a romantic liaison. They had a mutual passion – poker – and were both fanatical players. They later left together to be parachuted into France and, according to Bob, they didn't sleep in the plane on the way over as they'd been advised to do, they played poker. The despatcher joined in and turned out to be better at the game than they were, with the result that the two agents ended up broke! When the plane arrived at the landing ground, there was no reception committee waiting for them, so the pilot turned and headed back home. Since the two agents had been 'fleeced' by the despatcher, there was no longer any point in playing poker on the way back. So they slept.

When Bob and Violette climbed into the plane that June night and soared into the dark sky, they were unaware of the momentous event which was about to unfold. On 5 June that *message personnel* every organizer had been eagerly awaiting was finally broadcast. 'Les carottes sont cuites' ('The carrots are cooked') came over the air waves loud and clear, announcing the imminent landing, the following morning, of Allied troops on French soil. It was the eve of the Normandy landings! The next morning, when they awoke, they learned that at dawn Allied troops had landed on the Normandy beaches. It was D-Day. The long-awaited invasion had finally happened! 'Thousands of little ships had sailed by below us. Hundreds of aircraft had thundered past us,' Bob said dejectedly. 'And . . . we had slept right through it.'

Between the time of the message and the landing, nine hundred and sixty sabotage attacks against railway lines had been carried out, and every train between Marseilles and Lyons conveying German reinforcements to the front derailed at least once. During the following days, the Germans brought in Army

Chapter 10

We three women were used as decoys so, for obvious reasons, we never met or had any contact with the students who came to Group B before we linked up on exercises. Had they known us, the whole operation would have been futile. Jean worked in Southampton; my pitch was Bournemouth. Like the other occupants of the block of flats at Orchard Court, the inhabitants of both those large coastal towns hadn't the remotest idea, I don't think they even suspected, what was going on under their very noses.

A student would be let loose in Bournemouth and told that a young girl wearing a headscarf and a dirty mac and carrying a shopping bag would probably be walking along the sea front opposite the pier pavilion at a given time. He was told to detect her and, once he had found her, to follow her and discover where she was going and whom she might be meeting, without her suspecting anything. This also worked in reverse when they were taught how to detect if someone was shadowing them and then to shake them off without any suspicions being aroused.

My job was much easier than theirs. A young man, in or out of uniform, wandering around a seaside resort in the middle of the day was much more conspicuous than a young woman with a shopping basket. They were everywhere. We always carried shopping bags wherever we went in case we came across a queue which we could join and, hopefully, buy something 'off the ration'. It didn't matter what it was: if it was 'off the ration' it was worth having . . . and worth queuing for!

Once decanted in Bournemouth, I used to head for the appointed spot, then walk along a street facing the sea, which was lined with shops, and stop to look at the window displays – not that there was a great deal to display in those lean wartime years! This way, from the reflection in the plate-glass window, I could see anyone passing me or more importantly lingering behind me. Sure enough, my victim would sooner or later saunter into view and, if he spotted me, would stop and gaze into the window of the shop next door. But I outgazed him, and eventually he moved on. If my judgement had been right and he was my 'victim', he usually halted after a few yards to tie a shoelace which wasn't undone. This was my cue. I knew I had spotted my man. So I would head for a large department store called Plummers, the only department store in Bournemouth at the time, and make straight for the ladies' lingerie section.

I don't know whether modern men like wandering alone around a ladies' lingerie department, but in the early 1940s they most certainly didn't. They were usually highly embarrassed. I knew that and, when I saw him slink furtively in, I invariably held up to the light a few 'unmentionables' in order to embarrass him even further. When I felt I had taunted him enough, to put him out of his misery I would stroll across to the lift and press the button. I knew exactly what he would do next. So, when he casually reached the lift, at the last second before the doors closed I would either change my mind and leap out or not get in at all, but run down the stairs on the other side to another department which was more crowded. On the way down I would whip off my headscarf and mac and stuff them into my shopping bag so that when, breathless, he arrived at the top of the stairs – he'd probably had to go to the next floor and race back down – the girl he had been tracking had disappeared. And only a girl in a tweed suit, her hair flowing out behind her, was visible walking briskly towards the street door, through which she rapidly disappeared. Even had he spotted me it would have been pointless to try to catch up with me, because there were several roads joining outside the shop, and I could have dived down any one of them.

I also used to wait at a bus stop until my victim joined the queue. When the bus arrived, I'd loiter on the platform and leap off just as it was gathering speed. He couldn't follow me – it would have been too obvious, and also dangerous – so the poor, frustrated man had to sit and fume till the next stop, by which time, when he hared back, there was no sign of me. This exercise would have been much easier on the London Underground because if one leapt out just as the doors were closing, one knew that one had lost him for good. But we didn't have an underground in Bournemouth, so I had to make do with buses.

We also taught the future agents to pass on messages without being noticed, and without moving their lips. I would be told that at around three o'clock that afternoon there would be a man in the pier gardens, sitting on a bench facing the sea reading a newspaper, who had a message for me. So I would stroll to the pier gardens, hoping that other people would not have crowded onto the bench before I arrived. That would definitely queer the pitch. If it was all clear, I would sit down, open my handbag and take out a cigarette. I have never been a smoker, but I made the supreme sacrifice during the war and puffed my way to victory. After a while, without any sign of recognition having passed between us, he would put down his newspaper and walk away. I would then casually pick it up and flick through the pages. This was not unusual, and in no way remarkable. Newspapers were in very short supply, and everyone wanted to read them, so whenever one was abandoned it was always immediately spotted and grabbed. Every newspaper must have been read by at least twelve people. Somewhere inside this newspaper there would be a message. Perhaps part of the crossword, if there was one. As soon as I found it, I would fold the paper and put it back on the bench for the next person who sat down to read.

We often passed messages to trainee agents in telephone booths. This was not as easy as linking up on the park bench. There were very few private telephones during the war, and everyone wanted to make calls, so public call boxes were in great demand and always had a line of people waiting to use them. We were asked, or rather told, by the authorities not to make a call last longer than three minutes. If it was a long-distance call every three minutes the pips would sound, the operator would come on the line and, if one didn't immediately put more coins in the box, the call was cut off.

This exercise was much more complicated for me than the bench operation, because I had to be absolutely sure I had spotted the right man. And also contrive to squeeze in behind him in the queue, and not behind someone else. Otherwise, the outcome could be embarrassing, even disastrous, if I muttered a compromising message to a complete stranger, especially if he was with his wife! Our rendezvous would often be in the telephone booth in the pier gardens. For me this entailed a great deal of time wasted lurking in bushes in order to be sure to leap out as soon as I spotted my 'victim'. Luckily, there was a clump of bushes beside the pier gardens telephone box.

Once we had shuffled into line, he would go into the booth and search for a number in the telephone directory, put his twopence in the slot, pick up the receiver and make a fictitious phone call. After few seconds, he would replace the receiver and, since he hadn't pressed Button A to put him through to the person he was calling, he would then press button B to retrieve his money. This sounds unbelievably complicated in this modern age of mobile phones, but it was the way things worked in those days. On leaving the booth, he would smile at me – no doubt desperately hoping I was the person he was supposed to contact – and say, 'I'm so sorry to have kept you waiting.' We were very polite in those days. Then, without moving his lips, he would hiss through the side of his mouth, 'H for Harris.' I would smile back, murmur, 'It's quite all right,' and hiss back, 'OK. H for Harris,' then enter the booth and re-enact the same comedy, except that when I flicked through the pages of the telephone directory to H, I would surreptitiously read or slide out the message, continue the pantomime to the bitter end and leave, smiling my apologies to the next person in the queue.

I often performed this rigmarole in cafés and restaurants. A favourite place was the tea-room above the Gaumont Cinema, where I would order morning coffee and a bath bun, or, should it be after three o'clock, tea and toast and occasionally a poached egg, if my 'victim' didn't immediately loom into view, thereby stringing the operation out until I was absolutely sure I had spotted my man. Any mistake on my part – murmuring a message out of the corner of my mouth giving a rendezvous, or dropping a note onto the lap of a total stranger indicating when and where we were to meet – could not only be embarrassing, but could even lead me into serious trouble with the police for soliciting.

But I think the most 'James Bond' exercise – hardly surprising since James Bond's creator, Ian Fleming, worked for Naval Intelligence during the war, and his brother Peter was an SOE agent – took place in hotels, without anyone even suspecting the drama being enacted before their very eyes.

There were two very pleasant hotels in Bournemouth, the Royal Bath and the Lincoln. I preferred to operate at the Royal Bath, because adjoining the dining room was a large terrace overlooking the sea which, on a warm, moonlit evening, lent itself to a very romantic scenario, making my task much easier. The Lincoln unfortunately didn't possess such a commodity. Very often, on a student's last night of the course before being returned to his Section in London, where his fate would be decided, his conducting officer would invite him out for dinner to celebrate. The conducting officers sat in on many of the classes and watched the students closely, studying their different reactions to situations, their relationship with other students, whether they were level-headed, practical, gossips, volatile or knew how to 'hold their drink' or 'keep their cool'. Every student wasn't favoured with an invitation to dinner, so I can only think that the officers chose those whom they suspected might 'talk'.

Beforehand a little one-act play was worked out between the officer and myself. When he and the future agent were in the hotel lounge having a drink before dinner I would stroll in, and the officer would exclaim in surprise, 'Noreen, how lovely to see you. What are you doing in Bournemouth? Come and have a drink. Meet my friend.' Or he might say to the agent when they linked up, 'An extraordinary thing happened this afternoon. I bumped into a girl I hadn't seen since the beginning of the war. I was at school with her brother.' My little brother was still at school at the time, so that was stretching it a bit far. But the bod wasn't to know that. 'She's staying in Bournemouth for a few days, and I've asked her to join us for a drink. You don't mind, do you?'

If the future agent were a Brit he usually minded very much. He'd been looking forward to a boozy evening with the boys, and here was this wretched woman coming to put a damper on things. But the foreigners were often very pleased, since they didn't have that many opportunities to meet English girls. When the second glass of sherry arrived the officer, as planned, would ask me to join them for dinner, and after a few blushing protestations I would gracefully accept his invitation. But when it was time to put down our glasses and stroll across to the dining room, there would be a telephone call for the officer. He would return, apologizing profusely: something had happened which had to be dealt with immediately. 'But you two go ahead and start dinner. I'll join you as soon as I can.' Of course, he never did, or only when the meal was over. Then it was up to me. This is where the Royal Bath's superior facilities came into play. If it was a warm, moonlit night, and I could edge my victim out onto the terrace overlooking the sea, there was more of a chance that he would relax, possibly become sentimental . . . and talk.

The Brits mostly remained mute, saying, 'Oh, I'm on some boring old course for the War Box,' and smilingly refuse to elaborate, putting a finger to their lips if ever I insisted, whispering 'careless talk costs lives', a slogan written up on posters all over the walls. One man said he was a salesman for toothpaste, which was ridiculous. We didn't have any toothpaste: we cleaned our teeth with soot or salt. But it was his story, and he stuck to it. With a foreigner it was often easier, and some of them talked, especially the young ones. I understood them. They were lonely and must have often felt isolated, far from their families and their countries, not knowing whether their friends and relatives were alive or dead, or whether they would have a home or family or even a country to return to when the war was finally over.

I remember one student in particular. I don't think I shall ever forget him. His reaction on learning he'd been betrayed affected me deeply. I think it was then that I realized that my life in SOE was based on deception, on lies. I lied to my mother. I lied to my friends. I lied to everyone I met outside of F Section. It was inevitable. I was unable to tell them the truth, reveal what I was doing. This particular student was a Dane, a gorgeous blond Adonis, not unlike the Norwegian I had found so attractive in the BBC canteen. We met at the Royal Bath Hotel on a warm spring evening with a full moon, and I managed to persuade him to wander out onto the terrace. To be honest, he didn't need an awful lot of persuading. I think he was rather attracted to me. At the time I weighed twelve kilos less, didn't have white hair and didn't need glasses to read the small print! Once propped against the balustrade, gazing at the sea, he became sentimental. They often did. It was to be expected. On a glorious moonlit evening, with the silver-tinted sea lapping gently against the shore below, the scene was set for it. He asked me whether we could spend the following Sunday together, and I accepted his invitation, knowing full well that there was not the slightest chance of my being able to keep my promise. But his invitation gave me my lead, my chance to probe further, enquire about his next move, his activities, his final destination . . . and his intentions. In the end he talked: he told me what he was doing and where he was going.

Before their departure the following day, Colonel Woolrych received every student in his office. All the reports from the various schools they had attended were in front of him on his desk, and, having thoroughly studied them, it was up to him to give his opinion as to whether the prospective agent should be infiltrated or not. The final decision did not rest with Woolybags, but was the prerogative of the head of his country section. For those leaving for France, it was Buck who decided their fate: but Woolybags' report carried a lot of weight.

If the student had 'talked' during our dinner together, at one point during the interview the door would open and I would walk in. 'Do you know this woman?' Woolybags would ask. Mostly they took it well, shrugged and realized that they had been fools and made a stupid mistake, thereby putting in jeopardy their chances of leaving and carrying out their mission, the mission for which they had undergone such a long and arduous training. But this Dane was different. I shall never forget his face. He looked at me, stunned, then disappointment, I would almost say pain, clouded his eyes, to be quickly replaced by a terrible anger. He half rose from his chair and spat: 'You bitch!'

No woman likes to be called a bitch. I didn't. And I was upset. But it was then that I discovered Woolybags' compassionate side beneath his stern exterior. 'It's no good your upsetting yourself,' he said kindly to me afterwards. 'If he can't resist talking to a pretty face over here, he most certainly won't once he's over there. And it won't be only his life he'll be risking, but the lives of many others as well.' I knew he was right, but I couldn't help feeling sorry for the poor young man. He had survived six months' strenuous training, eight or nine months if he were destined to be a radio operator, learning escape tactics, how to rid himself of handcuffs, react under torture and during an interrogation, handle explosives, make bombs, live off the land, shoot at a moving target. And Beaulieu was far from being a holiday camp. This young Dane had survived all that yet, because of one stupid slip on a moonlit evening, he might not be allowed to carry out his mission, that mission he had worked so hard to achieve.

When confronted with this dilemma, Buck, taking into account all the other reports on the student's capabilities from the different schools he had attended, sometimes said: 'They've learned their lesson. They won't make the same mistake again.' And he allowed them to go. But I don't know whether the other section heads were so understanding.

After leaving Beaulieu every agent had to go on an exercise lasting ninety-six hours simulating a situation similar to those he would probably encounter once behind the lines. He would be given a temporary English 'cover story' – as opposed to his real cover story, to be used when he was in the field – and told to go to a certain place and carry out different tasks. Harry Rée had to 'clock on' at a factory for a few days and glean as much information as he could from the conversations going on around him while he worked. Another had to spend a couple of days in a hotel with some mission or other to accomplish, without being told that a beautiful young woman, sent for the purpose, would do her best to pick him up on the first evening and try to discover what he was up to. His task was to resist her charms, which were apparently considerable. He said he did!

Yet another agent faced with the same temptation reported on his return that on the evening he arrived in the town he'd been sent to he had wandered into the bar of the hotel where he was staying to be greeted by a beautiful woman who had turned round on her bar stool as he approached, smiled and addressed him by his real name. He had affected not to hear, but she had pursued him, whereupon he had explained that she must be mistaken and introduced himself using the false name with which he had signed the hotel register. They had spent that evening, and perhaps even that night, together. In fact, they were inseparable during the few days he was in the town on his mission. But on his last afternoon, during a passionate embrace in a wood where they had gone for a romantic meander, he had pretended to strangle her. When she was in extremis, her eyes bulging and her face blue, he had released her. Once she had regained her breath he told her to be sure to mention in her report to Colonel Buckmaster that she'd been murdered in an isolated wood by an unknown man! Realizing that her ruse was up, she had confessed that she had been sent to trap him and that she was, in fact, the sister of the commandant of one of the schools where he had trained. In spite of her close shave with death, they parted friends. But, all the same, she must have denounced him to the police because, as he was leaving the hotel later that afternoon to return to London, the police were waiting for him. He was apprehended and taken into custody. Seeing the black

Maria waiting outside, a group of middle-aged housewives had gathered at the hotel entrance. When he was led, in handcuffs, to the waiting police van the unfortunate student was obliged to submit to their jeers and abuse. 'You should be ashamed of yourself,' they cried. 'Why aren't you in uniform? Our brave boys your age are risking their lives to keep criminals like you safe.' The jeers rang in his ears as he was bundled inside the black Maria. Proof that one shouldn't always judge by appearances!

Chapter 11

One Saturday afternoon I accompanied a young major, a future agent, to London. The major's false address, where he was supposed to have a flat, was in Ashley Gardens, near Westminster Cathedral. Since he wanted to be sure he could answer any questions about his 'home' accurately, off to Ashley Gardens we went. It was there that I think I lived the most terrifying half-hour of my life. The Blitz was peanuts in comparison. I had imagined we were going to stand on the pavement and gaze at the flat from the outside, or perhaps venture up to the fourth floor in the lift and take note of the front door. We had no authority to do anything else, to go any further. And even doing that could have looked suspicious had a neighbour happened to pass by. But these details didn't appear to worry him. Once we left the lift, he walked boldly to the door with 'his' number on it and picked the lock, then strolled inside and looked around, gazing admiringly at the elegant furnishings. Had we been caught inside the flat, SOE would no doubt have denied all knowledge of us and, temporarily at least, left us to our fate. We would have been accused of illicitly entering with intent to commit a burglary, and taken into custody.

Hoping against hope that the owners wouldn't suddenly appear from the bathroom or come up in the lift, I stood trembling on the landing outside the door, ready to bolt in a cowardly fashion, and wait for him outside on the pavement, should such an eventuality arise. But he turned round and waved his arm in my direction. 'Don't stand there dithering,' he said. 'Come on in.'

'But . . .' I stammered.

'No buts,' he said firmly. 'Just come in and shut the door.' So I did! It was terrible. Instead of a quick peep, he bounced on the beds, opened kitchen cupboards, turned on the bathroom taps, examined the lining of the curtains and the chintz covers to find out where they came from. 'Ah . . . Sanderson's,' he said, turning to smile knowingly at me. 'I thought so.' I didn't care if they'd originated in the flea market, I just wanted to get out. In the sumptuous drawing room, while the perspiration poured down my back in torrents, he played a chord or two on the beautiful baby grand piano cluttered with photos in silver frames of exotic people wearing trailing ball gowns and tiaras, clutching fans made of feathers, and military gentlemen with twirling moustaches, their chests bristling with medals, lethal-looking swords hanging at their sides. Every time the lift rose I shut my eyes and prayed, convinced that we were both headed for Wormwood Scrubs.

After what seemed at the time to be about ten years, but couldn't have been more than half an hour, he turned to me with a smile, saying: 'Right. Now I'll take you to the Bear Garden. It's where I used to go with the rugger team on a Saturday night when I was at Cambridge.' By that time I was in shreds and felt that the only place I was fit for was the casualty department of the nearest hospital. He may, or perhaps he may not, have sensed my imminent collapse. Taking me by the arm, and ignoring the lift, he raced me down the four flights of stairs, perhaps to strengthen my wobbly legs or to get the blood, which had certainly stopped flowing, thrashing about in my veins again.

But I was young and once out in the street I soon recovered. When we got to Piccadilly Circus he bought me a bunch of violets from an elderly flower-seller wearing a shawl and a black straw hat. She was sitting, with a large basket full of the dainty flowers on her knees, on the steps of the statue of Eros, which was now boarded up. 'Lovely vi'lits,' she called, as we passed. 'Buy a bunch for the pretty lady, mister.' So he did. It was all very romantic. And I enjoyed the Bear Garden which, in spite of its strange name, turned out to be a delightful basement pub some-where near Piccadilly Circus. We got back to Beaulieu very late that night because, in order to make up for my earlier terrifying experience, he took me to the theatre.

I don't know what mission this particular agent had been assigned. All I know is that he had to go down to Wales for the weekend. While there he was arrested by the police and locked in a cell for the night – until HQ had him released. He had made a silly, but understandable, slip. His real name was Wilson, but his temporary cover name was Wilmot. When signing the register at the hotel where he was to stay, the first three letters being the same, he had made a fatal mistake and automatically written 'Wilson'.

The local police were always warned, in a roundabout way, to be on the lookout for these prospective agents facing their final test, without any details being revealed as to their real identity or mission. I believe the police were warned to look out for enemy agents whom the authorities suspected to be in the area. In this case the police only had to ask to see the agent's identity papers and check them with the signature in the hotel register in order to be suspicious and arrest him. Throughout the war we were all obliged to carry identity cards. They were as much a part of our daily apparel as our gas masks. We would never dream of going anywhere without first hitching over one shoulder the cardboard box holding the gas mask which most people – certainly most women, I'm not sure whether men were so fashion-conscious – encased in an attractive cover. Identity cards were usually carried inside the gas-mask case, so as to be sure to always have them on hand.

There had certainly been other reasons why the police had been able to arrest this future agent. Perhaps he also had succumbed to the charms of another 'Mata Hari' working for F Section who had been sent to seduce or trap him, and had then denounced him. Perhaps he had been given a mission to break into a building, retrieve documents or seek information and been caught in the act. All these suppositions were possible. Whatever it was, he was arrested and spent a night in a police cell, furious with himself for being caught. But, even so, he must have passed the test, because he was parachuted into enemy territory two months later.

Chapter 12

Time and distance must take away the edge of pain because, as I look back, I cannot help remembering the 'good' times: and there were some good times. There was the unity we felt during those traumatic years, when we were all together fighting for the same cause, a unity which sadly evaporated with the end of hostilities. And the wonderful people I met. These memories weave together to make up the tapestry of my life.

I think the war brought out the best and the worst in all of us. It certainly brought out the best in those young men and women who were so ready to sacrifice their lives in order that we might be free today. But it also changed those who remained behind. The war honed us, burned away the dross, made us realize and value the things in life which were really important, often the simple things which today in our world of plenty many take for granted, or ignore.

During the war hardly a day passed without our hearing of someone who had lost a loved one. We lived so closely with death that every new day was precious, a gift from God. We had so little, we were willing to share. People left the tube stations and air-raid shelters in the early morning to discover that the row of shops they always went to for their meagre weekly rations had disappeared under a pile of bricks in the night. The local hospital had been reduced to a heap of rubble. They no longer had a home, a school, an office. Then those whose homes were still standing usually said, 'Salvage what you can from the rubble and come to us. We'll fit you in somehow.' I'm sure the war hastened the beginning of the breakdown of the rigid English class system. There was an atmosphere in London at that time which I had never felt before and sadly have never experienced since. A closeness, a togetherness. The barriers of race, colour, religion and class seemed to have disappeared. We were all united, fighting together for the same cause.

Life went on. It had to. The war lasted nearly six years. People married. Those agents married. In this age of opulence, it might be difficult to believe that the best present anyone could give a girl who was about to be married was a few clothing coupons. What a change from the lists we receive with our wedding invitations today!

On the day before her wedding, I remember asking a friend of mine what she was going to wear. 'Oh, Mother's lent me a dress and a hat she wore to a wedding in the summer before the war. My aunt gave me coupons to buy a pair of shoes, my cousins have used theirs to offer me gloves and a handbag. And I've cashed in mine for a nightie and some underwear.'

'But it's January,' I exclaimed. 'You'll freeze to death in a summer dress.' She laughed.

'No, I won't. Grannie's lending me her fur coat. I'll be fine.' She was marrying an agent who was about to leave on a mission. He was supposed to have three days' leave, but in the end they only had twenty-four hours.

'Oh, Sally,' I cried, putting my arms around her when she

returned to the office the day after her brief honeymoon ended. I was almost in tears, knowing how she must feel. 'It's so hard to have to say goodbye after only twenty-four hours, isn't it?' She smiled, but only with her lips. The smile didn't reach her eyes, which reflected a deep sadness and the trace of recently shed tears.

'You can live a lifetime in twenty-four hours,' she said quietly. Then, shaking off her melancholy, she dimpled and added with a mischievous grin: 'Provided you don't sleep.' The slight tension electrifying the air between us abruptly disappeared, and we burst out laughing.

Anyone who has ever been in love knows that wonderful feeling of gently floating on a cloud to another world where the sun always shines, the grass is always green and life is perfect. It must be difficult to imagine nowadays what it is like to be terribly in love and know that all you have is twenty-four hours. I think those wartime marriages were as God meant marriage to be. They were truly marriages made in heaven. The moments they shared were so precious that each one sought only the other's happiness. They wanted a cameo of a perfect love which they could carry with them during the long months, perhaps years, when they would be apart.

After the war some people said that it was selfish of agents to marry, knowing the dangers they faced. But I can't agree. We all faced dangers during the war, from the blackout, the air raids, the lack of food and medication, etc. Admittedly those agents' chance of survival was infinitely less than it was for most of us. But I think marriage gave them a stability they might not other-wise have had, preventing them from doing foolhardy things and taking unnecessary risks. They knew they had someone who loved them, who was waiting for them, that there was a future for them once the conflict was over. They had a reason to survive, and return.

Many women working in SOE had their hearts broken, and I was no exception. On the eve of my nineteenth birthday I fell madly in love with an agent who had just returned from a mission. Oddly enough, he fell in love with me. I never understood why or what attracted him to me. He was charming, handsome and twelve years older than I: he must have met many more attractive, more sophisticated, more elegant women than I. But it was love at first sight, an irresistible pull one towards the other. I'd read about it, every young girl had, but I didn't believe it ever really happened except in Hollywood or between the pages of glossy magazines. Yet it happened to me. Our idyll lasted three months. Then he left on a last mission, assuring me that he was a survivor and would come back and we could be together again: grow old together.

The day Bill left we had lunch together in a Chinese restaurant in Soho. Just the two of us. It was the first time I had tasted Chinese food. Although we both knew that it would be our last meeting for perhaps a very long time, the last time we would be together, it was not an emotional lunch. We carefully kept emotion out of it. Bill talked about his family. He told me about his mother, who had died of a sudden heart attack when he was on his last mission – he had arrived back just in time to attend her funeral; of his elder brother, who had been killed at Dunkirk – and produced snapshots of his two young orphaned nephews, of whom he was very fond. I thought what a good father he would make. Among the snapshots was one of him with a beard, his blond hair almost down to his shoulders, taken when he came out of hiding. I asked him if I could have it. He seemed amused by my request. He smiled and gave it to me. I cherished that photo and kept it at the back of my wallet until one afternoon on Interlaken station a few years ago when my wallet was stolen out of my handbag. I only discovered it was missing when we were approaching Basle, the frontier town between France and Switzerland, and the inspector came to check the tickets. I was left to cross the border with no ticket and no identity papers. It took some explaining. I had hoped that whoever stole it would keep the money and return the wallet, or at least its contents. But they never did. It was the only photo I ever had of him.

After he left I was handed a letter he had written to me. It was a beautiful letter. He gave me his father's name and address, which was his home base, and asked me to get in touch with him. I never did. Perhaps it was discretion on my part, but more likely shyness. I still couldn't understand why, out of all the women Bill had met, he had chosen me.

That afternoon after our lunch together he left me at the door of the office. I don't think we even said goodbye. Then, with a smile and a wave, his hand raised to his maroon beret in a final salute, he leapt on a bus. It was the last time I saw him. I was left with a little cameo of a perfect love. Perfect, perhaps, because it had been so brief.

But that was life during the war. One took the rough with the smooth, eagerly grasping happiness with both hands. We lived the fragile moments to the full . . . and hoped for the best. It was all we could do. And, should our worst fears be realized, we picked up the pieces and carried on.

Some of my friends married when their future husbands in the Armed Forces were on embarkation leave, about to sail to an 'unknown destination', either the Middle or Far East. And that was hard. Five days was the most anyone in the Armed Forces could hope for as marriage leave; often it was only three. To have to part from your young husband after such a brief spell, knowing that it would be a very long time, probably not until the war ended, before you would meet again, was heartbreaking. But those brides had the consolation of knowing that, although far from home, their husbands would not be alone. They would be travelling with friends in their regiment, or squadron, or on board ship, comrades who would often be in the same situation as themselves. The wives left behind could track their husbands' journeys by listening to the BBC's bulletins or watching the Gaumont British newsreels which usually went out several times a day before every cinema programme. And once their husbands arrived at their 'unknown destination', the destination became known, and they could follow the regiment's or the ship's movements through these same news channels. They could write to them, giving them family news, telling them how much they loved them, how much they missed them, knowing that the letters would be delivered. And hopefully they themselves would receive letters in return. They might not arrive very frequently, and often only in batches, and would certainly be censored, but at least there would be some communication. They were not completely cut off.

The anguish they felt at parting was acute, but it was different from that of a woman who married an agent, because, once he had left, and been infiltrated into enemy-occupied territory, all communication between them ceased. He went alone, cut off from all he held dear.

Chapter 13

The refusal of MI6, and others, to cooperate with, or even to recognize the existence of, SOE resulted in lives being lost unnecessarily, since operations under the auspices of SOE were often duplicated, causing mayhem and confusion. A classic example of this is the Frankton affair, the story of the 'Cockleshell Heroes', an incredible feat, orchestrated down to the last detail by Major 'Blondie' Hasler of the Royal Marines. It involved more than six months' secret, intensive training, in which twelve marines took part, and only four survived. It was a tremendously daring and courageous venture, where loss of life could so easily have been avoided had the SOE agents planning the same operation scheduled for the following night, but to be carried out from inside the port of Bordeaux, been involved, or even been informed of the canoe intervention planned to take place from the estuary, which had been authorized by 'Combined Ops'.

On Remembrance Day 1942, the submarine *Tuna* slid down the Clyde, carrying with its crew six canoes and twelve Royal Marines commandos. On an evening early in December, ten of the marines were lowered in five canoes into the dark, swirling waters at the mouth of the Gironde estuary. The remaining two, unable to disembark with their comrades since their canoe had been damaged en route, returned to Scotland with the *Tuna*.

The mission of the ten remaining commandos was to make their way, silently paddling their canoes by night, to the port of Bordeaux and place limpet mines under the six German warships anchored there. Five days later, only Blondie Hasler and his crewman Sergeant Bill Sparks were still alive. Two marines were drowned on the first night; four others managed to make it to the shore, after their canoes capsized: two were arrested on landing, the two others managed to get away but were later caught. Although in uniform, and therefore entitled to be treated by their German captors as prisoners of war, all four were shot. The two remaining marines, Bert Laver and Bill Mills, who had lost sight of Hasler's canoe some days before, made it alone to the entrance of the port of Bordeaux, where they then linked up with Hasler and Sparks, who had already arrived. They managed, with Hasler, to place the limpets, but Laver and Mills were captured and shot.

Blondie Hasler and Bill Sparks hurriedly scuttled their canoe and escaped. But they were soaking wet and totally unprotected. They no longer had any supplies, money or change of clothes, and more than once had to resort to stealing food in order to remain alive. Had it not been for the charity of the occasional French farmer on whose door they dared to knock, they would certainly have been captured and executed like their fellow marines. As it was, knowing no one and not speaking French, the two of them made a horrendous journey on foot by a circuitous roundabout route to avoid towns and villages and crossed the Pyrenees at night. They finally arrived back in England late the following April, almost six months after their departure.

In September 1942, unaware of the Combined Ops venture,

Buck sent orders to Claude de Baissac, organizer of the Scientist *réseau*, to make preparations to go into action against the shipping in Bordeaux harbour. Charles Hayes, a demolitions expert and sabotage instructor, was parachuted into the *réseau* on 26 November 1942 to prepare a complicated series of limpet attacks on the blockade runners (German destroyers) anchored in the Gironde; a large amount of ammunition arrived shortly afterwards. De Baissac had an extremely efficient local agent, Jean Deboué, a wealthy self-made man who owned the Café des Chartrons situated right on the quayside, a wonderful 'lookout post', which served as de Baissac's temporary HQ. The ammunition, which had recently arrived from London, was hidden in the cellars of Deboué's country house at Lestiac. The entire Deboué family was involved in the operation, since Suzanne, his eighteen-year-old daughter, acted as de Baissac's courier.

Deboué also had many contacts among the workers at the port and had recruited some who worked on the quayside and others who actually worked inside the ships doing repairs and were therefore in a key position to place explosives in a place where they would do the greatest damage. The whole operation was highly organized and had been meticulously planned. There were about fifty local recruits involved and, with the saboteurs actually working inside the ships and not outside, as Hasler was obliged to do, the sixty pounds of explosives Hayes intended to use would have been more than enough, and could have inflicted far more damage on the warships had it taken place. Sadly, the damage Hasler and his team inflicted on the warships was minimal, and, with the usual German efficiency, within a few days it was easily and swiftly repaired.

Scientist's operation, which was ready and about to take place when the marines' Operation Frankton aborted it, would have been carried out more efficiently and been far more successful. Instead, Claude de Baissac and his team, who were gathered, prepared and waiting to attack, were left angry and confused when they heard these sudden explosions coming from the blockade runners in the harbour. It would also have spared the useless loss of young lives which the Hasler operation had incurred. In addition, Mary Lindell's escape line, which would have taken Hasler and Sparks, the only two survivors, through Tarbes and into Spain and would have been quicker and safer, began only three hundred metres from the port. Had they known of its existence and used it, with luck Hasler and Sparks could have been back home in England in time to celebrate the New Year!

The complete story of the 'Cockleshell Heroes' is told in Paddy Ashdown's book *A Brilliant Little Operation*, published in September 2012, and in a documentary based on the book which was televised in November 2011, with Lord Ashdown giving the commentary.

But the story does not end there. Early on the morning of 14 October 1943 the Deboué family and Charles Hayes were at the house in Lestiac, upstream from Bordeaux, where the ammunition, parachuted in for use in the operation against the blockade runners, was still stored, when Madame Deboué noticed Germans prowling around the gardens and approaching the house. The family alerted, they stationed themselves at an upstairs window and began firing. Hayes and the Deboué son held the enemy off for about three hours, firing until their ammunition ran out, by which time Charles Hayes had been badly wounded. Suzanne apparently held up his right arm when it received a bullet in order to enable him to keep firing. And when he was also hit in the leg and bleeding profusely he sat on a chair, and Suzanne held up his left arm, his right arm now being useless, to enable him to reach the end of the ammunition.

Madame Deboué, also wounded, got out through a back door but was later captured and taken to a prison hospital. Escaping from there, she wandered in the vines near the village for days, refusing to go back to Lestiac, since both she and her husband had been convinced that all the villagers were collaborators. She was discovered by the local priest, who took her in and cared for her until the end of the war. Jean Deboué, Charles Hayes and Suzanne were captured. Jean Deboué was sent to Buchenwald concentration camp, from which he returned, minus a leg, an embittered man. Charles Hayes was executed, probably at Gross Rosen, in August 1944, and Suzanne, who had refused to answer any questions put to her by the Gestapo, was sent to work in a German officers' brothel, from which she returned at the end of the war, not surprisingly, also very bitter.

Although there was a sixteen-year gap in their ages, Suzanne had fallen madly in love with Hayes, who had promised to come back to Lestiac after the war and marry her. She did later marry and have a family, but remained convinced that Charles Hayes would one day return to make her his wife. Refusing to believe that he had not survived, she pined for him for the rest of her life.

When he was researching his book, Lord Ashdown went down to Lestiac to meet Suzanne, by now well into her eighties, and being cared for by her son, Yves Leglise, named after Charles Hayes, whose codename was Yves. Her son warned him that his journey might be fruitless, since his mother was losing her mind. But Paddy went all the same. On his way back to London he stopped over in Paris and came to lunch with us when he told us about his visit.

Suzanne had cowered in a corner, refusing to speak to him. 'But, Maman,' Yves had pleaded, 'this gentleman has come all the way from England just to see you.'

But her only response was to glower at Paddy and say, 'He's not English. He hasn't got an English face.'

'That's probably because I'm Irish,' Paddy laughed. But she wouldn't be cajoled, insisting that he was German, convinced that he was a member of the Gestapo come to arrest her. Paddy had asked Yves if there was anything his mother particularly liked which he could bring her. 'She loves macaroons,' Yves had told him. So Paddy offered her the macaroons he had brought. She apparently grabbed them and stuffed them into her mouth all at once, terrified lest anyone else in the 'concentration camp' should snatch them from her hand. Paddy later heard from Yves that his mother had sunk deeper and deeper into dementia and one day had escaped from the house and disappeared. Was Suzanne searching for her lover? She never forgot Charles Hayes, or gave up hope, refusing right to the end to believe that he was dead, convinced that he would one day come back and marry her. All attempts to find Suzanne or her body have now been abandoned. A tragic family . . . or just another casualty of war!

Sadly, Suzanne Deboué was not the only person who had been unable to pick up the pieces after the war and face reality.

Every year at Valençay, where we meet to commemorate the memory of those F Section agents who did not return, Mlle Fontaine, a sad, pathetic figure, used to join us. I never saw Mlle Fontaine smile. She always came to the 'Brits' dinner' held in an old *auberge* the evening before the ceremony, and always provided the wine. And very good wine it was. She was brought by a couple who were devoted to her and cared for her until the end of her life. He was a chef and his wife a nurse, and every year they drove Mlle Fontaine to Valençay for the commemoration.

When we gathered in the bar before dinner Mlle Fontaine used to drift in, her eyes searching the assembled guests for a new face. When she spotted one she immediately latched on to him or her, waving under their noses a faded sepia photograph of a young man. 'Do you know my fiancé? Did you ever meet · him? Can you tell me where he is?' she would plead.

Most of us could give her the answer. But it wasn't the one she wanted to hear, and she would drift on to the next person, holding her faded photograph. Jean Renaud-Dandicolle, her fiancé, had escaped to England in 1943, been recruited by F Section and trained as a radio operator at the same time as Marcel Jaurent-Singer. In 1944, as 'René', Renaud-Dandicolle was parachuted into France near Caen. On 7 July a detachment of German soldiers was seen surrounding the farm where 'René' and a few members of the *réseau* had spent the night. René gave the order to disperse, but only one of the men managed to dodge the German gunfire and escape. René, together with the farmer and his wife who had sheltered them, was captured, taken away and never seen again. In all likelihood they died of their wounds, but since their bodies were never found, there was no actual proof of death.

Marcel Jaurent-Singer, who went to visit Mlle Fontaine when he returned to France and kept in touch with her, said she was an intelligent woman who had held an important post in local government. He is convinced that she knew perfectly well that her fiancé was dead and would not return. She was informed of this years earlier. I only met her in later life, after she had retired, when she was a pathetic figure living in the past, like Suzanne Deboué, refusing to face reality, clinging to the hope that she might one day find someone who could give her news of her fiancé's whereabouts. Perhaps, living alone after her retirement, she had let herself slide into this fantasy world, convincing herself that Renaud-Dandicolle was still alive, out there somewhere waiting for her, if only she could meet the person who could give her news of his whereabouts.

One year her 'couple' arrived alone, but they still brought the wine. Mlle Fontaine had sunk into dementia. The following year they came to tell us that she had been taken to a nursing home, where she could be given professional care. She has since died: a sad, lonely, pathetic woman. A wasted life, in fact.

As I have already remarked, we cannot know in advance what

our reactions will be if faced with tragic circumstances. Some survived, some didn't and became merely 'casualties of war'.

Could Mary Herbert be put into this category? Perhaps not. She had arrived by felucca at Cassis on the south-west coast of France on 31 October 1942 together with Odette Sansom and George Starr. Mary was sent as a courier to Claude de Baissac's Scientist *réseau* in early November shortly before the aborted operation on the German blockade runners in Bordeaux harbour. But a few months after her arrival, de Baissac was recalled to London for rest and debriefing. He left without knowing that Mary was pregnant by him. The pressures and tensions agents in the field laboured under meant that there were many unofficial 'love affairs'. In most cases these affairs were not serious and rarely came to anything once the agents returned to base. In Mary's case, it was apparently deliberate. She was thirty-nine years of age when she arrived in occupied France and realized that time was running out for her. And she wanted to have a child.

When Mary's condition became obvious and she was no longer able to carry out her duties, Lise de Baissac looked after her until Claudine (after Mary's codename) was born, after which Lise returned to London. One morning, while sitting up in bed in Lise's flat, feeding her baby, Mary was surprised by the Gestapo, who burst into the room and arrested her. Claudine was placed in an orphanage and Mary was taken to Gestapo HQ. She succeeded in convincing them that she could not possibly be an SOE agent since she had just given birth to her daughter, sticking to her cover story that she was a widow whose husband had abandoned her in Alexandria – her knowledge of Alexandria and the fact that she spoke Arabic gave authenticity to her story – and in the end they believed her and let her go. They had mistaken her for Lise, the agent they had really come to arrest.

She managed to find baby Claudine and, with the help of two

old ladies Lise had introduced her to, found accommodation in Poitiers with a couple who agreed to take in her and Claudine as lodgers. There she laid low until she left for England. When she returned, Claude recognized the child as his and married Mary. But it was a marriage of convenience in order to give Claudine a name, an arrangement which suited them both until 1960, when they divorced. For their daughter's sake, in spite of the fact that Claude later married, they remained in close contact, and Claudine remembers having a very happy childhood, loved and cared for by both her parents.

Mary never remarried and in January 1983, at the age of seventy-nine, she was found hanging from an apple tree in her garden. She left no note and had given no signs of being anxious or depressed, and there was no obvious reason for what appeared to be her suicide, though both Claudine and her cousin Clothilde, Claude and Lise's niece, another Mauritian now living in Paris who has become a friend of mine, vehemently refute the idea. Unfortunately, although they both refuse to believe that Mary committed suicide, they can offer no other explanation. It would be interesting to know what the doctor who signed her death certificate thought.

But the story doesn't end there. Only a few weeks ago, at a reception in London, I was introduced to a young man whose face seemed familiar, but I couldn't immediately place him. 'This is Claudine's son,' I was told. What a bombshell. Then the penny dropped, and I exclaimed: 'You look exactly like your grand-father!' He was the image of Claude de Baissac at the time he had married Mary Herbert. The young man smiled, then told me his story. He had been adopted at birth by a wonderful couple who gave him not only their name but also a very happy childhood yet didn't hide from him the fact that they were not his birth parents. But it wasn't until he became a member of the Special Forces Club in 1990 and saw photographs of both Lise and Claude de Baissac on the wall that he began to wonder about his real mother and to ask himself whether there might be some family connection between himself and these two famous agents, since the name on his birth certificate was 'Jean de Baissac', not a common name in England. But it wasn't until 2009 that he seriously looked into his true parentage. That year he met Claudine in Los Angeles, where she had lived for the previous fifty years, and learned that not only was she his mother but that he was indeed Claude de Baissac and Mary Herbert's grandson.

What a series of revelations! He is now interested in tracing all his 'lost' Mauritian relatives and was anxious to begin his search by contacting my friend Clothilde. So when I returned to Paris I excitedly rang her to give her the news of her long-lost cousin – and almost gave her a heart attack! 'But Claudine never had any children,' she protested. Then the story came out.

Claudine was very young when her son was born, studying ballet in London with high hopes of becoming a ballerina. I don't know why she gave up her child: perhaps because of pressure from her mother, who disliked the idea of a scandal in the family, or perhaps because it would have been difficult to continue her career and look after a baby at the same time. Whatever the reason, he was adopted at birth. Not long afterwards Claudine was involved in a car accident and very badly injured, which ended her hopes of a career as a dancer. Did she ever regret giving up her baby now that she had been obliged to give up her career? One cannot help wondering. She later married an American and left for the New World. But she never had any other children.

Her son, who since their meeting is now in regular contact with his mother, is shortly coming to Paris to meet some of his new-found Mauritian family living here. The revelation has caused a tremendous stir, not only with those members of his family living in Paris but also with those in Mauritius, and the telephone lines between the two countries have been buzzing non-stop ever since the news broke: they are all dumbfounded by it. Like her birth parents, Claudine would obviously have been a good recruit for SOE had the occasion arisen, since she clearly knew how to keep her mouth shut and, in a way, live a double life. Once again an SOE story proves the veracity of the old saying: 'truth is stranger than fiction'.

I think the women agents who survived mostly recovered. Yvonne Baseden, who at over ninety is now very frail, is able to talk calmly about her traumatic wartime experiences: being arrested, tortured, imprisoned first in Dole, and finally, in August 1944, in Ravensbrück concentration camp, where she remained under appalling conditions until repatriated the following April. The only moment in her story when she shows any emotion and seems upset is when she talks about her organizer, Gonzague de Saint-Geniès, and remembers how he took his life rather than risk giving away information to the Gestapo and thereby betraying his friends.

Nancy Wake was another one of F Section's larger-than-life, colourful characters who, once the war ended, seemed to survive life in peacetime, seemingly putting the past behind her and embracing the future with open arms. Nancy was a New Zealand-born Australian journalist married to a French business-man. They were living in Marseilles, her husband's home town, when France fell. Nancy immediately went to work organizing an escape line across the Pyrenees into Spain for downed Allied pilots and escaping British prisoners – until the Germans got wind of her activities. Urged by her husband, with whom she was very much in love, to leave the country and make her way to England, with his help she escaped into Spain by the same route, leaving Marseilles only a day before the Gestapo came to the house to arrest her. Her husband denied all knowledge of her whereabouts or her clandestine activities, whereupon he was arrested in her place and taken into custody. When he refused to speak he was terribly tortured and, according to a priest who was in the prison cell next to his, on the night before he was executed his back was so raw from the beatings he had received that his kidneys were exposed. Knowing that he was to be shot the following morning her husband managed to tap a message through the wall of his cell to the priest, who gave it to Nancy when she returned to France after the war, hoping to be reunited with the man she loved. 'Tell Nancy that I love her and that I didn't betray her,' it read.

It is perhaps not surprising that when Nancy returned and learned of her husband's terrible end she is reputed to have said, 'I love killing Germans.' At first, I hesitated to put this comment onto these pages: it could portray her in such a hard, cruel light, and Nancy was neither hard nor cruel. But very recently I met, quite by chance, an Australian who had been one of Nancy's great friends, and he put the remark in context. He told me that, there no longer being anything to keep her in Europe, after the war Nancy had returned to live in her native Australia, where she frequently spoke in schools about her wartime exploits. He often accompanied her on these speaking engagements and, one afternoon, when she had held her young audience spellbound for almost an hour and a half, a young teenage girl, of obvious German extraction, got up and challenged her, remarking: 'You once were heard to say that you loved killing Germans. Is that true?' There was a deathly silence in the audience, followed by an embarrassed shuffling of feet.

Nancy looked at the girl sadly, shook her head and replied, 'You silly girl. I don't hate Germans. I have been many times to Germany, where I have two German godchildren and many German friends.' She paused and looked straight at her. 'But I hate Nazis. And all they stand for.'

This hatred of the Nazis had been born before the war, when Nancy was Reuters correspondent in Paris. On an official visit to Germany in 1938, when she was travelling with a group of foreign journalists, the bus had passed through a village where Nancy noticed what looked like a large Ferris wheel, with people attached to it, turning round and round. When she asked the guide what was happening he glanced out of the window of the bus and replied dismissively, 'Oh, they're only Jews!' At that moment an intense hatred of the Nazi element in Germany was born, and she vowed to do something to stop the massacre.

Nancy was an agent who thrived while carrying out her clandestine activities and was perfect for the work she had been chosen to do. She didn't know the meaning of fear, was never arrested and was called by the Germans 'the White Mouse' because she always managed to slip through their fingers. George Starr, a man not given to over-enthusiastic comments about a woman's charms once remarked, possibly echoing the thoughts of countless other men who didn't express them vocally, that Nancy was the sexiest woman he had ever met.

She admitted in her daring, audacious way that in the field she had had a German officer as a lover. 'Of course, I shall have to kill him,' she was heard to remark at the height of their affair. And she did. Not personally. She betrayed him, which led to his execution. She could be a warm, loving, loyal friend but also ruthless when the occasion demanded. I don't know how she felt about his death but I do know of one case where she had to pronounce the death sentence, which upset her deeply. She had made friends with a Dutch girl who was a member of her Resistance group. There were not many women in these Resistance groups, and if one met one with whom one felt an immediate bond it was a bonus, and a very special relationship. Sadly, the 'Dutch' girl turned out to be not Dutch at all but a German agent working for the Abwehr. When her true identity was revealed, she was sentenced to death by the members of the *réseau*. Nancy did not carry out the execution herself, even

182

though she had pronounced the sentence, but she was there to witness it. When the girl was led out and passed Nancy, she spat on her. Then, just before the bullet which ended her life rang out, she looked at Nancy and said, 'I am a patriot too.' It was perhaps this last remark which upset Nancy more than the loss of her friend.

I last spoke to Nancy a couple of years ago. It was on her ninety-sixth or ninety-seventh birthday, I can't remember which. She was back in England, having married an Englishman, a former pilot. Now widowed for the second time, she was living in a Star and Garter home in Richmond. Tim Buckmaster, Buck's son, was with her to celebrate and help her cut her cake. Tim had apparently mentioned that he had seen me the month before, and Nancy had said she would love to see me again. So Tim rang me up. At first she seemed to be just as perky as ever, but after a few minutes the conversation faded out, and the line went dead. Tim picked up the receiver. 'She's dropped off,' he explained. Perhaps at ninety-six or ninety-seven I shall 'drop off' in the middle of a sentence too!

Nancy died just two weeks before her ninety-ninth birthday and had a very impressive memorial service in St Clement Danes, a beautiful old church in the Strand opposite Australia House. It was a wonderful ceremony: three robed clergy officiating, a magnificent choir, a flurry of FANYs showing an impressive number of distinguished guests and top brass to their reserved seats. The Duke of Edinburgh had sent his equerry to represent him, and I recognized Viscount Slim sitting at the other end of the pew with a lady MP whose face I knew, but whose name I couldn't recall, sitting behind. An assortment of military attachés in full regalia from various embassies read the lessons or said the prayers, and the Australian high commissioner gave the address. The church was packed to the rafters, with many celebrities present. But it wasn't Nancy! The Church of England wasn't her 'cup of tea' at all. I don't think any church was. Had her spirit been present, hovering over the elaborate ceremony, she would have roared with her raucous, throaty laughter and doubtless used some unrepeatable epithet to describe the occasion.

When the service ended the high commissioner gave a splendid reception, and, as we left the church and crossed the road to Australia House to attend, the bells began to ring, peal after peal of joyous chimes, which seemed to echo and reverberate all over London. A wonderful goodbye and a wonderful tribute to Nancy, an exceptional woman, the most decorated woman in the Second World War. I think Nancy would have liked that.

On 10 March 2013 Nancy's ashes were taken to Verneix in central France, where she had operated during the war and where she is still remembered. They had been brought from London by Brigadier Bill Sowry, the Australian defence attaché. In a splendid ceremony attended by the local mayor, the military attaché from the Australian embassy in Paris and two FANYs who had come especially from London, as well as other local dignitaries and ordinary folk, a few who remembered Nancy, Brigadier Sowry scattered her ashes in the woods outside Verneix. 'We are here today to pay our respects and give her the tribute she deserves,' he said. During the splendid lunch, hosted by the mayor, which followed, the mayor said that this little part of France was now also part of Australia and announced that later in the year a plaque would be unveiled in the centre of the village in memory of Nancy. But it was far from being a sombre occasion. Nancy was a woman who loved life and lived it to the full. She also was very partial to an early-morning gin and tonic. So, after her ashes had been scattered, there was, as she had requested, a drinks reception in the town hall.

Eileen Nearne was made of a different fibre. She was tough in one way, but fragile in another, surviving arrest, hard labour and two concentration camps. But once she returned to peacetime life her life seemed to go to pieces, and it was a long time before she was able to recover her former joie de vivre.

Born of an Anglo-Spanish marriage and brought up in Boulogne-sur-Mer, Eileen was the youngest of four children, three of whom – Jacqueline, Eileen, or Didi as she was always known, and Francis – became F Section agents. We know very little about her brother Francis's activities. Her elder sister Jacqueline, the more beautiful of the two beautiful sisters, seems to be the one who is better known. Like Eileen, Jacqueline trained as a radio operator; she had one successful but uneventful mission, from which she returned unscathed. Didi's exploits were much more spectacular, so spectacular in fact that she took a long time to recover from them, whereas in 1946, immediately the war ended, Jacqueline went on to begin a successful career with the United Nations in New York.

As 'Rose', Didi landed by Lysander in March 1944 to work as a radio operator for Wizard, a small réseau outside Paris. She was arrested the following July, just after transmitting. In spite of telling a fairly convincing story about being a governess, she was given the 'bath treatment', imprisoned at Fresnes and then sent to Ravensbrück and on to Torgau, the nearby concentration camp. Here she was sent to work in the fields, dig roads and work in factories, before being sent back to Ravensbrück and ending up at Markkleeberg. Managing, with another woman prisoner, to escape from a death march, she was finally discovered by the advancing Allied armies hiding in a belfry and taken into care. But on her return to England after the liberation in 1945 she was in such a state of physical and mental shock that she was hospitalized for over a year. During this time she painted abstract pictures in vivid colours, which might have given a glimpse into her mental state at the time. When she was discharged she took up a position as an auxiliary nurse in a hospital and after her mother's death in 1950 returned briefly to France, but came back to England after a few months and went to work as a care nurse in an old people's home. This position she held until she retired.

Although the two sisters were close and kept up a steady correspondence, their lifestyles were very different, and each remained independent of the other, though occasionally Jacqueline did help Didi out financially. Didi recovered from her horrendous experiences and was able to live what one might call a normal life. In her later years she became a recluse, knowing no one, having few visitors, living a solitary life with her cat in a flat in a seaside town in Dorset. She kept very much to herself, and the neighbours seemingly knew nothing about her. When she was found dead from natural causes in 2010 she was about to be buried in a pauper's grave when the authorities, searching her flat seeking some evidence of next of kin, stumbled across her medals, an impressive array, and her citations and realized that she was a 'forgotten war heroine'. Then, all the stops were pulled out. She was given a wonderful funeral, with standard-bearers, flags, magnificent wreaths, lots of top brass and splendid newspaper coverage.

But it was too late for Didi. She had died alone and, apart from her niece who lives in Spain and visited her when she could, forgotten. What a pity the authorities had not enquired of her welfare while she was still alive. In Didi's case, taking into account all she had suffered, it was surprising that her mind had not flipped. Some people can endure the most dreadful mental and physical torture and survive.

The terrible massacre inflicted by the German Army in Oradour-sur-Glane is well known, but few people realize that this was not the only village in France to experience such a dreadful fate. Castelnau-sur-l'Auvignon in the Gers also suffered, and another massacre took place in St Pathus, a village outside Paris, shortly afterwards. After the liberation of Paris in August 1944 twenty-year-old Jeannine Pernette, having recently qualified as a nurse, decided to follow the retreating German Army in order to tend any wounded they had left behind. She went to St Pathus, east of Paris – where Henri Diacono had been radio operator for the Spiritualist *réseau* – with a jubilant lorryload of résistants, who believed that only a handful of Germans, whom they could engage and easily defeat, remained in the area. But when they arrived they were met by an entire contingent of German soldiers, and a fierce battle took place. The résistants, hopelessly outnumbered, were quickly defeated, leaving many casualties on both sides. Jeannine was busy tending the wounded when the remaining résistants, together with the villagers, were lined up to be shot. Jeannine was with them when one of the Germans recognized her. 'Don't shoot her,' he shouted. 'She looked after our wounded.' On his testimony, her life was spared, and she was told she was free to leave. But she didn't leave.

'I am a nurse,' Jeannine replied with as much dignity as she could muster. 'I tend the wounded. I do not ask their nationality.' And she insisted on accompanying the wounded of both sides who were being loaded onto a lorry, in order to look after them on the journey to wherever they were going. She did not know whether she was heading for Germany or not!

After a long, tiring journey they arrived at the Red Cross camp at Armentières-sur-Brie, to the east of Meaux, where the French were put into prison camps and the Germans taken to a German military hospital. Jeannine thought that she was now free to leave and return to Paris to resume her nursing career. But she was arrested and sent to Metz and later imprisoned in the fortress at Queuleu, where she remained until the following April, when the Americans, together with Leclerc's army, liberated her.

After the war we became friends. Jeannine was a lovely woman, a typical *parisienne*, very slight, scarcely more than five feet tall. She died in June 2012, aged eighty-eight, and it was only at her funeral in a crowded church overflowing with magnificent floral tributes, and standard-bearers, with many dignitaries present, that I realized the extent of her bravery and learned of the decorations she had received, including the prestigious Chevalier de la Légion d'Honneur. Like all true heroines Jeannine was very modest and had hardly ever mentioned her dramatic wartime experiences.

A few years ago I met Honoré d'Estienne d'Orves's daughter, and her story both moved and impressed me. Her father was a regular naval officer who, when France fell, left his wife and family and escaped to England, where he trained and returned to France to organize a Resistance *réseau*. He landed on the coast of Brittany, a dangerous operation, since the beaches and the sea were heavily mined, and there was also a ban stretching the length of the coast forbidding civilians from going within twenty-five kilometres of the shore. So, even when they landed, agents arriving by this route were not 'home and dry'. On a pitch-black, moonless night the Royal Navy would bring the agent or agents as near to the coast as possible, where a fishing boat, usually manned by Breton sailors, would be waiting to take them ashore. The transfer in the dark was perilous and made more so because a sea which on that coast appeared to be as calm as a mill pond could suddenly erupt, causing violent waves to dash against the rocking fishing vessel, threatening to overturn it.

D'Estienne d'Orves landed safely one night and immediately set about organizing his *réseau*. But he was eventually captured, together with several of his men, and condemned to death.

On the night before his execution his wife somehow managed to get permission to visit her husband in his prison cell to say goodbye. 'I was eight years old at the time,' his daughter Rose, now a middle-aged married woman with a family of her own, told me, 'and my mother took me with her.' I was horrified.

'Wasn't it awful?' I asked. She smiled.

'No,' she replied, 'it wasn't awful at all. We weren't allowed to stay with my father for long, but we were able to say goodbye.' She paused. 'That evening I witnessed my father's courage and his calm and composure confronted with what was inevitable. And I also witnessed the love my parents had for each other, and the dignity with which both my mother and my father faced this situation. I think it taught me something which has stayed with me ever since, something I shall never forget. And perhaps the memory of that evening gave me courage when I later faced difficult situations in my own life. The following morning my father was taken to the fortress at Mont-Valérien and shot.' Mont-Valérien, where so many résistants were taken to be shot, stands on a hill in the shadow of a beautiful American cemetery where hundreds of US soldiers from the First World War lie beneath the impeccably kept white crosses. It is almost ironic.

Rose seems to have survived what can only be described as a traumatic experience for a little girl of eight. I don't know whether I would have had the courage to take my daughter, or whether I would even have been able to face such a situation with dignity and courage.

Stéphane Hessel was a Jew born in Germany who emigrated to Paris with his parents when he was eight years old. In 1939, at the age of twenty-two, he became a naturalized French citizen. In 1941, agreeing with neither the armistice nor the Vichy government, he fled to England and joined General de Gaulle's BCRA, the Free French intelligence service. He returned to France in March 1944 to organize communications in the run-up to D-Day but was arrested the following July by the Gestapo, having been denounced under torture by one of his fellow résistants. Given the 'bath treatment', he himself broke down and talked.

In early August, together with thirty-six other British agents, he was deported to Buchenwald. By October, twenty-seven of them had been executed. It was then that Yeo-Thomas, with the help of résistants working in the infirmary, devised his ingenious escape system. Unfortunately only three of the remaining prisoners were able to take part. Hessel was one of the lucky ones; Harry Peulevé was the other. They exchanged places with three prisoners who had died of typhus. But, like Yeo-Thomas, once on the other side of the barbed wire Hessel became separated from the others and, wandering alone in the forest, was recaptured. He said that when he was taken to the camp commandant, who told him that the penalty for escaping was death, he looked him in the eye and replied in his native language: 'What would you have done in my place?' The commandant, startled perhaps not only by the audacious question but also by being addressed in perfect German, finally agreed that he would have done the same. 'And yet you are going to execute me for doing what you admit you would have done,' Hessel challenged him.

This account is not reported in any official document so cannot be verified, but it was told to me by Maurice Southgate's daughter, Patricia Génève, who heard it from Stéphane Hessel himself when they met and lunched together at a Buchenwald commemoration. The commandant did not order Hessel to be executed, he sent him to Dora, the extermination camp, from where he again made an unsuccessful attempt to escape and narrowly escaped his punishment, death by hanging, when he was despatched on the death march to Belsen. Escaping en route, he made his way to Hanover, where he joined up with the advancing Allied forces.

The war over, Hessel returned to Paris and, on the surface, suffered no ill effects from his experiences. He plunged into politics and went on to have a brilliant career, culminating in being nominated as French ambassador to the United Nations. Small and slightly built, his bright eyes always twinkling with amusement, in 2013, at almost ninety-six, he was still very active – lecturing, writing books, and much in demand as a public speaker – until the evening of 26 February when, his diary no doubt crammed full of scheduled lectures, and his mind full of articles half-written or waiting to be written, he went to bed – and never woke up. One of the 'survivors', he died as he had lived, bursting with life to the very end.

Maurice Southgate was with Hessel on that convoy to Buchenwald. One of F Section's agents, he had been parachuted into France in January 1943 to organize the new Stationer *réseau*, from where he built up a network which stretched across the Limousin and as far south-west as Tarbes. He did sterling work attacking railway targets, power stations and aircraft factories, building up an army of 2,500 men. But the Gestapo were looking for him. He was eventually arrested on 1 May 1944, badly beaten up by his Gestapo interrogators and taken to avenue Foch, where the torture continued. When he arrived there, John Starr, a fellow agent who had apparently defected to the Germans, was in the hall and greeted him by name. Southgate must have felt betrayed. But he affected not to hear or to understand, and in spite of being tortured he never broke. He, too, was then sent to join the convoy.

Southgate had had a traumatic time before joining SOE, having served with the BEF (British Expeditionary Force) at the beginning of the war. Evacuated from St Nazaire at the time of Dunkirk, the ship on which he was sailing, the *Lancastria*, was sunk by air attack with a loss of over 3,000 lives. But Southgate was a strong swimmer and managed to stay afloat until he was picked up by another vessel and brought back to England.

When Yeo-Thomas had to choose the prisoners who would be 'allowed' to escape, was he aware of what Southgate had gone through? I certainly thought he should have been a candidate for the group, possibly more so than Stéphane Hessel, who was younger, unmarried and had had so little time between his arrival in France and his arrest to prove his worth. I couldn't help wondering how Yeo-Thomas made his choice. Admittedly, it was a very difficult decision to make. There were nine agents from the original convoy still alive: six of them had to be left behind. One might almost say six had to be sacrificed. Did they draw straws? I knew Yeo-Thomas; he was a very kind, fair-minded man. Why he chose Hessel and left Maurice Southgate to face almost certain death baffled me for a long time. And I couldn't help wondering what Southgate's feelings must have been when Yeo-Thomas, his compatriot and comrade-in-arms, chose a BCRA agent and not him to be one of the escape team. The entire group had been under threat of execution since their arrival, and those remaining would be even more vulnerable once news of the escape broke.

Then I met Patricia Génève, Maurice Southgate's daughter, and I saw the whole picture in a different light. She and her brother have since become friends of mine and have told me that they knew virtually nothing about their father's wartime activities. He refused to talk about them or give his children any indication of what he had done. That is not unusual: many agents were reluctant to share their experiences and by doing so relive the clandestine role they had played. From what Patricia told me at the time I had the impression that her father was remote, almost withdrawn at times, and could be very taciturn. And I asked myself: was it unresolved anger or bitterness at what he must have felt to be the unjust choice Yeo-Thomas had made? Then Patricia and her husband, Marc, who has taken a great interest in his father-in-law's wartime activities, enlightened me.

'It was Papa's choice,' Patricia said. When talking with Hessel she had discovered a lot she didn't know about her father. Hessel told her that on arriving at Buchenwald, Southgate had discovered a group of Polish prisoners to whom he had taught English in London before being infiltrated into France and he immediately gravitated towards them. 'Don't worry about me,' he had apparently told the other members of the group, 'I can manage. You look after yourselves.' The Poles had hidden him and kept him safe when the others were executed. So there was no question of his being part of Yeo-Thomas's escape plan.

'Professor Foot wrote that your father came back a broken man, which would not be surprising considering what he had suffered. And you say your father could be remote, almost withdrawn,' I queried. 'Do you think he was suffering the after-effects of all he had gone through during the war?'

'Not at all,' Patricia smiled. 'He may have been "broken" when he returned, but he had certainly recovered by the time my brother and I were born. He wasn't really remote, just naturally reserved, like all Englishmen. As far as we could see, there were no unpleasant after-effects. When the war ended, he went home to his wife and picked up their life where he had left it in 1939. My parents were married in 1937, but because of the war they had to wait ten years before they had children, so when I arrived in 1947 and then my brother was born shortly afterwards, he was immensely proud and took a great interest in us. It was always Papa who plaited my hair every morning before I left for school. And when our daughter was born he and she were inseparable. He took her everywhere with him. No, Papa seemed to be a very happy, contented family man.'

'If you don't think he suffered any consequences from his wartime activities, why do you think he was reluctant to talk to you about them?'

'I may be wrong,' Patricia's husband interrupted, 'but I have the feeling that my father-in-law was still working "behind the scenes". He had connections with the British embassy and was responsible for gathering the names and keeping in touch with British nationals living over here whom he should inform and arrange for their evacuation if ever there were another crisis. This was during the "Cold War" period.'

It seemed to be a plausible answer. There is no official verification of this, but if it were the case that Southgate had never really abandoned his wartime training, then he wouldn't be the only member of SOE to do so!

I only met Maurice Southgate once, at a lunch party here in Paris in the mid-1970s, well after the end of the war. He seemed normal enough, charming in fact, without any outward signs of psychological damage.

Without making comparisons or wishing to be critical or judgemental, but remembering the traumas some people had lived through and survived, one cannot help wondering whether, as far as Suzanne Deboué and Mlle Fontaine are concerned, wallowing in what can only be described as their self-imposed misery and refusing to face up to reality was really a luxury they indulged in and may even have enjoyed. Had they perhaps lacked what we used to call good old-fashioned 'guts', and should they have been told that, even though knocked down by life's blows, they needed to 'pick themselves up, dust themselves down and start all over again'?

We can only conclude that some survive, and some do not.

Chapter 14

SOE was not a large organization, and recruitment was mainly by word of mouth, therefore it could pick and choose those it accepted for training. Perhaps that was its strength. Unlike de Gaulle, SOE was not interested in a prospective agent's present or former political opinions. The general was terrified of a communist takeover in France once hostilities ended, and refused to consider any candidate who had, or had ever had, communist leanings. SOE looked for qualities in a candidate such as intelligence, discretion, determination. To them, these were what mattered. Their political opinions, past or present, were of no interest. When recruiting future agents they also needed to be sure that they had not volunteered for the 'wrong reasons' – to escape from an unhappy marriage, a broken relationship or perhaps from a desire to commit suicide as honourably as possible. This was the case of George Millar.

George returned to England after serving in the Middle East to find that the wife he adored had left him for a naval officer. In despair, he volunteered for SOE. But during the long training he met and fell in love with the woman he later married, and no longer wished to 'honourably' end his life: he now had a reason to live! He could have turned back, changed his mind, refused to leave: but he didn't. He was parachuted, in uniform, into France after D-Day as a member of a 'Jed' team, to help the resistance and to stir up trouble. He managed to do it very well and survived. At one time he lived for several hours – or was it days, I can't remember – in a sewer! I believe Michel de Bourbon-Parme, a descendant of one of the last kings of France, was part of George's team. Michel was incredibly handsome. I thought he was twenty-two but apparently he was a hardened veteran of nineteen. He'd put up his age and volunteered at sixteen, there being no way the authorities could check his age, since his birth would have been registered in France.

George looked unbelievably English, one couldn't mistake him for anything else, with his blond hair, blue eyes and fresh complexion so, before he left, his hair was dyed black. But when he returned it had grown and now half was golden and half black – he looked like a two-flavoured blancmange! After the war George wrote a highly successful book entitled *Maquis*, recounting his experiences as a 'Jed'. I typed the first rough draft, about a dozen pages, which he later worked on and expanded into his bestseller.

Some did inevitably 'slip through the net'. Perhaps Cecily Lefort was another one of them. An Englishwoman, she was married to a French doctor who, when France fell, despite her protests, insisted that she leave for England. But she was desperate to return to France and be reunited with her husband. She joined SOE and, after having trained as a radio operator under the codename 'Alice', was sent to work for Francis Cammaerts's Jockey *réseau* in the Drôme, far from Paris, where her husband had his consulting rooms. In June 1943, just as the Prosper group was about to explode, she and Noor Inayat-Khan arrived by

Lysander at one of Déricourt's chosen landing grounds outside Paris.

Was 'Alice' another one of Déricourt's victims? She may have been trailed, as Noor was trailed, from the time she arrived all the way down to Marseilles, her first stop before joining her *réseau* in the Drôme. 'Roger' said later that, after a very short time, he realized she was quite unsuitable for the work and, had it been possible, he would have had her sent back. According to him, she was very frightened and apprehensive about her mission, nervy, pessimistic, convinced from the start that she would not survive. Had she had some premonition, or perhaps a warning? She may well have contacted her husband before making her way south. We don't know with whom, if with anyone, she had been in touch in Paris. Sadly her fears ended by being justified: she was arrested three months after her arrival in France, tortured and finally executed at Ravensbrück.

How had she slipped through the net? I don't know. I do know that Buck often trusted his intuition, his 'feeling' about a student's capabilities, even when the instructors from the various schools they had attended gave an adverse report. Perhaps that was the case with Cecily Lefort. On the other hand, the reports sent back to him about Francis Cammaerts were far from reassuring. He was described as pleasant, hard-working, having an easy contact with the other students on the course, but totally lacking in the initiative and the necessary leadership qualities required of an agent. But, in spite of this, Buck backed him, and he left for the field. Full marks for Buck's intuition. Cammaerts returned from France covered in glory. He was one of F Section's finest agents.

Chapter 15

As already mentioned, the head of MI6 and his close associates disapproved of SOE. They didn't care for our guerrilla tactics. They resented this 'upstart' army composed of amateurs who behaved in a nasty, noisy, ungentlemanly fashion – making bangs, killing Germans – and they did everything in their power to frustrate and hinder SOE's efforts, sadly, themselves often resorting to 'ungentlemanly schemes' in order to achieve their goal. In this, they were ably assisted by General de Gaulle, head of the BCRA. Malcolm Muggeridge once remarked that MI6 and General de Gaulle's joint hatred of SOE was stronger that their hatred of the Abwehr (the German intelligence unit). And Winston Churchill was reported to have said that, of all the crosses he had to bear during the war, the Cross of Lorraine (the symbol of the Free French) was the heaviest.

In this tangled web of tensions, antagonisms and rivalries, one might almost say SOE's problem was that it did not belong to the Ministry of Defence, or the 'War Box', as it was then known. So, as we were not their responsibility, they did nothing to help us. We were the responsibility of the Ministry of Economic Warfare, not under the control of the British Military Intelligence Service, and answerable only to Winston Churchill. The Foreign Office could perhaps have helped or protected us, but unfortunately MI6 was an important player in their hierarchy, and MI6, disliking us so intensely, refused to cooperate in any way. They saw SOE as an upstart army seeking to usurp them. But they were wrong. SOE had no desire to usurp them. We were fighting a very different war from them, a war far removed from the velvet-glove policy of bona fide espionage.

SOE was Churchill's 'baby', and Churchill was the supreme authority. Since we were under his protection, as long as he was in power not even the combined efforts of MI6 and General de Gaulle were able to remove us from the scene. But, after the war ended, Churchill was no longer in power. At the general election in July 1945 he was ousted, and SOE lost its protector.

Unfortunately the spirit of unity and the *entente cordiale* that characterized F Section did not stretch to our links with General de Gaulle's BCRA. Although both organizations were working to free France from Nazi occupation and oppression, they did not work together. On the field level, members of F Section were on friendly terms with their opposite numbers in the BCRA. It was General de Gaulle who was the problem. Having refused to accept Pétain's armistice with the Germans, the general had decided to continue the fight from a base in England, prophetically stating in his now historic call over the airwaves of the BBC on 18 June 1940 that 'France had lost a battle, but had not lost the war', hence his idea that he was incarnating France, not a defeated nation, but a future victorious country.

At first, Winston Churchill admired de Gaulle's courage and determination. When Pétain signed the armistice with Hitler and France fell under German domination, he sent a plane to evacuate the general and his family to England. 'General, you are all alone,' Churchill declared. 'Well, alone, I stand with you.' ('Vous êtes tout seul. Eh bien, je vous reconnais tout seul.') On 2 August, on Pétain's orders, the Permanent Military Tribunal at Clermont-Ferrand not only stripped Colonel (acting General) Charles de Gaulle of his military titles and his French nationality, but also confiscated his property and condemned him to death for treason, for deserting his country for a foreign power in time of war. Churchill immediately gave both the general and his staff all the help and assistance they needed, not least by allowing him access to the French Service of the BBC.

But the talented team behind the BBC French Service's broadcasts to occupied France, composed mostly of well-known journalists, were treated with 'veiled hostility' by de Gaulle's staff. The general later faced strong opposition in London itself from many fellow countrymen who had initially supported him. They objected to his rigid, dictatorial attitude, and *La France Libre* and other non- (or anti-) Gaullist newspapers began to appear on the London news stands.

Strangely, the more dependent de Gaulle was on the British, the more determined and belligerent he became, behaving as if he were a head of state. It was therefore unavoidable that de Gaulle's relationship with Churchill would quickly deteriorate. Clashes between these two men, both with strong personalities, became more and more frequent and acrimonious. In 1943, after one of their violent exchanges, Churchill exclaimed: 'Look at this man. He's alone. He has nothing. He has no country. He has no army. Yet he behaves as if were as powerful as Stalin.' What the general failed to understand was that all he possessed he owed to Churchill, and that without Churchill he would be nothing. He appeared to have forgotten, or perhaps he preferred not to remember, the French saying 'Qui t'a fait roi?' ('Who has made you king?').

General de Gaulle was a fiercely proud, patriotic, chauvinistic man. He strongly objected to any interference by a foreign power in France's affairs and refused to allow English to be spoken at his HQ in Carleton Gardens. Any person crossing the threshold, should they not speak French, was obliged to go through an interpreter. This rule was absurd, since his second-in-command, Colonel de Wavrin, spoke perfect English, and most of his officers were fluent in the language of Shakespeare. Leo Marks, who frequently went to Carleton Gardens to instruct the officers in coding, said that he knew most of them understood what he was saying since he always introduced an amusing anecdote into his lectures, and they always laughed before the interpreter had got round to interpreting it.

In an effort to wipe out SOE and be solely responsible for organizing clandestine operations in France, de Gaulle allied himself and worked closely with MI6. He declared that any French citizen fighting under the British flag was a traitor sold to foreign interests, and that once France was again free, any French man or woman who had been a member of SOE would be court-martialled for having served with a 'foreign power'! Mercifully I don't think he carried out his threat.

The contemptuous name 'amateur bandits' by which MI6 referred to us was the brainchild of Claude Dansey, the famous 'C', head of MI6. It is even reported that he delighted in SOE's failures, and rejoiced at the collapse of the Prosper *réseau*. Can it be true that Dansey rejoiced at this barbarity, this terrible tragedy? What is true is the dislike, which almost amounted to hatred, between Dansey and General Gubbins, head of SOE. Unfortunately, neither made any attempt to disguise the fact, which must have warmed the general's heart.

A few years ago I was horrified to read, in a British Sunday newspaper, the Maurice Dufour story. According to an investigation conducted by Michael Bilton, a journalist, Dufour, a Frenchman working for MI6, was posted in 1941 as a supervisor at a Vichy government internment camp for British prisoners of war. From there he organized the escape to Britain of dozens of downed RAF crews. Believing the Germans to be suspicious of his activities, Dufour fled to Lisbon, and from there was flown to England.

According to the journalist, Dufour, having cooperated with British Intelligence, was brutally tortured by BCRA security agents in the basement of 10 Duke Street, one of de Gaulle's headquarters in London. Bilton claimed that several other Frenchmen were submitted to the same ordeal. According to the records, Paul Manuel, after being tortured, committed suicide in this cellar. But the distinguished forensic scientist Sir Bernard Spilsbury, who performed Manuel's autopsy, declared that suicide was not the cause of death. Manuel had been strangled before being strung up from a pipe in a corner of the cell in order to simulate suicide. After these facts came to light, the cellar at Duke Street where these atrocities had been committed was officially closed by the investigating British authorities. But the British government, wishing to avoid further conflict with General de Gaulle, is said to have covered up these crimes.

Whether this story is true, I cannot say. Many French people I have spoken to doubt it. But Bernard Spilsbury was a well-known and highly respected pathologist, perhaps the most respected pathologist of the time, so it is difficult to imagine that the story is a complete fabrication.

The general, who, from what the account stated, was aware of these crimes committed in, and against, a country which had protected and sheltered him, appeared to have forgotten that France was a defeated country, now under the German boot. He ignored the fact that if he had an organization, any power at all, it was because Britain, the 'foreign power' he so fiercely opposed, had granted him refuge, given him an HQ from which to operate and fed, clothed and financed his Free French Army and the members of his organization.

Michael Foot's official history of SOE was published in London in 1968, and the French translation completed shortly afterwards. But its publication was banned by the general. As far as he was concerned, SOE had done nothing. It was his set-up, the BCRA, which had organized and carried out all the resistance in France. Consequently, the French edition of *SOE in France* only appeared on the shelves of bookshops in France in 2008.

When the general returned in triumph to France in 1944 he tried to crush any mention, and erase any memory, of SOE; and his treatment of some SOE agents he met was despicable.

'Hilaire' – George Starr – had been infiltrated by felucca and fishing boat into south-west France in December 1942, from where he made his way to the foot of the Pyrenees to set up the Wheelwright *réseau*. He had worked tirelessly for more than two years, arranging drops of materials, recruiting and training Resistance members into a fighting unit, always one step ahead of the Germans. He was never caught. In a victory parade before General de Gaulle he marched at the head of his army of 1,000 résistants. This did not please the general. He was incensed that an Englishman should lead a group of French fighters, so, when Starr was presented to him after the ceremony, de Gaulle ordered him to leave France immediately. In other words, he was summarily told to get out! Starr apparently replied, '*Je vous emmerde*' ('To hell with you'). Stunned that anyone could speak to him so disrespectfully, de Gaulle gasped, 'I beg your pardon?', whereupon Starr replied, 'General, have you been away from your country for so long that you've forgotten the language?', turned on his heel and walked away.

Roger Landes, who headed an army of 5,000 résistants, was given by the general two hours to leave France. 'Xavier' – Richard Heslop – organizer of the Marksman *réseau*, a remarkable man, but then they all were, who had become almost a legend in the Ain, where he operated, was given by the newly formed administration thirty-six hours to leave the country. Yet another agent, who had worked in the Bordeaux area, was pushed forward by his Resistance group to be introduced to General de Gaulle, who was making a victory tour of the area. He was told by the general in no uncertain terms that he was not welcome in France and given ten minutes to leave. He apparently asked the general if he might reply, was granted permission, said, 'Merde,' and walked away.

General de Gaulle was very afraid his countrymen would believe that it was not his 55,000-strong Free French force alone which had brought about the final victory and the liberation of France, and he did everything in his power to suppress, if not erase, the memory of SOE – ably assisted, no doubt, by MI6. When he became president of France in 1945 de Gaulle showered medals and decorations on his BCRA agents and office staff, even down to the typists. But SOE agents were ignored. They received nothing – and were even denied pensions.

As far as I was concerned, the French Ministry of Defence has consistently refused to grant me the status of veteran. The reason given? The UK, where SOE operated, was not a war zone, and SOE not a fighting unit! But the real reason is that I was a member of SOE. Had I belonged to the BCRA, the general's organization, I would have been given a veteran's card over twenty years ago.

However, out of the blue in March 2013 I received an un-expected call from the veterans minister's PA inviting me to lunch with the minister, Monsieur Kader Arif, at the Ministry, when he would be pleased to give me my veteran's card. After almost twenty-two years of constant refusals I couldn't believe my ears. So I accepted his invitation. It was a delicious lunch in a beautiful setting with the only woman general in the French Air Force and a delightful French naval captain present. To my astonishment I was given the seat of honour at the table, on the right of the minister. He was charming and not only gave me my card, but also an enormous bouquet of flowers and the Médaille des Volontaires de la Résistance as well. It was a special card, I learned afterwards, which goes with the medal. I know that this is thanks to that 'little girl' who almost suffocated under the blanket when listening to the BBC during the war. Sabine, who is now a doctor of law, has become my friend. Since she often works in close collaboration with the government, I know she spoke to the minister about my frequent requests and refusals. Sometimes life works in strange, mysterious ways!

Radio operator Henri Diacono, who had behaved so courage-ously in the face of danger, received his Legion of Honour decoration when he was in his seventies. And then it was not pinned on his chest by the French president at the Elysée Palace, but by a former F Section agent, during a simple ceremony at the Free French Club in Paris.

Despite their outstanding acts of bravery, no member of SOE was named to the prestigious roll of 1,038 Resistance heroes known as the Compagnons de la Libération, even though General Eisenhower had stated in May 1945 that the disruption of enemy rail communications, the harassing of German road transports and the continual, increasing strain placed on German security forces throughout Europe by SOE's organized resistance played a very great part in our complete and final victory. Military historians credit SOE, along with other Resistance fighters, with delaying the arrival of large numbers of German reserves for the Battle of Normandy, but SOE was not honoured in the com-memoration of the battle in 1994.

This dismissive, disdainful, one might almost say cruel treat-ment, this refusal to acknowledge or even believe the British contribution to the Resistance and the Allied efforts towards the final liberation of France, extended even to local French-born members of the Resistance, recruited by SOE on the ground. It was not only British-trained agents who were ignored, but also de Gaulle's own compatriots, those who had responded to his call from London in June 1940 to resist and join in the struggle against Nazi Germany. They had indeed answered his call and resisted but had joined SOE – the 'wrong side'.

What the general could not deny, though he made every attempt to prevent the facts from being known, are the following figures. They were quoted, during a conference held at the residence of the British ambassador to France in December 2008, by Jean-Louis Crémieux-Brilhac, who had been a close adviser to General de Gaulle when he was in London. He is now not only the best-known but also the official historian of clandestine operations from England during the Second World War.

> 480 F Section agents were infiltrated into occupied France by the RAF. Of them, 30 were women, 15 of whom never came back, executed, after being horribly tortured, in one of the infamous concentration camps – usually Ravensbrück. Altogether 104 F Section agents gave their lives for France whilst on missions. This figure does not include those agents who disappeared without trace and whose fate is still unknown.

> 329 high-risk pick-up and landing operations (224 successful, 105 failed), with 446 passengers landed and 655 (including rescued air crews) flown to England.

> 470 résistants were picked up and 211 agents landed by the Royal Navy.

> 425,000 résistants were trained into fighting units, and equipped with tons of supplies, parachuted in by the RAF: Sten guns; millions of cartridges; mortar rounds;

hand grenades; radio transmitters; combat boots, clothing; food; and enormous sums of money.

The RAF also dropped millions of tracts over occupied France.

During the Normandy landings in June 1944, SOE's prior undercover operations and sabotage behind enemy lines saved the lives of thousands of Allied soldiers.

But in November 1970, General de Gaulle went to his grave still denying SOE's immense contribution to the liberation of France – and even its very existence.

PART TWO

The Aftermath of War, the Dream – and the Reality

Chapter 16

The war ended and the 'peace' began. But not the peace we had dreamt of during those turbulent years. The Second World War changed everything beyond recognition. Some former agents who had performed heroic acts never really recovered from their traumatic experiences. They found it hard to accept this 'peaceful' world, which was far from the peace they had fought for, and to which they had hoped to return.

Many agents received very poor post-war treatment. For the most part they were ignored, not only by General de Gaulle but also by the British authorities which had sent them into the field; their value and their contributions to the war effort were never recognized.

Lise de Baissac, Yvonne Baseden and Pearl Cornioley had to wait until they reached a ripe old age before receiving their wings. Lise had hers pinned on her breast at ninety-nine! She died shortly after. I remember seeing a photograph of the ceremony, Lise standing to attention, as slim and upright as ever, smiling happily as the wings were at last fastened to the lapel of her jacket. Pearl and Yvonne were in their eighties before they received this deserved recognition. In February 2012, one month after her ninetieth birthday and more than ten years after receiving her British 'wings', Yvonne's wartime activities were finally recognized by the French authorities. At a private ceremony in London, where Yvonne now lives, Admiral Edouard de Coriolis, the French defence attaché, pinned her French wings onto her dress. But I don't think the French ever honoured in this way Lise and Pearl or any of the other F Section women agents who had parachuted into France.

Radio operator Henri Diacono, after having performed heroic deeds while working in occupied France, discovered on his return to London that he had been demoted from captain to lieutenant! And it was as a lieutenant that he retired. Perhaps it is not surprising that, when he was approached and asked to join Force 136 operating in the Far East, parachuting agents behind the lines into the Burmese jungle to fight the Japanese, he declined the offer.

Like Henri, Krystyna Skarbek, known as Christine Granville, was also poorly treated by the authorities after the war. A Polish countess who had carried out undercover work with her husband in her native country, she escaped to Egypt after her husband was killed, from where she was recruited by SOE's Cairo office and sent to England for training. She was parachuted into France to work as a courier for the Jockey *réseau*, where she carried out amazing and courageous acts of bravery. It was she who orchestrated the eleventh-hour release of Jockey's organizer, Francis Cammaerts ('Roger'), and his two companions from a prison cell in Lyons, where they were awaiting execution at dawn that morning. When the war ended, she was no longer able to return to her native Poland, where both her own and her husband's estates had been confiscated. Almost penniless, Christine was obliged to work as a chambermaid in a hotel, before taking a job as a stewardess on a cruise ship. In 1952, she was murdered: stabbed to death in the foyer of the third-rate London hotel where she lived.

Nancy Wake, who was awarded the George Medal and three Croix de Guerre with palm and one with star, the Médaille de la Résistance, the American Medal of Freedom and the insignia of a Chevalier of the Legion d'Honneur, the Order of Australia and the New Zealand Returned Serviceman Gold Medal, was the most decorated woman agent of the war. But when in 1997 Nancy left her native Australia and returned to England, she was obliged to sell her medals in order to live.

As in the case of Nancy, Christine and also Didi Nearne, many of the agents' contributions went unrecognized and were only acknowledged when it was too late. Impressive funerals were held, attended by high-ranking officials and bemedalled officers, but sadly that did not help the agents – by then they were beyond recognition – though the grieving families might have derived some measure of comfort.

Many returning agents found it difficult to settle down to life in peacetime. Trauma doesn't suddenly go away, it lives with you, maybe even colours the rest of your life. There was a psychological trauma as well as a physical one, and some committed suicide. I don't think the agents received any medical help; they were left to cope with their hallucinations, their nightmares, their flashbacks, their depressions . . . and their bewildered families. Their lives spiralled out of control, and many marriages suffered, some irrevocably. Other agents seemed to slip back easily into their former pre-war existence, with its normal relationships. It was a question of personality, a person's make-up, and in some cases the severity of their experiences. Like everyone else, those agents were individuals with their differing characters, and some were unable to come to grips with peace.

War had been so much part of our lives. We had cruised

along not thinking about tomorrow, not thinking about anything except the job in hand. For those agents in the field, their
mission would have been impossible if they had done otherwise.
We couldn't afford to stop and wonder what the future might hold
because, had we done so, we would have realized that for many of
us there would be no future We couldn't waste time speculating
on life after the war or lamenting the 'might have beens'. Then
suddenly it was all over. SOE was disbanded with undignified
haste, and we were all 'out on the street', wondering what to do
with the rest of our lives. A chapter had now closed, and we were
not sure what the next chapter held. Or even whether we wanted
to open it.

But one's war doesn't abruptly disappear from one day to the
next. People cannot suddenly turn the page on six years of their
lives. Even after the bunting had been removed, the patriotic
songs had faded, the blackout taken down and the streets were
once again flooded with light, the agents' wartime memories
stayed with them . . . sometimes for a very long time. Nothing
was urgent any more. Nothing seemed important. It was all over.
For some agents the war never left them. They realized that the
'new world', the world fit for heroes for which they had believed
they were risking their lives, was not going to happen.

The 'new world' we had fought to create and, once hostilities
had ended, stepped confidently into was not very different from
the one we had left behind in 1939. The old tensions, the rivalries,
the snobberies and the struggle for power which, if not absent,
had been only underground rumblings during the war, sprang to
life again. No longer united as a nation fighting a common cause,
society once again became fragmented, torn with the desire for
power and self-gain, and we became the 'me' generation. It was
hard for many who returned to realize that those who had stayed
behind, the 'chair-borne brigade', had climbed the ladder to success, while those who had risked their lives were left standing

with a foot on the bottom rung, obliged to start again. And, for some, bitter disillusionment set in.

At the time there were no psychiatrists, psychologists or counsellors on hand as there are today, waiting to treat victims of wartime stress. Or if there were, we didn't hear of them. When a difficult situation arose, or tragedy struck, as it so often did, we just picked ourselves up, dusted ourselves down and got on with life. We had no option. And perhaps it wasn't such a bad philosophy after all.

Had SOE survived, instead of being more or less annihilated, the files mostly destroyed by a 'mysterious' fire in December 1945, I think the authorities might have looked after returning agents, and they would have received better treatment. No one knows how or why, or in some instances even where, the fire started. Records don't seem able to agree on the exact location though it was most probably central London, possibly at the HQ in Baker Street. However, some hazard that it was at nearby Michael House, the property belonging to Marks and Spencer which had sheltered Leo Marks's team of coders. Some theories say it was arson. Others blame MI6, and still further accusations have been made that two officers weeding through the files carelessly threw a lighted cigarette butt into a waste-paper basket. All these theories are possible, though none can be proved. But suspicions were aroused at the time, and rumours circulated that it was not an accident.

Was this arson? A deliberate attempt to completely wipe out any trace of SOE's wartime activities? If so, who or what authority was responsible? One can only surmise. There is no proof. As it was, many were left angry, often embittered, by the offhand treatment they received. General Eisenhower said that the work of SOE agents had shortened the war by at least eighteen months. How many civilian and armed forces lives did that save? And the late Professor Michael Foot estimated that, when at its highest, the total strength of SOE was that of a weak Army division, and added that no single division in any army exercised one-tenth of SOE's influence on the course of the war.

For women who had lost loved ones the post-war period was very difficult. As long as the fighting continued, no one had had time to mourn. But when peace came, and they saw their friends' husbands and fiancés returning, they suddenly came face to face with reality, and the brutal truth hit them. Their men were not coming back.

I think that for women with children it must have been the hardest. Their children saw the parties being organized for returning dads. And when the long-awaited day finally arrived, they watched as their friends excitedly hung across their front doors or garden gates improvised banners made out of old sheets with 'Welcome Home Dad' painted in gaudy letters: and they knew it was a celebration which would never take place in their home. They saw their friends playing ball in the park with their fathers, and they knew their fathers would never come home to play games with them. They would never again swing from his hand on a Saturday afternoon as they went off together to watch a football match. He would not be there to cheer them on when they played in the school eleven, applaud them when they acted in their school's end-of-term play . . . or just be a father. That was something which was now denied them for ever. And those women had to bear not only their own pain, but a double pain. The pain, even the envy, they saw in their children's eyes when they watched families leaving on holiday or fathers and sons setting out on expeditions together.

Those women had to be father and mother at the same time. And sadly, I saw some of them lose their femininity. Especially mothers with sons. They realized that there was no father figure in the home, no man to be not only loving, but stern at times, and lay down the law, no role model for their boys to look up to and follow, and they almost forgot that they were mothers and became surrogate fathers instead. So the bewildered children sometimes 'lost' both parents.

Abraham Lincoln said: 'The only good part of a war is its ending.' Francis Cammaerts aptly remarked when it was all over – was it with bitterness or an ironic smile? – 'War achieves nothing.' And Winston Churchill summed it up, hitting the nail on the head, when he advised: 'To jaw-jaw is always better than to war-war.' How right they all three were.

Chapter 17

When the war in Europe ended, it left a desolate void for many people. Once the church bells had stopped clanging, the dancing and singing in the streets had come to an end, the shrieks of 'We want the King' coupled with the cheers of the crowds clamouring outside the gates of Buckingham Palace had faded, the street parties were over and the balloons and bunting had been removed, we came down to earth with a bump: and were confronted with peace. And many didn't know what to do with it. It was bewildering. All the landmarks had disappeared. People had lost their anchor, that prop which had kept them going, despite all the odds: now they had to face the reality of a country, often a life, devastated by war, which would need to be rebuilt. And they didn't know where to begin.

Men came back from the war believing they could take up their lives where they had left off in 1939, that the wives they had left behind would be waiting to go back to the domestic round they had followed in the 1930s. But for four or five years many wives had carried the weight of the responsibility of the family on their shoulders – they had had no option. They had worked outside the home, driving buses, working in factories, acting as special constables, fire-fighters, air-raid wardens, and some were reluctant to relinquish their new-found liberty. They had discovered independence and they didn't want to go back to being the 'little wife', waiting at home for their husband's return from the office each evening.

Other young women, dazzled by a uniform and caught in the heat of passion, had married hastily, sometimes after only a few days' acquaintance. It had happened with some SOE agents about to leave for the field. The uncertainty of anyone surviving the war had added an urgency to these marriages, a desire to grasp whatever happiness they could while they had the chance. It had been thrilling, romantic; the scent of danger and the proximity of death had added excitement to their passion, and they were unable to look beyond today: nothing was permanent, nothing lasting, and they had lived only for the moment. Later many realized that getting married had been one of those mad, impulsive things people did in wartime. Since no one knew whether they would still be alive the following week, or even the next day, the thought that marriage was not a step one took lightly, without reflection or forethought, which might later prove to be a mistake, didn't come into it. One grabbed happiness as quickly as possible, when and where one could, without considering the consequences, since tomorrow might be too late.

But with the end of hostilities, the handsome pilot with wings on his chest, the dashing young army or naval officer came home to them in an ill-fitting 'demob' suit, and many realized that their hasty marriage had been a mistake. This wasn't the man who had swept them off their feet, the glamorous daredevil they had fallen in love with. No one would notice him in a crowd; they would no longer be given the best table in a restaurant; her friends would not now glance at her enviously as she walked down the street with her handsome hero by her side. They had been in love with love, and the heart-stopping precariousness of life in wartime. The danger had been an aphrodisiac forcing them, blinded by passion, to snatch at happiness. But once peace came, many couples realized they no longer had anything in common. Some of these marriages survived after the war. But many didn't, and in the late 1940s divorce petitions, which ten years before had been something which only happened to film stars in Hollywood, blocked the law courts.

In June 1945 I was sent to work at SOE HQ in London, there no longer being any need for 'decoys' at Beaulieu. In early August, I received a letter from General Koenig commanding the FFI, the Free French Forces of the Interior, thanking me for my services, after which my time as a member of Churchill's Secret Army came to an end. I was left wondering what to do with the rest of my life. It was as if a vital part of me had suddenly been torn away, ripped out, leaving me wounded. No one had had time to mourn during the war, not openly. Now one had all the time in the world, but it was almost too late. We no longer knew how to cry.

My mother left Bath and returned to London when my father, after four years in the Far East serving with the Royal Navy, came home. When he turned up unexpectedly one Sunday evening in December 1944 on his way from Greenock, where his ship had docked, to his base in Portsmouth, he didn't recognize his only son. Four years in a teenager's life can bring about startling changes. When he had left, Geoffrey had been a little boy, but on his return, he discovered a man. It also worked the other way round. My cousin's small daughter crept into her mother's room in the early hours of the morning and suddenly shrieked, 'Mummy, wake up! There's a man in your bed!' Her father, whom she scarcely remembered, had returned home from the Middle East during the night.

Although she rarely voiced them, I know my mother had had fears about my father's survival. William Joyce, the American-born British traitor, nicknamed Lord Haw-Haw, had defected to Germany and throughout the war years had been actively involved in Goebbels' Political Warfare broadcasts. He frequently announced, on his radio programme from Berlin, *Germany Calling* – 'Jairmenny carling', as he pronounced it, affecting what he must have imagined to be an upper-class British accent – that the *Adamant*, my father's ship, had been sunk. The ship – and my father – survived, but our family had been decimated.

In June 1940 my twenty-year-old cousin had gone down at Narvik with his first ship, the *Glorious*. My father had been in Narvik at the time the *Glorious* was torpedoed and met the few survivors who were brought ashore. Jack was not among them. Although my father said that no one could have survived for more than a couple of minutes in those icy waters, my aunt continued to hope that after the war Jack would return. But when less than a year later her husband's ship was also hit by a U-boat, and his father followed their only son to the depths of the ocean, I think her stoic attitude began to falter.

It was Eastertime, and I was on holiday from school when we received the news. 'Clifford's ship has gone down,' my mother announced bleakly, her eyes scanning the letter. 'He's missing, believed killed. We must go to Eleanor at once.' She looked up, her eyes misty. It was late March. The weather had been grey and stormy for some days. 'No one could have survived in the Atlantic at this time of year,' she ended sadly.

When we arrived, my aunt opened the door to us, her face creased with pain, but true to the British 'stiff upper lip' tradition all she said was: 'Wasn't one enough?' and continued to present a brave face to the world. I cannot help thinking how much more natural, more healthy it would have been had she released her anguish in a torrent of tears and emotion.

221

Another cousin had survived Dunkirk only to spend his leave digging for his young wife after her block of flats received a direct hit on the night he arrived. Knowing that her husband was on his way home, and wanting to be there to welcome him, she had refused to go to the shelter when the air raid began. On the day which would have been their first wedding anniversary, his week's leave over, John rejoined his regiment, his frantic search for his wife having revealed only a torn fragment of her blood-stained nightdress. My aunt, my father's elder sister, had lost her husband, daughter and son-in-law, and my grandparents had lost their home: the home in which my father had been born.

So, coupled with the fact that food was still strictly rationed and would continue to be for almost another ten years, and in spite of the joy of the four of us being once again united as a family after four long years, Christmas 1945 was a rather sombre affair, though my mother did manage to persuade the butcher to give her a rabbit, which she roasted, and we pretended it was a turkey. And she somehow made a Christmas pudding out of carrots!

Shortly afterwards, my brother went to Sandhurst, one of the first post-war intakes, and two and a half years later we said goodbye to him when he left for Singapore. So, for our family, life continued to be a reminder of war . . . and goodbyes.

That dreary February day when Geoffrey left, the bands were playing, the kilts of Scottish regiments were swinging and the crowds were cheering and frantically waving as the troops were marched through Waterloo station to board the train which would take them to Southampton to embark on their long sea voyage. But Geoffrey was not among them. He was to travel alone, only leaping into his compartment when the guard blew his final whistle. The Green Howards, the regiment he was joining, were already in Malaya, fighting a desperate war. That afternoon, as the train departed and the crowds slowly dispersed and walked away, many wiping their eyes, some openly weeping, Waterloo station, reminiscent of so many heart-breaking goodbyes, resembled a scene from a First World War film. I was feeling miserable at the thought of possibly losing my little brother to a sniper's bullet in the steamy jungles surrounding Kuala Lumpur. The age gap between us had become less significant as we left our teens behind, and we had become very close. And I couldn't help thinking, 'Not again': we had fought a war to end all wars, or so we had believed. What had it all been for?

Now that I have sons of my own, I cannot help wondering about my mother's feelings when she watched the train slowly draw away from the platform taking her only son, 'her baby', on a journey to fight a bloody war which could go on for years. Being British, like my aunt, and true to her Victorian upbringing, she said nothing: she showed no emotion, unable to release the anguish which must have risen deep inside her. And I followed her example. Perhaps it would have been better had we both given vent to our feelings and cried together, as so many leaving the station that afternoon were doing.

Thanks to 'Vinegar-face', I had been forced to decline the offer I had received during the war to work at the BBC, but, sensing my disappointment at what I considered to be Vinegar-face's callous refusal, the head of the French Service had assured me at the time that there would be a job for me once hostilities were over. So, at the end of August 1945, when I left Baker Street, I presented myself in his office. I don't know whether he remembered me or whether he was even particularly pleased to see me but, being a 'gent', he kept his word and took me on. And so began a few interesting but turbulent years, years when the environment, and the turbulence, were not so very different from my time in SOE. I had left the French Section there to continue my life in another French Section, equally exciting, though in a less dramatic way, and peopled with equally fascinating characters.

I was sent to work first of all in the News Room, a hive of

frantic activity, especially when the hour for the regular bulletins to go on the air approached: telephones ringing non-stop and the clatter of old-fashioned Royal and Remington typewriters going hammer and tongs as we became submerged by the news items being sent up from the Central News Desk. On receiving the papers the sub-editors hastily glanced through them, selected the relevant ones, then rushed across the corridor to us and practically hurled the papers at the seven or eight translators already hard at work. Sometimes a 'flash', an important item of news, arrived after the newsreader had left for the studio. Then it was action stations all round. The 'flash' was speedily translated, usually with a sub-editor standing over the poor translator, who was desperately typing, dictating the flash to him or her at the rate of knots, while a secretary hovered in the background ready to grab the page the second it was ripped from the typewriter and hurtle with it down the four flights of stairs to the basement studio. No time to wait for the lift.

One particularly hectic evening a secretary, who should have been hovering, was writing a letter to her current boyfriend. Thoughtfully sucking the end of her pen, she looked up and enquired of the tense sub-editor standing impatiently over the poor harassed translator: 'Does passionately have one or two *n*s?' I thought he was going to hit the roof.

We worked in shifts round the clock. When we were on the 'dawn shift', preparing the early-morning bulletin or press review, we began at around three in the morning. Since in the 1940s few people had cars, we had to rely on public transport, which didn't run all night. So we used to arrive at Bush House at some time during the evening, go to 'Bed Bookings', collect our sheets and pillowcase from a rather austere lady called 'Phil', who lived in a cubbyhole on the ground floor, off reception, and go to a communal unisex dormitory for a few hours' sleep. We didn't get much. People were coming and going all night and snoring in a variety of languages. Just as one was dropping off, a commissionaire would tiptoe in and shake the person in the next bed, it could be a man or a woman, and whisper: 'Your call, sir/madam. It's two o'clock,' or three or four or whatever time they had asked to be roused. Groans and creaking of bed springs would follow as the person shook themselves awake and heaved themselves to the floor.

On the other hand, when finishing a 'shift' at some impossible time of the night, if one lived in London, a BBC car would take one home. The chauffeur had orders to always wait until his passenger had actually entered his or her house or block of flats and closed the door before driving away. It was all very civilized.

Being on the late shift, I walked into the News Room one afternoon to find Lise de Baissac busily typing. We looked at each other in surprise. Introductions were made, and we mentioned that we had already met, without going into further explanations. It was only later, when we escaped to the canteen, that we were able to take a trip together down memory lane.

One day, Buck appeared in the corridor. He had been asked to do a series of talks and had come have his paper vetted before recording the first one. Once again we neither of us mentioned where we had previously met. When he came as usual to the office one evening I noticed him chatting amicably to a girl I vaguely knew. She was secretary to one of the 'high-ups' in the Section. Her name was Rée, but I hadn't liked to ask her whether Harry Rée, one of F Section's better-known former agents, belonged to her family. Harry was a great friend of Francis Cammaerts. I think they had been at university together, and both been schoolmasters before the war. It was Harry who had introduced Francis to SOE. So, after Buck ambled off to the recording studio, I tentatively approached her. She looked up and smiled when I entered her office. 'Are you by any chance related to Harry Rée?' I ventured. She gave me a curious glance.

'Yes,' she replied. 'I'm his niece. Why do you ask? Do you know him?' The ice was broken, and I told her I had met her uncle during the war, but didn't elaborate further. The secrecy rule still held fast! I glanced down at her left hand. She was wearing an engagement ring. 'He's Czech,' she explained. 'But there's no news!' I gathered that her fiancé was an agent, but one who would probably not come back. She obviously realized that I knew more than I had revealed about 'the racket'.

When the series of talks Buck had been commissioned to give ended, he held a Christmas party in one of the larger base-ment studios at Bush House. It must have been in December 1947. He invited former F Section agents to gather there and send greetings over the air to the Resistance workers they had recruited in the field in France. I think it was on that afternoon that I realized that human reactions can often work in reverse. Having heard so many courageous stories, usually modestly told, from returning agents during their Y9, and been amazed at their incredible bravery in the face of terrible danger, I came across the reverse reaction. I can only compare it to the elephant and the mouse syndrome.

I was one of the last to arrive in the studio for the party and was met by Odette Churchill, who as Odette Sansom had been Peter Churchill's courier in the Vosges area. 'We are 'aving a terrrrible time with Peter!' she whispered, her eyes rolling theatrically, and her delightful French accent more pronounced than ever. I raised my eyebrows in surprise. ''E is terrrrified,' she announced dramatically.

'What of?' I enquired, puzzled. I couldn't imagine Peter being terrified of anything. Odette looked at me as if I were a complete nincompoop, obviously thinking I should have immediately understood why he was afraid.

'The microphone!' she declared. 'We've 'ad to give 'im two stiff whiskies. And . . . look at 'im.' She pointed to where her husband was sitting in a far corner on the edge of a table, his knuckles white as he grasped its sides, literally shaking with fear.

I'm afraid I laughed. I couldn't help it. It was unbelievable that this highly decorated man, who had become almost a legend, after having dropped twice by parachute into occupied France, been infiltrated there by submarine and then survived a concentration camp, was nerve-racked at the thought of having to speak into a microphone. As I once heard a wise old Yorkshire farmer say, 'There's nowt so funny as folk!'

During the war, and in the immediate post-war era, Bush House, the home of the BBC World Service, was known as 'the best club in London'. It was staffed by multinational, often eccentric people not unlike those I had worked with in Norgeby House. The best brains in Europe were gathered there. As in F Section, at every turn in the corridor one met interesting people racing around in what appeared to be a great hurry. Like the Crazy Gang, they were all very pleasant and easy to get on with, which made my transition from one French Section to another remarkably easy. A friendly, but rather vague, member of staff was the poet Louis MacNeice, a strikingly handsome man with a shock of prematurely white hair who worked at Central Desk, the News Room on the second floor. He always seemed to be darting in and out of it, looking wild, his magnificent mane bouncing in all directions. He was often followed by Joanna Scott-Moncrieff, looking tragic; but then she always looked tragic.

Intellectuals, the 'brains' of all the occupied European countries, many fleeing from the Nazi terror, as well as émigré Russian aristocrats, 'White Russians' as they were called, had flocked to London, and many had found their way into the World Service. As in my time with SOE, I don't think I realized how privileged I was to meet so many Hungarian counts, Russian princes, unusual, irresistible people. There was a splendid Russian prince, slightly older than I, whom all his Section declared, with much eye-rolling and clasping of hands, was the image of Peter the Great. If that was the case, then Peter the Great must have been a remarkably handsome man. Valerien was a bona fide prince, with an illustrious title, but hated to be addressed by it. He preferred to be known as 'Jook', or that's what it sounded like, claiming it was the nickname his mother had given him when he was born, because she said he looked like a beetle! One of my friends always insisted on introducing him as Prince Obolensky, which annoyed him greatly, and even more so when she asked for a message using his full title to be broadcast loud and clear over the tannoy in the canteen.

My father had been in Russia during the Revolution, sent there as part of the naval brigade, so I already knew a great many White Russians who had fled the terror and settled in London. My friend Tamara had been brought up with Jook in the south of France before the war, their respective families having been friends during the imperialist days of old Russia. Having a White Russian mother and an English father, Tamara was completely trilingual and never appeared to be aware of which language she was speaking, jumping haphazardly between English, French and Russian according to her audience. But when she dived into Russian, she changed completely, adopting slurred vowels, speaking through her nose and gesticulating wildly. Her grand-father had been a general in the Czar's Imperial Army. In 1940, after the Germans invaded France, she had fled with her family from Nice wearing shorts and a tennis shirt, her only luggage her grandfather's sword, which she had reverently carried to safety. It now graced almost an entire wall of their Kensington flat.

Tamara and I were often invited to the same parties, and when that happened I usually stayed with the family overnight. I cannot imagine what our very English escorts must have thought when they arrived to collect us. The door was opened by Olga, an old retainer who had stayed with the family when they left Russia during the Revolution. Olga didn't appear to speak any known language. Once admitted, they were then vetted by Grandfather Postovsky, who must have stood almost two metres in his socks. He was adorable, but could at first glance be a forbidding figure, with his clipped white beard and heavy gold watch and chain draped across his waistcoat. Invited to take a seat, our bewildered escorts would be offered a glass of sherry and a cup of steaming consommé. It was impossible to convince Olga that we were not about to cross the frozen steppes on a sledge pulled by huskies!

The members of the Russian section, whose head was Carleton Greene, another man of impressive stature, brother of the well-known novelist Graham Greene, lived on the floor below us. They were all terribly Slav, pessimistic and melodramatic, given to bouts of hysteria. I invited myself into the cubicle when a well-known Russian pianist was to give a recital and arrived early at the same time as the studio manager, hoping to hear the pianist rehearsing before performing live on the air. Peering through the plate-glass window, to our horror we saw the lady flat on her back on the studio floor. Rushing in to administer first aid, not that I knew much about it and I'm not sure the SM did either, we discovered the pianist's English husband sitting unperturbed, reading the evening paper. He seemed surprised at our panic. 'Oh, don't take any notice of her,' he said dismissively, when the SM suggested calling the emergency service. 'She always throws one of her tantrums before a concert.' He poked her prostrate form with his foot, and she opened her eyes. 'Pantomime over,' he declared. She leapt to her feet, sat down on the piano stool and crashed into a series of resounding arpeggios, to the immense relief of the SM and the anxious programme producer, who had joined the first-aid team.

Gyorgy Mikos was a member of the Hungarian Section. He had a very beautiful Hungarian actress wife, who occasionally was to be seen with him in the canteen. She must have specialized in tragedy, since she never smiled and always gave the impression that the end of the world was imminent. In the late 1940s, as George Mikes, Gyorgy, who looked like a surprised baby, with his round face and protruding eyes, won fame in the literary world when his highly entertaining book *How to Be an Alien* was published. The Hungarians, or 'Hunks' as they were known, were also very pessimistic, but marginally less dramatic than the Russians.

The Poles lived on the floor above us. They were enormous fun and always seemed to be laughing, though at the time I don't think they had a great deal to laugh about. They 'adopted' me, and when Marian Sigmund, the Polish Army officer with the magnificent bass-baritone voice, gave a recital, knowing my foible for him, they invited me into the studio to listen. He turned up in uniform, a splendidly handsome man who also must have been almost two metres tall.

The German Section was across the corridor from the French. We shared the loos but, unlike the dormitory, they were not unisex. The men's loos were on the German side, the ladies' on the French. Whenever I went to the cinema to see a war film I had the impression that the entire German section was on the screen, strutting around in Nazi uniforms. Most of them had fled the Nazi terror, so it was perhaps their revenge, and must have been very satisfying for them, since in the immediate post-war period the war films that were made never portrayed the Nazis as anything but idiotic. Ferdy Mayne, who later featured in many very amusing Louis de Funès films – he was a perfect foil for the well-known French comedian – and Marius Goring, whom I idolized at the time, were frequently seen roaming the German Section corridors.

I became friendly with Albrecht, one of the young Germans in the Section, who had been cleared of any Nazi affiliation. His grandfather, or perhaps his great-grandfather, I don't remember which, had been the German ambassador (not von Ribbentrop!) to the Court of St James before the war. Albrecht taught me to ice-skate. We used to go to the Bayswater ice-rink every Thursday morning. I'm sure we should both have been working, but discipline in the Sections was very lax, one might say almost non-existent. I had been promoted to 'Programmes' by this time, and as long as the programme was ready and went out on time, no one seemed to bother over much how or when it had been prepared. On my first visit to the rink, I wobbled about on the edge, clinging desperately to the rail, until Albrecht sailed over, grasped both my hands in a figure of eight crossover movement and swung me out into the middle of the rink. I was terrified but soon became exhilarated as, through his expertise, we did fantastic movements, twisting and turning, practically looping the loop – until the day he decided I needed to 'stand on my own two skates'. He waltzed me into the middle of the rink and left me stranded, tottering precariously and crying out for help, until he came to my rescue. I don't know what he was trying to prove. Perhaps that Germany was the 'master race' after all!

After we became friendly, he seemed to spend more time stalking the corridors of the French Section than the German and used to park himself against our open office door, completely blocking it, he was very tall, reading love poems out loud. Our friendship was entirely platonic, we were merely skating partners, so I was surprised when one afternoon my 'boss', a delightful Frenchman, said with a deep sigh, 'Noreen, why don't you marry the poor fellow and put him out of his misery?' adding *sotto voce*, 'And get him off my back.'

I could only reply, 'Because he's never asked me, and I don't think he has any intention of doing so. And even if he did, I'd say no. We are, as all the film stars say, "only good friends".'

The French Service was not without its celebrities. Our head was Tangye Lean, brother of the film director David Lean, who made many epic films. The well-known actress Peggy Ashcroft's brother, Edward, was another member of the team. Jean Dutourd also belonged to the Section. Later, on his return to Paris, he became a well-known writer and broadcaster and ended as an *académicien*, a member of the prestigious Académie Française, the highest literary accolade in France. He had a high-pitched, rather squeaky voice which didn't go with the pipe-smoking, tweedy masculinity he wished to portray. His secretary always insisted that the door of their office be kept wide open, saying she felt safer that way, since he was known to be a *coureur de jupons*, a 'womanizer'. He used to prowl the corridors, puffing at his pipe and, according to rumours, seeking out his prey, though I never had personal experience of his amorous advances. The fact that he was married didn't seem to bother him one iota, even though his wife used to sometimes appear and hang around in an attempt to catch her husband in the act.

Michel Saint-Denis, who, as Jacques Duchesne, had been part of the wartime team – it wasn't only SOE who used codenames! – later went on to become a very well-known and respected director at the Old Vic and at all the Shakespeare festivals.

One of the sub-editors in the News Room was Vyvyan Holland, Oscar Wilde's younger son, whose book *Son of Oscar Wilde* had just been published. I don't think Vyvyan, a gentle, courteous, quietly spoken man, ever got over the tragedy which had ruined his family when, as a young boy, his mother had fled with him and his brother to France after her husband had been condemned for homosexuality and imprisoned in the infamous Reading Gaol. Vyvyan had a very beautiful Australian wife, much younger than him. When he was on duty she often wheeled Merlin, their little son, in his pushchair into the Section to say 'hallo' to his dad.

With a few exceptions, all the men working for the French Section, in fact in every section, appeared to drink a great deal.

They were encouraged by the numerous correspondents of French newspapers who seemed to circulate endlessly in the corridors, urging them to come and have a pint with the boys. There was almost a groove in the street running across the back of Aldwych from Bush House to Finch's, the pub on the opposite pavement. If ever a newsreader didn't appear on time, the cry was always: 'Ring Finch's, that's where he'll be.' And he invariably was. I remember one newsreader staggering back from Finch's at the last minute, totally oblivious of his surroundings. Once in front of the microphone, he spelt out every word, full stop, comma and question mark in the bulletin, until the horrified editor, who always sat beside the announcer, in case he said something seditious or blasphemous, pressed down the censor key and put an end to his antics.

One memorable Sunday evening, in the same state of inebriation, he almost ruined a programme. It was pre-recorded on discs, large versions of the old 78s we used to listen to on wind-up gramophones. He wasn't reading the news that evening, thank goodness. But as the programme assistant appeared in the corridor on her way to the studio with the discs in her arms, he snatched them from her, threw them onto the floor and jumped on them, shattering the lot. She screamed, burst into tears and was led away in hysterics.

The producer grabbed me, the only person in sight, and, without wasting his breath on explanations, raced me down to the studio. We arrived, gasping for breath, in the narrow passageway separating the studio manager's cabin from the studio itself, just as the news bulletin was ending.

'We'll have to improvise,' he panted, when our breathing began to slide back to normal. 'We're in a genteel guesthouse in Brighton. OK?' I nodded dumbly. 'And we're two of the residents. I'm pompous old Colonel Ponsonby; you're Miss Thistlethwaite, an elderly strait-laced spinster.'

The newsreader noiselessly left the studio, nodded to us as we all collided in the passage, and we heard the presenter announcing the programme, *La Vie à Londres et en Angleterre* (*Life in London and in England*). We tiptoed into the studio, the light flashed on, and Robin, the producer (he later went on to become someone terribly important in television) plunged in. Somehow I managed to continue the 'conversation' when he paused for breath and pointed at me to take over. Standing opposite each other, on either side of the microphone, we improvised for the full half-hour. I don't know how we did it. Had I been warned beforehand, I'd have had hysterics too, but, taken by surprise, we just went ahead and carried on. Perhaps my wartime training came to my aid that evening. According to Miss Peacock, the result was very much appreciated by the listening public.

Miss Peacock, a delightful middle-aged lady, plump but tightly corseted, had an office on the third floor, which she shared with a bevy of 'debs' manning the telephones, and her assistant, a bosomy, deep-throated woman with a sexy voice and a come-hither look. Miss Peacock was in charge of 'Listener Research' and enthusiastically announced – she was an enthusiastic kind of person – that reports on the programme had declared it very lively and well constructed. It was certainly lively, I'll grant her that but . . . well constructed? Well, I suppose everyone is entitled to his or her opinion – even the listener!

The hard-drinking newsreader, who had a particularly melodious voice and knew it, thought he was invincible. But that second episode signalled the end of his career at the BBC. When we turned up for work the following day, he was no longer a member of staff.

Another member of the French Section staff who disappeared overnight was a French journalist who was supposed to be preparing the early-morning press review. Perhaps he needed a break from reading the pile of first editions of the next day's newspapers which were always delivered to Bush House shortly before midnight, but whatever the reason, the night watchman, doing his early-morning rounds, discovered him and a secretary, who was supposed to be working on the press review with him, lying on a sofa in the head of Section's office – the only item of clothing between them a pair of dark glasses. The unlucky journalist made the fatal mistake of trying to bribe the night watchman to keep his mouth shut. Without that offence, he might have got away with it. As it was with his colleague, both he and the secretary were out on their ear by the morning.

I later bumped into him on my first visit to Paris. He was then working on a French 'daily' – the French are more broadminded about these youthful lapses! He offered to show me Paris, lent me his sister's bicycle, and we spent a pleasant Sunday cycling round the city, seeing the sights. That was in 1949. I'm not sure I would venture to cycle round Paris today!

In a similar vein a well-known English newsreader was arrested in the early hours of the morning and taken into custody by the police. He was drunk. Cooling off at around six o'clock, he rattled the bars of his cell, insisting loudly that they must let him out, since he had to get to Broadcasting House in time to read the seven o'clock news. The police officer was unimpressed.

'Oh yeah?' he replied. 'And I'm Father Christmas.' Unlike television, radio is faceless, so the poor newsreader wasn't recognized. Shortly afterwards, an amusing cartoon was posted on the noticeboard in Bush House showing a dishevelled, bare-foot announcer, with tousled hair, open-necked shirt, collarless, no tie – an unthinkable sin at the time – standing in front of the microphone, one hand clutching the bulletin, the other holding up his trousers, bunched together at his waist, with the caption: 'Here is the seven o'clock news, and this is Frank Phillips reading it – because nobody knows where the hell Freddie Allen is!'

The French Section was not unlike Montague Mansions, my first glimpse of SOE. A windmill – all the office doors wide open, and interesting people whirling incessantly in the corridors. One morning, when I'd advanced into 'Programmes', I was asked to look after Joyce Grenfell when she came to record a talk. She was a charming lady, very tall. I felt quite petite trotting along beside her. I also once went up in the lift with Laurence Olivier, just him and me. I didn't immediately recognize him – in person he seemed much smaller than on the screen. It was only when he removed his dark glasses, smiled and said 'hallo' in that un-forgettably beautiful voice of his that I realized who he was and almost missed my floor!

Like SOE, the World Service in those immediate post-war years was a true democracy, where everyone was equal. In the canteen, heads of sections could often be seen sharing a table and chatting animatedly with one of the many ex-servicemen who operated the lifts. I particularly remember one of them, because he had lost an arm in the war. Many years later I met him again. He was working in Broadcasting House, where I had gone to record an interview after one of my books had been published, and I was very touched when he recognized me. He greeted me warmly, like an old friend. 'Bush 'Ouse is not like it was in the old days, miss,' he confided, as we rose to my floor. 'Different clarse a' people working there nowadays.'

In 1950, just before I left the BBC, I voted in a general elec-tion in England for the first and last time. In those days before computers it took ages, possibly days, for the final election results to be announced. I remember sitting on the stairs outside the Central Desk News Room on the second floor – there no longer being any more room inside – listening to the results as they came through. I was with Pam, one of my friends from the French Section, the daughter of a well-known filmmaker. Pam was married to a chappie in the Dutch Section. I think he was there too; we were quite a crowd. We were all biting our finger-nails, being frightfully dramatic and wailing, 'What shall we do if they don't get in?', 'they' being the Labour Party. We'd all voted Labour, simply because our families were staunch Conservatives. Pam's father-in-law was a minister in the recently formed Dutch government, so her husband would most certainly have been a Labour supporter, just to be different. He may even have influenced his wife's choice. None of us having had time to work through our rebellious stage and indulge in our teenage crisis during the war, we were no doubt being ridiculous and having it then, fiercely opposing everything our families stood for.

Now I understand the routine. Our five children did exactly the same, in rapid succession, one after the other.

Chapter 18

When I joined the BBC in late August 1945 I decided to put the war and my time in SOE behind me, but I discovered that I couldn't. People from the past kept 'popping up' in unexpected places, as Buck and Lise had done. And it was inevitable that meeting them again, and being able to share in a way one was never able to share with anyone who had not been part of 'the racket', kept that past alive.

In 1939, when war was declared, I had been a happy, self-assured teenager with my future mapped out. I knew exactly what I was going to do. I planned to go to Oxford and take an arts degree before going on to study medicine: doctors in those days were often literary people. Then, after stunning the world with my incredible medical expertise, I intended to marry a tall, dark, handsome man who would whisk me off to a thatched cottage in the country, suitably staffed of course, with a pony poking its head over a paddock gate, and there produce six boys, all with red hair. I'd arranged it all, even down to the wedding, imagining myself floating down the aisle lost in a mist of tulle and old lace, the cathedral bells clanging, the organ thundering, and a cloud of little pages and bridesmaids tripping along behind me. The only thing I hadn't organized was the bridegroom! But I considered that a minor detail which could be sorted out at the last minute!

Then Herr Hitler decided otherwise and . . . the lights went out all over Europe. When they went on again, I was no longer a happy, carefree, self-assured teenager, I was a woman, a woman who had suffered, a very different person from the girl I had been in 1939. We were all different. It was impossible to be otherwise.

I had thought I could turn my back on the war, close that door and start afresh. But the memories seemed to colour my every waking moment and sometimes my dreams. In an effort to forget I refused to join the club which former members of SOE had started. I shunned old friends, those I had worked with and especially those young women whose men had survived. I didn't want to share in their happiness. I realize now how foolish and selfish I was. But perhaps it was my way of coping.

The youth who had survived the war went crazy. They were heady with the newfound freedom peace brought, blinded by the brilliant lights blazing and flashing across the city again, drunk with the sudden release of tension and fear, and the heartbreak of war. And I joined the crowd. London was swinging in those immediate post-war years. A spate of musicals had arrived from the United States: *Oklahoma!*, *Annie Get Your Gun*, *Carousel*, each one more gay and colourful than the one before. The Café de Paris came into its own again, and in order to attract a younger clientele they founded the Guinea Pig Club, offering Sandhurst cadets and young subalterns an evening with dinner and the cabaret for a guinea. And, of course, 'ringside' tables to show the world how young and swinging they were. Geoffrey immediately became a guinea pig, and I often made up the numbers when their party needed an extra woman.

There were rumours at the time of a budding romance between the young Princess Elizabeth and Prince Philip, a handsome naval officer, and every time they arrived, or even if the princess came with a party of friends without her handsome prince, the band would immediately break into: 'People Will Say We're in Love'. It was reported that one evening in the ladies' powder room Princess Elizabeth rebuked her younger sister, Princess Margaret Rose, as she was then known, for putting on too much lipstick, whereupon Margaret was heard to reply, 'You look after your Empire and leave me to look after my face.' Though how true this is, I cannot say.

A couple of days before he left Sandhurst I received an SOS from my little bro. 'You remember Archie, don't you?' I didn't. 'He was one of the party the last time we went to the Café de Paris,' Geoffrey explained. 'Henrietta was with him. Well she's let him down. He's frightfully cut up about it. He was taking her to the passing-out ball on Friday and she's changed her mind: decided at the last minute to go to her best friend's engagement knees-up instead. It's too late now for him to invite anyone else, so I've offered him you. You're coming to the passing-out parade, so you'll be there anyway. I told him you're terribly old. Twenty-four. But, as he said, "I can't be fussy at this stage, old chap. I'll have to take what I can get."'

So I swallowed my hurt pride and went. And had a wonderful time. Archie picked me up in his old boneshaker, which appeared to be held together with bits of string and sealing wax. We almost made it to the top of the hill when it fell to bits. Archie got out, opened the bonnet, poked about, scratched his head, then gave the engine a few resounding whacks with a shooting stick. 'I must have run out of petrol,' he announced apologetically, when his efforts produced no visible result. He gave me a sweet smile. 'If you wouldn't mind getting out and giving the old girl a push, once we get to the top of the hill we can roll down to the garage at the bottom.' I did mind but I didn't see I had any choice. The other alternative would have left us stuck there so, hitching up my trailing ball gown, I got out and pushed.

Several chauffeur-driven limousines carrying the season's 'debs' to the passing-out ball cruised by, treating us to astonished stares. But no offer of help. We finally slithered to the garage, where Archie asked the attendant for a pint of petrol. He looked at him scathingly, shook his head and cast his eyes skywards – I think he was used in impecunious Sandhurst cadets – before complying with his request. When Archie handed him the money, he sniffed and said, 'I s'pose you wouldn't like me to cough in your tyres as well while I'm at it?' Archie assured him that it wouldn't be necessary. We finally spluttered through the Sandhurst gates and made it to the ball in one piece. I danced till dawn to the lilting tunes of Humphrey Lyttleton's band, which later was not allowed to play at Sandhurst, since Humphrey had been at Eton with so many of the cadets that he was treated as one of the party. After a splendid evening, which I wouldn't have missed for anything, in the pink and golden light of early morning we all punted down to Bray for breakfast.

I was pleased afterwards that I had accepted this rather un-usual invitation, since not long after Archie left Sandhurst to join the Gloucesters in Korea he was taken prisoner. Even in my miserable, self-centred state, I'd have had the grace to feel guilty if I'd got on my high horse and taken umbrage and deprived him of his passing-out ball.

Shortly afterwards, in Copenhagen, I met a young Dane who asked me to marry him. Bjorn and I became engaged but merci-fully, before we married, the whole situation exploded. I was terribly unhappy, and so was he. I didn't understand what had happened, and I don't think he did either. I had thought I was in love with Bjorn. Perhaps I was. I realize now that I was desperate to find the love I had lost. To be loved again. I thought that with

Bjorn I could replace the love I had lost when Bill did not return, which is where I made my mistake. One cannot replace one love with another. Each is separate and special.

Before I came to my senses, I was to go through this experience again a few years later when one of my brother's fellow officers, who had been with him in Malaya, proposed to me. I met Andrew at a New Year's Eve regimental ball. I danced with him, but no more than with the other men in our party, so I was surprised when, the following morning, he rang me at the hotel where I was staying the night and invited me to lunch. Lunch drifted into tea and, finally, he offered to drive me back to London. He said he was going that way, and that it wasn't a detour, but I don't think that was strictly true. Before we parted he asked me whether I would care to accompany him on the following Saturday to a point-to-point meeting near where he was stationed. That meeting drifted into dinner and another drive back to London. I didn't enquire where he got his petrol coupons from. Petrol was still in short supply and strictly rationed. The following weekend he was on duty but he invited me to the traditional curry lunch in the mess after church parade.

By now I was getting to know his fellow officers, some of whom were married. Offers of beds in married quarters whenever I was there for a weekend began to flow towards me from every direction. I was enjoying Andrew's company; we laughed a lot, I liked his friends and I gradually began to wonder whether I hadn't fallen in love. So when, one Sunday afternoon, while having tea in the River Room at the Savoy, Andrew produced a small black velvet box with a beautiful five-diamond ring inside and told me, 'Those five diamonds mean "Will you be my wife?"', I accepted his proposal. As he slipped the ring on my finger I truly believed I was in love and had finally wiped out the past and found happiness. But one Saturday afternoon, when we were discussing the plans for our wedding, to his bewilderment, I gave

242

Andrew back his beautiful ring. I don't know what went wrong. I, too, was bewildered. He took it very well. Perhaps he had also begun to realize that we had both made a mistake. Nonetheless, I was desperately unhappy, not understanding why all my friends seemed to sail through engagements into happy married life, while mine tended to disintegrate at the last moment.

Between my two engagements I had fallen in love yet again, this time with a German, a former Luftwaffe pilot. I met Franz through my father, who had been part of a reconciliation programme called the World Friendship Organization. I don't think it was very well known or had a very long life, but my father was involved in it for three or four years. I remember meeting Dutch and Danes and Germans who passed through his hands, and I helped him entertain them. Franz was slightly older than the others, twenty-eight at the time, and had come on a study tour. My father asked me to show him the sights. There was an instant rapport between us, and I think, had he been allowed to settle in England or even been prepared to emigrate to the New World, as so many young people were doing immediately after the war, I would have married him. But he was fiercely patriotic, viscerally attached to his country, in spite of the fact that his father and his brother-in-law, both Army officers, had lost their lives because of their anti-Nazi sentiments. He wanted to rebuild Germany, put it back on its feet with a new regime. And I wasn't prepared to help him. Quite apart from my feelings, in 1949, marriage to a German was unthinkable, especially if I wanted to put the war behind me and live a 'normal' life. I realized, too, that I would have hurt my family, who had suffered such tragic losses, and also lost most of my friends, who would have either condemned me or shunned me. It occurred to me that Franz might even have flown the plane which dropped its bombs the night my cousin's wife was killed, or those which destroyed my grandparents' home. But apart from that, deep down I knew I could never marry a man whose countrymen had tortured and killed so many of my friends; nor could I go and live in Germany and become what was still considered one of 'the enemy'. At the time, the 'no fraternization' rule between the local population and the British occupying forces in Germany was strictly enforced. How different it would have been today! So, once again, there were two unhappy people.

Confused and uncomprehending, I began to wonder whether this was to be the pattern of my life from now on: finding love and then seeing it evade my grasp. A couple of years later, when my second engagement was broken, I asked myself how many more lives I was going to damage before I either found the right man or gave up the idea of marriage altogether.

Now, looking back, I understand why my engagements always ended in disaster and heartbreak. The men were wiser, more far-sighted than I. They realized before it was too late that I was marrying a ghost, that I was using them as a substitute for the man I had lost and never forgotten, and they didn't want to be loved in that way. They wanted to be loved for themselves, and at the time it was something I was incapable of doing. I not only made myself very unhappy, but I also made them unhappy. It was some years before I discovered that love had been there all the time. But like so many things which are under our noses, I didn't realize it.

I had met Jacques in February 1946 shortly after he had been demobilized from General de Lattre de Tassigny's First French Army, for which he had volunteered in June 1944 after the Allied landings in Normandy. One afternoon, when I walked into the News Room, he was sitting at a typewriter, hammering away with two fingers. We became friendly, but not more friendly than I was with a lot of other people at the time, and although I enjoyed his company, he was more interested in me than I in him. I wasn't romantically interested in anyone at the time, and

I don't think I had any wish to be. He invited me to Paris to visit his parents and then to holiday with the family in the south-west, where his grandmother had a farm.

I shied at the thought. I was quite happy with the idea of going to Paris, but for me a farm in south-west France meant an old peasant woman with no teeth, wearing clogs and a black apron, spreading grain for the hens. The thought of perhaps being asked to get up at dawn and help swill out the pigs did not appeal. So I refused. Had he told me that his grandmother's 'farm' was a vast wine-growing estate where all the family, uncles, aunts and cousins gathered in the summer, I would have been more enthusiastic. But in spite of my lukewarm response to his attentions, when he left the BBC the following year to work for the United Nations at Lake Success we kept in touch through Christmas cards.

Through a meeting at a party, I was offered the chance of going to Bucharest, then very much behind the Iron Curtain – Stalin was still in power – to teach in a small school for diplomatic children who were too young to go to boarding school in England. I protested that I knew nothing about teaching, but was assured that it was all done through a correspondence course. So I accepted the challenge and found it very interesting. On my return, as I believed at the time, to London I decided to stop over in Paris, where my brother was on a course for the Army. It was quite an experience travelling from Bucharest to Vienna – I think the train only went once a week, and Romanians had to leave it at the Hungarian frontier. Only the one carriage, that day I travelled, carrying the two British Queen's messengers, the Swiss courier, the Israeli ambassador and me was allowed to proceed. It took ages to cross the frontier into Hungary, which at the time was also under Russian occupation. While we waited, guards high up on lookout posts had their machine-guns trained on us in case any unauthorized person had concealed himself in the train in an attempt to cross the border and escape, hopefully to freedom. The formalities took at least an hour, during which time our compartments were turned upside down by Russian soldiers. It was frightening. The two Queen's Messengers, who were in the next compartment to mine, asked me to join them, which made me feel a little more secure. They also fed me, since I had brought no food for the journey. There was none to be had on the train, but since the QMs made the journey once a fortnight, carrying the diplomatic bags back and forth, they were prepared and had a primus stove and all the equipment necessary for preparing makeshift meals.

We went through the same hair-raising performance all over again on reaching the Hungarian border with Austria, where the train was halted, in the middle of the night, in a kind of no man's land before being allowed to cross the frontier and enter Austria. I think that halt was even more dramatic than our experience at the Romanian/Hungarian border, which had been carried out in daylight. Unfortunately, on the night I travelled, while the train was waiting in Budapest station, a man had inserted himself between the rails underneath the train in an attempt to escape to freedom. He was discovered by the soldiers doing the search and tried to make a run for it. We were unaware of this until suddenly, while our *wagons-lits* were being literally turned upside down by the soldiers searching perhaps for more fugitives, several shots rang out, and I imagine the person attempting to escape was killed. By the time the train finally got on its way and shunted into Vienna I was suffering from violent stomach cramps, brought about solely by nerves. The journey had certainly been an experience, one I don't think I shall ever forget. Nor shall I forget the feeling of relief, almost exhilaration, I felt when we finally crossed the frontier and entered freedom.

But our troubles didn't end there. We were caught up in an avalanche outside Salzburg and nobody, not even the British embassy in Paris, seemed to know what had happened to us. Geoffrey went backwards and forwards to the Gare de l'Est on false alerts all day, and, finally, when the embassy telephoned him at one o'clock in the morning to say that the train had been located and would be arriving in an hour, he asked Jacques, who had a car, to accompany him to the station. When the train finally arrived, at two o'clock in the morning, four days after leaving Bucharest, they were both at the station to meet me. My trunk had disappeared in the avalanche so, in the hope that it would eventually reappear, I stayed on for a few days in Paris. By the time it did arrive I'd caught German measles!

It was April, a magical time in Paris. The air was like champagne, and I was condemned to view through the open window of a fourth-floor flat the heady spring and the young couples gazing into each other's eyes and exchanging kisses as they strolled entwined along the banks of the Seine. I was sitting up in bed, covered in spots and feeling very sorry for myself, when a friend I had known at the BBC came to visit and commiserate with me. She was now working at a press agency in the rue de la Paix and told me she was looking for an assistant. She offered me the job, and, being at a loose end, I accepted, only returning to my parents' home to sort out my affairs. I didn't know it at the time, but I was never to live in my home country again.

When I returned to Paris, Geoffrey had already left to rejoin his regiment. I had visited the city only once before, for a few weeks in 1949, so I didn't really know my way around: but Jacques was there, and we renewed our friendship. He was endlessly helpful and seemed to be always available for me when I needed advice or assistance, and I came to rely on him.

He found me accommodation and coped with the mountain of paperwork necessary at the time in order to get temporary residence status. He even joked that, rather than wading through this lot, it would probably be easier to marry him and thereby obtain French nationality, a solution which would solve all my problems. I laughed and took it as a joke, but I realize now that he was only half-joking: he was in fact 'testing the waters'. After a while he did ask me to marry him, but I hesitated. Scenes of my previous engagements, and the pain, not only that I had endured, but that I had also inflicted on others, flashed through my mind, and I wasn't sure I wanted to repeat the experience. I liked Jacques enormously and had come to rely on him. I enjoyed his company and was grateful to him for all his help. But was that enough?

Jacques assured me that it was enough, and that he could make me happy. I was still a selfish beast and didn't consider whether I could make him happy. I was only thinking of my feelings, and again I hesitated. But perhaps, after all this time, something was melting inside me and, in the end, I realized that I did love Jacques. It was not at all the love I had expected. In my search for some wild passion, I had hoped to recapture the blinding feeling of adoration I had experienced during the war with Bill. I had not considered the simplicity of the union of two souls. In Jacques' company I no longer felt alone. I felt complete. Now, looking back, I can see more clearly what attracted me to Jacques. He is not unlike Bill in so many ways: quiet, unassuming, courageous, amusing, not easily ruffled, and he gets on with everyone, the qualities Bill possessed. One of my husband's favourite sayings, which I have now adopted, is: 'Any fool can fight. It takes an intelligent person to keep the peace.' I gather from that that he must be very intelligent, since he refuses to quarrel with anyone!

But my heart had been dead for too long for it to instantly spring back to life, and I was troubled with doubts. I was, after all, no longer a starry-eyed teenager rushing blindly into marriage; I was a mature woman who saw the pitfalls not only of marriage, but of marriage with someone from another culture, and I found myself wondering about the wisdom of the step I was about to take. I imagine most women have these same doubts at the prospect of sharing their lives, their most intimate moments, with another human being – in my case someone whose upbringing had been diametrically opposed to mine and who, by nature, was so different from myself.

I am impetuous, impatient, critical, inclined to judge and also to act first and think afterwards, often with disastrous consequences. Jacques is calm, unhurried, optimistic, seeing only the glass as half full, not half empty, as I am inclined to do. He looks only for the good, and usually finds it, in others. In the more than sixty, nearer seventy, years since February 1946, when I first met him, I have only twice seen him lose his temper, which I imagine must be a record. How could two people so fundamentally different, not only temperamentally, but also culturally, ever merge into one whole, I sometimes asked myself in the weeks leading up to our wedding. It was impossible. And yet we have achieved the impossible, largely thanks to my husband's forgiving spirit, and also perhaps because we share the same faith, proving that the old saying 'couples who pray together, stay together' is true.

Jacques is not at all the kind of man I had expected to marry. The four men I had been in love with had all been military types who towered above me, had blond hair, blue eyes, bristly moustaches, medal ribbons lined on their chests and enjoyed balls and parties. Jacques is the opposite. He is scarcely half a head taller than I, though with the advancing years he seems to have shrunk a few centimetres, with the result that we are now running neck and neck. I have never seen him with a moustache, though I know from photos that he did sport one briefly during the war. His dark-brown hair, once wavy and so abundant it used to flop into his eyes, is conspicuous by its absence, and his gentle hazel eyes are now hidden behind glasses. But his smile is still the same, that smile which so captivated my mother when she first met him and prompted her to exclaim, 'He's like a little boy!' He was twenty-six at the time and a hardened veteran of the First French Army!

Jacques can't dance, except on the toes of his partner, and he is not keen on parties, although he always accompanies me when we are invited; and he is not in the least bit interested in decorations. He can't even remember where he put the Croix de Guerre with Bar which he was awarded on the field whilst fighting in Germany towards the end of the war! I only found out he had the medal when, before moving from Paris, I was turning out a drawer and came across it. He laughed when I asked him why he had received this award. 'I chased the Germans out of France all by myself,' he teased. 'Didn't you know?' And he has never elaborated further.

He hates what he calls 'fuss', with the result that our wedding was original to say the least. We got married in the lunch hour! Well, Jacques' lunch hour. I'd stopped working two days before. It would have been unthinkable in the 1950s for an executive's wife to have worked outside the home. Jacques chose the date, bang in the middle of August, when absolutely everyone has fled to the coast for *les grandes vacances* and Paris is empty . . . of Parisians. My parents were staying at my brother's house in Connemara at the time and offered to come over for the occasion, but I told them not to bother. Being the kind of people they were, they didn't insist but took me at my word. Jacques' parents were in the family house in Narbonne for the *vendange* (grape harvest), where we later joined them. So we were a wedding party of four.

When my witness – an old Sandhurst friend of my brother who was in Paris for a few days on his way to Korea – and I arrived in the church porch, only Jacques' witness was there waiting for us. The bridegroom hurtled in, breathless, with about twenty seconds to spare. At the end of the simple ceremony the vicar said, 'Well, at least you can have the "Wedding March",' climbed up into the organ loft and played it himself. As we four marched, as solemnly as we could, down the aisle of this vast, echoing church with its 600 empty seats, we all suddenly saw the funny side of this bizarre situation and were overcome with helpless giggles.

Once in the porch, Jacques said, 'Sorry, I have to rush, I'm terribly busy at the office,' and disappeared into a taxi. So Hugh took Anne and me to tea at Rumplemeyer's, after which he tactfully dropped me at the entrance to the block of flats, saying: 'I expect Jacques will come home early and take you out for a celebration dinner.' It was only after he left that I realized Jacques had forgotten to give me the key to the flat. My frantic calls to his office were met with the stern reply that Monsieur Riols had given orders that he was not to be disturbed on any account. It was August and the concierge, who had a spare key, was on holiday, so I sat on the stairs outside the flat until nine o'clock that evening, when the lift disgorged my weary husband. He smiled at me, said, 'Weddings are exhausting, aren't they?' and collapsed on the bed in a comatosed sleep.

A few years later my brother married: a sumptuous affair with pages and bridesmaids, over 300 guests and a splendid reception to follow in his in-laws' garden. As the last guests drifted across the lawn to say goodbye, I collapsed onto a seat under one of the trees, enjoying the relative peace of this gentle April evening after the hectic past few days. My father came across and sat down beside me. 'I wish we had been able to give you a wedding like this, dear,' he said sadly. Remembering the exhaustion etched on the faces of my brother and his bride when they left on their honeymoon, I turned to look at him in horror, and exclaimed emphatically, 'I don't.'

My sister-in-law turned out to be the sister I had never had, and the four of us became great friends. My links with my brother, which had strengthened after the tribulations he had put me through during our early years, never lessened. I could always call on him when needed and know that he would be at my side, an invaluable asset when, in his early fifties, Jacques was rushed to hospital with cardiac arrest and suffered a coronary thrombosis. Christopher, our youngest child, was only nine at the time and I did not know where to turn. Suddenly Geoffrey was there, with his wife's blessing, coping with everything and almost carrying me through what proved to be a few traumatic weeks. I knew he would never let me down. But in the end he did. Three days after his seventy-fourth birthday he died. It was a terrible shock to us all. And the only time he didn't keep the promise he'd made to me some years before. I had been indignant after my mother-in-law's funeral at what I considered to be the offhand way in which the pallbearers had slung her coffin between them as they walked down the aisle. And I voiced my anger . . . loudly.

'I've got sons and nephews,' I said, 'when I die I want to be carried on their shoulders, reverently. I don't want to be waved about like that!'

'Don't you worry, old girl,' my brother soothed. 'I've organized many pallbearers at military funerals. I'll be there to see you are properly carried.' And I felt appeased. Now he wouldn't be there. But when he died what hit me most, I think, was the realization that, as far as our English family was concerned, I was now alone. Our last cousin on our mother's side had died the year before, at only sixty. Since he had never married, there were no nieces or nephews left to remind us that he had ever lived. My father had been the youngest of four children, so all our Yorkshire cousins were in their teens when I was born and had long since died. I was now the only one left: the sole survivor. It was a strange feeling. We had never been a close family, our links were very tenuous, but all the same, it was odd to think that whenever I went to England there would be no one to welcome me. It was then that I realized how lucky I was to have married into this close-knit French family, bristling with cousins and aunts and uncles who had all welcomed me wholeheartedly.

When Jacques and I married a whole new world opened up, and I was finally able to put the past behind me and start again. I feel so blessed when I hear other women complaining about their mothers-in-law, some with good reason, because I was so lucky with mine. Jacques' mother welcomed me, the 'foreigner' her son had married, with open arms, and once we were married I immediately became part of his large extended family. Jacques seemed to have cousins who were so far removed they were vanishing into the distance, who whenever we met always greeted me warmly with 'Bonjour, Cousine,' and a kiss on both cheeks. Being a part of this united family I had married into, so different from my reserved, one might almost say cold, English relations, I at last found the love and the security which, perhaps even without realizing it, I had always craved.

I had been brought up by parents who were kind, but remote. They themselves had been raised in the late Victorian era, when to show any kind of emotion in public was simply 'not done' in polite society. And they continued the tradition with my brother and me. Cuddles and spontaneous hugs were shows of affection I never experienced as a child. How different and how much better things are today. When I see my grandchildren being showered with love by their parents I understand how, during my own childhood, without even consciously realizing it, I must have missed the warmth and the wealth of affection my children give their offspring. They are so much wiser than I was. My children understand that, 'done' or 'not done', human beings at every age need love; and they also need roots.

When I married Jacques I 'adopted' Narbonne in the Languedoc, the *pays* in south-west France, near the foothills of the Pyrenees, where Jacques' father's family had been landowners since the thirteenth century: and finally I began to put down roots. I was born in Malta so never felt I had any roots in England and, my father being in the Royal Navy, I had never felt 'rooted' anywhere, since we moved around a great deal. My mother always complained that the curtains never fitted the windows in the next house. I have in fact inherited a trunk full of curtains which she collected over the years, always hoping that one day she would move into a house where the windows and the curtains matched each other; but I don't think she ever did. My father's base was Portsmouth, and my brother was born there, but although we had a house in Southsea, we only lived in it very briefly, and it was eventually sold.

When my father retired from the Navy in 1936 we went to live in Durham. But before we had had time to settle, much less put down roots, my father was recalled to the Service during the crisis in 1938, so we moved to London. In 1945, since the London house had been badly damaged during the war, not so much by bombs as by the tenants to whom my mother had rented it when she relocated to Bath, my parents sold that house and retired to Essex. So by the time I finally said goodbye to England, and settled in Paris, it was without any fond attachment to or deep regret for any particular region. There was really nowhere I could claim as 'home'. All the houses I had lived in had merely been places where my parents had temporarily settled.

How different my life is now. After five years in Paris, where Jacques was born, we bought a rambling seventeenth-century house in Marly-le-Roi, a village outside Versailles, the place I now call home. For more than fifty years we have lived in this delightful village and brought up our five children, now all 'flown'. We have filled the gap of the empty nest syndrome with outside activities, becoming active in an association, Entente Cordiale – shades of F Section! – which groups British with French people anxious to speak and improve their English. I joined the British

Legion and became a poppy seller, and I am now secretary general of Libre Résistance, or 'Amicale Buck' as it is called affectionately.

Libre Résistance was created in 1946, immediately after the war. It grouped together former F Section agents, something like the Special Forces Club in London, though not so grand – we've never had our own club house and survive on a shoestring. The organization has perforce dwindled to almost nothing as far as agents are concerned. I am the only woman survivor in France and there are now only three men. André Watt is, I believe, ninety-six or ninety-eight and no longer active. Marcel Jaurent-Singer is ninety-two and does all the administrative work for the association but does not feel up to attending ceremonies, although he still comes to Valençay and to the annual reunion before the memorial to the members of his resistance team who were massacred. And Bob Maloubier, now president, probably the greatest saboteur we had, is ninety but still active. He and I basically represent the 'upright' members of the group who attend ceremonies. We have many members: sons and daughters and other relatives of former agents, and also historians and writers who are interested in SOE but were not directly involved in it. Soon, the 'younger generation', who, if sons and daughters, are no longer young, will have to take over since we three are not eternal. We welcome new members, encouraging them to join through a 'colloque' (conference) held every year at somewhere grand – in 2012 it was at the École Militare in Paris and the year before at the Paris Town Hall – with speakers and usually a film, followed by a get-together dinner for those who wish to stay. Through these various activities, hopefully, Libre Résistance will continue to live and keep alive the memory of those who gave so much so that we might live in freedom today.

In all these activities, remaining quietly in the background, Jacques has wholeheartedly supported and encouraged me.

Without his help I could not have carried them out. After the children left home I began to write books, and Jacques became my unofficial editor. We didn't always agree on the changes he made to my manuscripts. And I often went into a big sulk when he slashed my favourite passages, stating that they were *hors sujet*, they distracted from the main narrative or, worse still, I was being self-indulgent! But on reflection, when I stopped sulking, I nearly always had to admit that he was right.

How inspired I had been all those years ago, in spite of my misgivings, to take the plunge out of the shadows of bewilderment, and the dark tunnel of unhappiness, to find fulfilment and contentment where the love I had been so desperately seeking, and not finding, was there where I least expected it: waiting for me to grasp with both hands. I had at last reached the end of the rocky road on which I had been stumbling and been led to the man who was able to restore my confidence, give me back my zest for life and would finally lead me home. The man who doesn't allow me to take myself too seriously, who has brought love and laughter to my sometimes troubled world, teasing out the knots in my churning stomach and giving me his peace. Like all couples, we have had our difficult times, our dramas and our tensions, but overriding them all is the memory of a hundred fragile moments showered on us like apple blossom in the spring. Moments to cherish, shared with the man who has become my other self, and of whom, even in the midst of my tormenting doubts before my marriage, I was sure of one thing: in his company, I would never be bored. And I never have been. Perhaps after all he was the man who was destined for me. What a lot of heartache I would have avoided, not only for myself but also for others, had I only realized that before.

Chapter 19

In the year 2000, when the secret SOE files were finally opened to the public, the media in all its forms pounced on us few survivors, and one of the questions they often asked me was: 'Did you know Fifi?'

'Fifi?' I puzzled. 'Who was she?'

'A very attractive woman who was used by SOE to find out whether prospective agents talked in their sleep.'

I ridiculed the idea. 'What nonsense,' I always replied. 'That's just a figment of someone's over-active imagination. There was no such person as Fifi.' But afterwards I began to wonder whether I hadn't known Fifi. Whether I hadn't in fact lived with her.

Dorothy, the third member of our team at Beaulieu, was older than Jean and I. She was also something of a mystery, though at the time it didn't strike me as strange. Our lives in SOE were a mystery from beginning to end, and the order I received on my first day not to ask questions, had become a habit. Dorothy never came with us on local exercises in Bournemouth and Southampton, but she often disappeared to London for a few days. 'Dorothy,' I remember asking her when she returned from one of her jaunts. 'Do you stay in your flat when you go to London?'

'No,' she replied. 'Usually in hotels.'

'Whatever for?' I pursued, in my innocence. Or was it ignorance? Probably just pig-headedness, not knowing when enough is enough.

She smiled enigmatically and replied vaguely: 'Oh, I do a bit of sleep-walking.' And left it at that. And so did I. I didn't understand. But something prompted me not to pursue the matter further.

But, intrigued by the media's persistent questioning, I began to wonder what Dorothy had been doing on her 'sleep-walking' jaunts to London. She was certainly not the kind of woman anyone could ever mistake for a 'tart': rather the opposite. But she knew a great many agents: their photographs in silver frames, with touching dedications to her, jostled for place on her dressing table. And I couldn't help wondering whether perhaps Fifi had existed after all and wasn't merely the figment of someone's fertile imagination.

After the war I met Dorothy by chance one afternoon in the Strand. I hadn't seen her since I had left Beaulieu in June '45, and we had tea together in Lyons Corner House.

'I'm giving a dinner party next week,' she announced, when the waitress arrived with our tray. 'I've invited several friends from our Beaulieu days. It would be lovely if you could join us.'

She raised her eyebrows expectantly. But I hesitated. When the war had ended all I had wanted to do was forget those dramatic years and attempt to make some sense of my life. My heart had been broken, an experience not uncommon to many women who worked for SOE, and I wanted to turn the page, pick up the pieces and start again. But it wasn't easy. Those years cannot just be blotted out, however hard one tries. Dorothy knew this.

She knew my story and let me pour out my pain, vocalize my impossible hopes . . . and my moments of despair. We had lived together in very close contact, but, looking back, I realize now that I had known very little about her . . . until that afternoon.

When the flow ceased and the teapot had run dry, she reached across the table and squeezed my hand sympathetically. 'Noreen,' she said softly, 'he's not coming back.' In my heart of hearts I knew that. He was one of those who had disappeared without trace. But I had hoped against hope for the impossible. Soldiers behind bars or in prison camps had turned up. And airmen who had been reported missing, believed killed, had survived incredible experiences and finally returned, sometimes to face tragic situations: their wives, believing them dead, having married again. 'If you find a good man,' Dorothy went on, 'marry him.'

I looked at her in surprise. Good men were two a penny at the time. There were so many of them returning from the war, tired of fighting, sick of strife, wanting only to settle down and be happy with a loving wife. Every presentable woman had her choice. 'Why should I marry?' I asked belligerently, adding bluntly, 'You didn't.' She must have been almost forty at the time.

She smiled. 'No. But I had lovers.'

'Then why shouldn't I?' I countered, sullenly picking at the remains of the scones and cherry cake. The war had brought out a bitter streak in me. Dorothy smiled again, that enigmatic smile which was so intriguing and which many people, especially men, found irresistible. 'Because,' she replied, 'you are different. You wouldn't be happy living my way.' She patted my hand affectionately and signalled for the bill. 'You're a born wife and mother . . . I'm not.'

I looked down at my now empty plate, idly sketching patterns in the crumbs with one finger. I liked her and admired her, and her revelation had not really surprised me. I think I knew. I also knew that she was right about me: we were different.

'Now,' she went on, briskly changing the subject, 'promise me you'll come to my dinner party next Wednesday. Harry and Donald and their wives and . . .' She mentioned a couple of other former agents who had ended up as instructors at Beaulieu, whom she'd also invited. 'They'd love to see you again.' She collected her gloves and handbag and stood up. 'You can't go on ignoring us for ever.'

I was reluctant to go, but I went. I was curious. I knew the officers she mentioned, but I had never met their wives, and I told myself it would be interesting to meet the women they had married. Dorothy had a lovely flat in a fashionable part of London, and the dinner was superb. She was right: they were all very pleased to link up with me again; we had spent many poignant and amusing moments together during those difficult years. They knew about my heartbreak and all confirmed what Dorothy had said: he was not coming back. I think that evening was the catalyst I needed which propelled me to turn the page. It need not have been difficult but, true to type, wrapped up in myself, I made it so. When the evening ended we promised to all meet again very soon. They urged me to join the club which fellow SOE members had created in 1946 in order for former members to keep in touch. I said I would. But I never did: not, that is, until many years later.

I never saw Dorothy again. I left for Copenhagen shortly afterwards, and we lost touch. I heard later that she had gone to South Africa, but wherever she was, our paths didn't cross. Now, I can't help wondering, was she the mysterious Fifi? If Fifi did exist, Dorothy was the only woman I knew at that time who could fit the description. The film company which made the documentary for the BBC never managed to track her down either, which was probably as well, should the few remaining agents have been watching the film with their wives. Even after all these years it could have caused friction.

Although at Dorothy's dinner party I had promised to join the SOE club, it was only many years later, urged by my little brother, that I did so. He happened to be lunching with an SAS friend at the Special Forces Club, and when they were leaving they bumped into the club secretary, a retired lieutenant colonel. When his friend introduced them, Geoffrey confided that he was sure I had been a member of SOE during the war. The secretary immediately asked him to persuade me to join. Having fought in Malaya with his regiment and spent his twenty-first birthday in a foxhole deep in the jungle had matured my little bro, and I think he guessed what my wartime activities had been. He gave me the address of the club with orders to present myself. So, remembering the promise I had made in 1947 at Dorothy's dinner party, the next time I was in London I resolved to visit the club and see for myself.

But I couldn't find the place. I had the address and I knew more or less where it was, but the street seemed to vanish after a few numbers. Puzzled, I decided to ask the doorman at Harrods. He scrutinized the paper I gave him, then looked furtively round, bent down towards me and whispered out of the side of his mouth: 'Do you mean the secret club?' I was startled and whispered back that I thought it was secret. He nodded conspiratorially. 'Were you one of them?' he continued, still hissing out of the side of his mouth in the best secret agent tradition. I blushingly admitted that I was, whereupon he drew himself up to his full height – and he was tall. I wondered what on earth he was going to do. 'Madam,' he said in a loud voice, 'allow me to shake your hand.' So I allowed him. It was midday. There were crowds of people milling about on the narrow pavement outside Harrods, and he was supposed to be opening doors for those who wanted to enter or leave. But the entrance remained inaccessible while we stood there, two elderly people holding hands, blocking the pavement so that shoppers could get neither in nor out of the shop. I don't know what passers-by thought. But I was very touched by his gesture.

Another touching experience linked to the club, and the activities of those who were its founders, happened to me only a few years ago. I had been staying at the club but was leaving that evening on the Eurostar to return to Paris, so I walked along to Harrods, where I knew I would find a taxi. I told the cabby I was going to Waterloo and asked him to stop at this address on the way, so that I could collect my luggage.

When he drew up outside the door of the club, he was anxious to come in with me to pick up my case, but I assured him that there was no need, someone would carry it out for me. He seemed disappointed and, as soon as the front door was opened, he strained forward in an attempt to catch a glimpse inside. 'That's the spies' club, isn't it?' he remarked, as he drove away. Again I was taken aback and asked him how he knew. 'Oh, at the taxi school we're told that's where it is. But I've never picked anyone up from there before.' He turned round and, echoing the words of the doorman at Harrods, said, 'Were you one of them?'

It was six o'clock in the evening. He was driving through the crowded rush-hour London traffic with his head screwed round at an angle of forty-five degrees, his eyes not on the road, but on me, eyeing me inquisitively, as if I were some kind of fossil he had picked up on the beach. I began to feel nervous, expecting a head-on crash at any minute, so suggested that he might keep his eyes where they should be: on the road ahead. But he didn't appear to hear, enthusiastically telling me that he was passion-ately interested in Second World War history, had read all the books on the subject he'd been able to lay his hands on and watched every film and documentary. 'My kids wouldn't do what you lot done,' he ended morosely. I assured him that they would if ever the occasion arose. But he didn't seem convinced. 'Nah,' he said. 'You was a special generation.' Not knowing his 'kids', I couldn't argue.

When we arrived at Waterloo – it was in the days before the Eurostar left from St Pancras – and I gave him the fare, he refused it. 'I couldn't take a penny, lady,' he said, to my intense embarrassment. 'You've made my day. I'm honoured to have met you.' I tried to insist he accept the money, but he was adamant in his refusal. He dived into the glove compartment of his car and brought out a card. 'Next time you're in London,' he ended, 'ring this number and ask for Dave, and I'll drive you anywhere you want to go.' He insisted on carrying my case right up to the ticket gate. We shook hands warmly, and I walked through moved almost to tears, feeling humbled and undeserving of his unstinted praise and admiration.

I remembered a conversation I had had one afternoon with radio operator Henri Diacono in the train on one of our journeys back home. We had been lunching in Paris with the other two F Section survivors, Bob Maloubier and Marcel Jaurent-Singer. And, of course, winning the war all over again! Bob nicknamed us 'les trois anciens et la gamine' ('the three old fogies and the kid' – me!). Henri and I took the same train home, his station being two stops before mine. 'If the opportunity arose would you do it again?' he asked as the train trundled through the outskirts of Paris. I looked at him.

'Would you?' I countered.

'I don't know', he reflected. 'We were so young, weren't we? We didn't realize the danger.' It was true. I don't remember feeling afraid or in any kind of danger, even during the air raids. We thought we were invulnerable, immortal. Death was something which happened to other people. It couldn't touch us.

Perhaps all young people think this way. Perhaps that's the way the agents felt when they left for the field. I don't know, but I hope so: it would have given them courage, buoyed them up to face whatever lay ahead. That could be the reason why I was so disappointed when I was not allowed to train as an agent. I had wanted to go into occupied France, but I was too young. Then, when I could have gone, the war was almost over. Perhaps, like Henri said, I didn't realize the danger.

I remember saying to Henri that afternoon: 'Do you think today's young people would do what we did?'

'Of course they would,' he laughed. 'You only have to see them at football matches. They love a fight.' I'm not sure those agents volunteered because they 'loved a fight'. But it's a theory. I like to think it was because we all had a stronger sense of patriotism than do the youth of today, an allegiance to king and country, and were prepared to take the risk because of our ideals and the values we believed in. Or was it just naivety? Perhaps today's youth see things more clearly than we did and are not blinded by the standards we lived by. Only the future will tell.

Two or three years ago the History Channel made a film for the BBC called *Churchill's Secret Army*, in which Marcel Jaurent-Singer, Bob Maloubier, Henri and I were featured. Towards the end, Bob, Henri and I were filmed sitting chatting at a table outside a café in my village near Paris. Henri had cancer, but was then in remission. On screen he seemed very well, but two months before the film was shown he died, and the production company dedicated it to his memory.

His death was very sudden and came as a shock. He had seemed fine just two weeks before. When I heard he was in hospital I went to see him, but he was already in a coma. I remember sitting by his bed, holding his hand and talking to him about the old days, clinging to the hope that he could hear me, telling him how much his friendship had meant to me and how much we all loved him – he was a very loveable person. That was a Wednesday afternoon. Early on the Friday morning his son rang to say that his father had died.

The funeral was held a few days later at four in the afternoon. I was due to speak at a big meeting in the *mairie* that evening, so Jacques didn't want to me to attend. 'Françoise [Henri's widow] will understand,' he said. 'You'll barely have time to get home and change before we have to leave. You can't do it; you'll be too upset.' But I knew I had to go. And I wanted to go. So my husband took me. 'You must have been one of the last people to see him alive,' Françoise said when we got to the crematorium. I had never met their son, who lives in New York, but when he got up to speak, I had a shock. He was an older version of the Henri I had known as the twenty-year-old who had parachuted 'blind' into France all those years before: the same mannerisms, the same build, the same thick black curly hair. When the service ended, Bob, who had been sitting on the other side of the crematorium from me, got up and left. He didn't wait outside to greet me as he normally would. I understood. We were both too upset.

That evening I gave my talk. I had given the same talk, albeit in English, a few years before. The *mairie* had been packed; the entire British colony seemed to have turned out. On that occasion, Henri and Françoise had been there, too. When I began to tell the audience about what the radio operators did, I had suddenly said, 'But we've got a live one here, sitting in the front row. Get up, Henri, and let us applaud you. You're one of our unsung heroes.' Reluctantly, Henri had risen to his feet and faced the room. The applause was thunderous.

'You shouldn't have done that,' he chided me afterwards. Like all heroes, he was a truly modest man.

Now, giving the talk in French, at the end I found myself recalling that moment and told the assembled gathering that I had attended Henri's funeral that afternoon. I don't think I showed any outward emotion, but what I said must have touched the audience. I got a standing ovation.

Chapter 20

A couple of years ago, there was an amusing incident connected with SOE, which supports the theory that one cannot judge from appearances! I received a telephone call from Help for Heroes, a charity I greatly admire, asking me if I would be willing to go to a small airfield near Dreux, in Normandy, where Tania Szabo, Violette's daughter, would be landing in a Second World War plane, the same kind of plane from which her mother twice parachuted into France – the second time never to return. The occasion was the annual Help for Heroes sponsored bicycle race from London to Paris. Three hundred cyclists – some of them soldiers still on active service, there were three generals among them, but most of them disabled ex-service men – would be arriving en masse at this airfield, their last leg before entering Paris, the following afternoon, and cycling up the Champs-Elysées to rekindle the flame at the tomb of the Unknown Warrior.

I readily agreed. I knew Tania and liked her: it would be fun to see her again. At over sixty she is still a very beautiful woman, but not as beautiful as her mother had been. All the men had been in love with Violette. Tania's beauty is different: she is very vivacious, bubbly, like a bowl of soap suds.

'It's an early start,' I was warned. 'The plane is due to arrive at nine-thirty, so we'll send a car for you the night before and put you up at our hotel. We're also inviting Bob Maloubier,' she ended.

But, when she telephoned Bob, he cancelled the arrangements. 'I'll bring Noreen down,' he announced magnanimously.

On hearing this, my heart sank. At eighty-seven Bob was still flying his own plane, and I had a horrible feeling that that was how he intended to transport me. The thought of hurtling through the clouds in the early morning sitting behind him in an open cockpit made me shudder. I was all set to refuse his offer when he announced that we would be driving down to Normandy. That idea was only slightly less terrifying. Bob drives a long, low, open sports car resembling a guided missile, the sort of vehicle James Bond leaps in and out of.

'I'm not going in that bomb of yours,' I said firmly. So he agreed to borrow his wife's more conventional vehicle.

The outing started badly. The day scheduled was Thursday, but at seven o'clock on the Wednesday morning our sleep was shattered by telephones and the doorbell all ringing at once.

'I'm outside your front door,' Bob announced. 'Where are you?'

'But Bob,' I yawned, shaking myself awake, 'we're expected tomorrow.'

He insisted I had made a mistake.

'Go down and give Bob a cup of coffee while I throw on some clothes,' I spluttered, shaking my comatosed husband awake.

My 'toilette' took all of ten minutes.

'Bob, are you sure it's today?' I queried, when I joined the two of them, slurping coffee. 'Have you got a contact number we can check before we rush off?'

The sleepy cameraman who answered the phone was not too pleased to be dragged from his bed at seven-fifteen. He'd been filming until four o'clock that morning and had hardly got to sleep. He confirmed that our rendezvous was for the following day. So Bob slurped some more coffee and went home. Jacques climbed back into bed but, since I was dressed, I didn't see any point in getting undressed only to start all over again, so I finished the coffee.

We drew up at the airfield the following morning and were greeted by the officials already on the tarmac waiting for the plane. When it was announced, I had imagined that Bob and I would, like everyone else, greet Tania when she alighted. Bob had dandled her on his knee when she was a toddler. But no such luck.

'Get in, Noreen,' the organizer said briskly, urging me forward, when the plane ground to a halt and the door was flung open.

I gasped. 'I'm not going up in that thing,' I protested. 'It's come out of the ark!' But I was already being propelled up the steps and into the cabin, where Tania was sitting together with a couple of FANY 'Queen Bees' and an Army officer. I sat down gingerly beside her, and we waited. After a while the telephone inside the cabin rang. 'Right,' the pilot announced, replacing the receiver, 'we're going up.'

Tania and I had been laughing and chatting, reminiscing together, but at his words my happy mood evaporated and panic took over. 'Lord,' I prayed, squeezing my eyes tightly shut when the engine whirred and I felt a jolt as the plane lifted off the ground, 'I'm coming!' When I dared to open them again we were circling round in a bright blue sky.

'There they are,' the pilot announced. 'Look out of the window. You can see them.'

Below us were 300 specks, the cyclists, standing below on the tarmac, waving at us. I felt a stab of disappointment. I wasn't in heaven after all.

We landed, and the door was opened. I was handed a poppy wreath and helped down the steps, where a piper in full dress uniform, bearskin and all, was waiting. Bob, standing in solitary state on the tarmac, came forward and embraced me warmly. It seemed rather silly, since I'd been with him for the past three hours. Tania, also carrying a wreath, and the officials followed, and a bugler appeared from nowhere. The piper put his best foot forward and began to pipe. Tania and I and the officials marched behind him in crocodile formation, with the bugler bringing up the rear, no one knowing where they were going or what they were supposed to do once they got there. So we blindly followed the bagpipes till they gave a last gasp in front of a barrier, where we were marshalled into line.

'Go forward and place the wreaths,' a voice from behind us urged, so Tania and I went forward and put them on the ground in front of the barrier, since there didn't appear to be anywhere else. The bugler sounded the 'Last Post', the piper puffed out his cheeks, went puce in the face and attacked his bagpipes, which spluttered into a mournful wail, and we all marched to where the cheering, waving cyclists were waiting to receive us. They escorted us, en masse, into a large hangar, where a splendid buffet was laid out. I didn't eat much because all these lovely young men, so many of them handicapped victims of recent wars, wanted to talk to us. It was a very humbling experience.

The next day the local paper carried a large front-page photo of Bob hugging me when I landed, with the caption: 'A touching reunion between two former agents.'

A lesson in subversion, showing not only how easy it is to deceive, but also how wrong it is to judge from appearances . . . and how foolish to believe all one reads in the newspapers!

Chapter 21

Every year on 6 May we meet at Valençay, in the Indre-et-Loire. It was on this day in 1941 that Georges Bégué, the first F Section agent to be dropped into occupied France, landed in the area. He dropped 'blind' near Valençay, and from this small beginning the whole infiltration system into occupied France of over 400 F Section agents, including thirty women, began.

We, the survivors of F Section, together with the families and friends of agents, gather to commemorate the memory of those whose names are inscribed on the memorial which stands on the outskirts of this small town in the Loire Valley. The simple memorial is dedicated to the 104 F Section agents who were executed in Nazi concentration camps, among whom were fifteen women. We welcome others with no connection to F Section or even to SOE, but who feel drawn to honour and pay tribute to those who so willingly sacrificed their lives.

At the 'Brits' dinner' on the evening before the ceremony, between twenty and thirty of us meet in an ancient *auberge* in Valençay. It's a wonderfully picturesque place, with low, raftered ceilings and creaky, twisting staircases. The plumbing in the bathrooms is antiquated, but somehow it adds to the charm of our two nights' stay. If the weather is fine, and it usually is, we meet beforehand for drinks in the courtyard and sit reminiscing under a canopy of wisteria before going in to a splendid, more than copious, regional meal.

At this dinner in May 2011, I witnessed a very touching re-union between a pilot and a wounded agent he had picked up from a field near Angers in Brittany. Ninety-two-year-old Leonard Ratliff, a former 'Moonlight Squadron' pilot who made more than forty landings in occupied territory during the war, met again Bob Maloubier, then eighty-eight, the badly wounded agent he had picked up in February 1945. Bob had been shot in a lung, his liver and his intestines in a gun fight while escaping from the Germans but had managed to swim across a stream and throw off the dogs pursing him, since they lost the scent. On arriving on the other bank, weak and losing blood rapidly, he had collapsed in a wood. In February in Brittany the water in the stream was extremely cold, but it was the freezing temperature that saved his life. The shock of hitting the icy water stopped the haemorrhage. Picked up by Leonard, Bob was repatriated to England.

These two men finally met again, sixty-seven years later, at our dinner party. It was a very moving moment when Bob walked into the room. Leonard rushed to greet him, and the two fell into each other's arms in a great bear hug. 'The last time I saw you,' Bob quipped, 'was when you cruised to a rapid standstill. Your head shot out of the cockpit and you yelled, "Get him on board quick before the Germans arrive." If I had to do it again,' Bob ended quietly, 'I would trust my life with you even now.' At that moment, there was hardly a dry eye in the room.

These poignant moments, full of memories, are not easy to erase. That is the story of a Lysander rescue which succeeded. But sadly it was not always the case.

The sixth of May 2011 was the seventieth anniversary of that memorable night in 1941 when Georges Bégué was dropped near Valençay, and also the twentieth anniversary of that rainy day in 1991 when Queen Elizabeth, the Queen Mother, unveiled the F Section memorial there. As it was a very special occasion, HRH Princess Anne graced us with her presence. On the death of her grandmother, the late Queen Mother, the princess succeeded her as patron of the Special Forces Club, and also patron of Libre Résistance.

To honour the occasion on that beautiful spring morning in 2011 there were many prominent people present. Sir Peter Westmacott, the British ambassador to France, Sir Colin McColl, president of the Special Forces Club, the *préfet* (rather like an English lord lieutenant) of the Indre-et-Loire, the mayor of Valençay, the defence attaché from the British embassy in Paris, various other embassy attachés, local dignitaries and a military band. A splendid array of standard-bearers, including two British representatives carrying the Union and Legion flags, marched into position in front of the monument. After the ceremony, they were all warmly greeted by the princess. But she seemed especially pleased to talk to a group of schoolchildren, some English among them, all waving miniature Union Jacks.

The local choir sang not only the National Anthem – all three verses – and the 'Marseillaise', but also 'Le Chant des Partisans', that haunting refrain which hostages and many members of Resistance groups sang as they were led away to be executed and even when tied to their posts before being shot. A guard of honour of French SAS commando parachutists was flown in from their base in Pau especially for the occasion. Their colonel and one of his men later jumped into an adjoining field, one waving a British and the other a French flag.

On that sunny morning, when we commemorated those sometimes forgotten, little-known or unacknowledged heroes and heroines of F Section who did not return, there must have been almost seven hundred people of all nationalities at the country crossroads outside the little town of Valençay, on which the monument stands. They were gathered on a grassy knoll which undulates slightly, giving way to the shelter of trees. Not being entirely flat, it allowed everyone to watch the ceremony. On the gravel space round the memorial were rows of chairs, but most of the people were standing, or sitting on the grass.

Sadly, out of the seven hundred people present, only Bob Maloubier and I were left to represent F Section. After the speeches, given by the princess, who spoke in both French and English, the *préfet*, the mayor, Bob, now president of Libre Résistance, whose speech was worthy of Winston Churchill, quoting at the end Winston's famous words: 'We shall never surrender', there followed the traditional laying of wreaths at the foot of the memorial. Each year since the monument was erected, surviving agents have read out, in turn, the names of their 104 comrades who gave their lives, inscribed on a tablet next to the memorial. As the years have passed, so the number of readers has dwindled. In May 2011, only Bob Maloubier and I were present.

When our names were announced we both went forward to the microphone. As we stood, side by side, Bob put his arm round my shoulders and held me tight. I was feeling emotional: we both knew so many of the people whose names we were about to call, and his affectionate gesture almost made the tears, which were not far from the surface, spill over.

'You start,' he whispered. Perhaps he was feeling emotional too. So, taking a deep breath, I began. As I did so, faces from the past, those whose names I was calling out, rose up and drifted in front of my eyes, then floated away to be replaced by others, all of them youthful and smiling as they had been before they left on their last fateful journey. After I had read fifty-two names,

Bob took over and read the remaining half. At the end we both said, 'Morts pour la France' ('Died for France'), and Bob added, 'And for England.' I then recited the exhortation, Laurence Binyon's famous lines, which, in Britain, are so often quoted on 11 November in front of war memorials.

> They shall not grow old, as we who are left grow old.
> Age shall not weary them, nor the years condemn.
> At the going down of the sun and in the morning,
> We will remember them.

Bob repeated those moving lines in French, after which the Last Post was sounded by a British military bugler. When we turned to go back to our seats, Bob gave my shoulder an affectionate squeeze and kissed my cheek. I managed to stumble back to my seat next to Wing-Commander Leonard Ratliff, the ninety-two-year-old former 'Moonlight Squadron' pilot who had flown into France to rescue Bob. Leonard had been listening intently as we read out the names: he also must have known some of those who had not come back – had even 'dropped' them from the night sky over France. When I sat down beside him, he placed his hand over mine. It had been another very moving few minutes for the three of us. So many memories had surfaced, and faded with the bugler's last quivering notes. I couldn't help thinking that, had I not been too young to be trained and parachuted into occupied France, my name might well have been inscribed on that memorial. Or perhaps, like Bob, I would have returned with only the memory of those I had left behind to pass on to the next generation.

At the reception in the Château de Valençay after the ceremony, many people told me that for them the most moving moment of the ceremony, the most poignant of all their memories of that day at Valençay, had been when Bob had put his arm around my shoulders and held me tight as we prepared to read out the names of many of our comrades who will not grow old as we who are left have grown old. They said his gesture had brought tears to many eyes. I understood. It had brought tears to mine. Such moments remind me that we will not forget, but will remember with pride those who will forever remain young in the hearts of all who knew and loved them.

Chapter 22
Beaulieu revisited

When the files were opened in the year 2000, Lord Montagu invited SOE survivors to a wonderful reception at his home in Beaulieu, the place which for so many of us held fond, often painful, memories. He himself did not share those memories. He had been at Eton at the time, ending his schooldays a short while before the Japanese surrender in August 1945, by which time the heart and soul of 'Group B' had become only a ghost. And all that was left of SOE's presence on his family's estate was rapidly being torn down as the houses which had sheltered agents from so many different European countries were handed back to their original owners.

On that glorious summer day we gathered as old friends in the grounds of Palace House. Princess Anne was present, as well as members of the Montagu family. Sadly, Lord Montagu's mother, who had been with us at the House in the Woods on that memorable evening when we had had a splendid party and rejoiced because the war in Europe was finally over, had died shortly before, aged 100. When I was presented to the princess she seemed to be genuinely interested in hearing about all that had happened at Beaulieu during the war. The Montagus are, after all, distant relatives of her family. While we were talking, three Hudson aircraft thundered overhead, giving the salute. People cheered and waved, and we all looked up and watched as they vanished then reappeared, dipped their wings and saluted us again.

'When I see those Second World War planes and hear them roaring overhead, I feel shivers going up and down my spine, don't you?' the princess enquired. I could only agree.

The following day, I went back to the House in the Woods to revive old memories. But it's strange how one's memory can play tricks. Everything seemed to be on a smaller scale than I remembered. The House in the Woods, which had been home to the twenty-five officer instructors, had seemed enormous in the early 1940s. But when I went inside more than sixty years later and stood in the beautiful drawing room where the grand piano, on which Colonel Woolrych had played every morning before breakfast, still held pride of place, I couldn't believe that this was the room where I had danced on the eve of VE Day. It appeared to have shrunk. How had we all crowded into it on that spring evening so many years ago? Yet we had. Now the house stood empty; only the ghosts of its former wartime occupants inhabited its rooms and corridors, and hovered on the wide staircase.

'The Rings', our rather ugly stockbroker-Tudor HQ, had been knocked down, and a large, modern bungalow, which I found equally ugly, now stood in its place, but the owners had kept part of the original name. I think it was called 'Rings Corner' or something equally twee.

Lastly I knocked on the door of the cottage where I had lived all those years ago. It was now inhabited by a market gardener, who was astonished and eager to know more when I told him how his little cottage had been involved in our activities on the estate during the war. The files had only just been opened and, like so many people, he had no idea even of SOE's existence, much less the important role the Beaulieu estate and his cottage had played during those dramatic years.

The sun began to sink, a fiery red ball slowly drifting towards the horizon, as I walked once again in the sheltered cloisters housing the Montagu family chapel, out of whose dim interior the Grenadier Guards' band had poured on the previous day to Beat the Retreat. On one wall of the cloisters a plaque had been unveiled in April 1969 by General Sir Colin Gubbins, former head of SOE, honouring the memory of all the trainee agents who had passed through this tranquil place, which had been perhaps their final glimpse of England before entering enemy territory. I stood in front of the plaque, remembering those men and women I had known, many of whom had not returned, and read the inscription: 'Remember before God those men and women of the European Resistance Movement who were secretly trained in Beaulieu to fight their lonely battle against Hitler's Germany, and who, before entering Nazi-occupied territory here found some measure of the peace for which they fought.' Those words commemorate over 3,000 men and women of at least fifteen different European nationalities, and a number of Canadians and Americans, who, during the Second World War, had been trained at Beaulieu.

And I remember thinking, and fervently hoping, that they had found peace, their last days of peace before they entered enemy territory to face the turmoil and tensions and fear of living undercover in German-occupied Europe. Peace, that peace which we all seek and long for, not only in wartime, when it is a vision we grasp and one day hope to achieve, but in our ordinary, everyday 'peacetime' life. Sadly, in this modern world, that peace for which courageous men and women fought and often sacrificed their lives still remains for many people only an illusion: a goal they never reach.

As I turned away from the plaque that Indian summer evening, the inscription imprinted on my mind, I realized that out of the six women who had worked at Beaulieu during the war I may be the only survivor. I looked around those sunlit cloisters and I think I understood a little of what those future agents must have felt when they too turned away from Beaulieu and faced with courage whatever fate had in store for them. They were so young . . . with their whole lives before them. What must have been their thoughts as they drifted down out of the night sky to face an unknown enemy?

When he returned, one agent told me with a smile that as he had dangled above the dark ground, not knowing whether friend or foe awaited him, he couldn't help saying to himself, 'What on earth am I doing here? I must be crazy. I could have been sitting in a bar in London, having a drink, spending a pleasant evening with friends, and enjoying the relative safety of a free country, instead of leaping alone into the unknown.' Then he had hit the ground with a bump, and out of the dark, willing hands had come forward to help him shed his parachute which, caught in the wind, was dragging him along the ground. And as he had looked up into so many unknown, but friendly, faces smiling in welcome, he had felt a sudden surge of emotion and knew that had he, at that moment, been able to change his mind and return to London, he would have chosen to be where he was, where he was meant to be, that what he was doing might be crazy, but for him it was right.

I can only think and hope that this is how most of them must have felt – that what they were doing was right, whatever the future might hold. I feel very privileged to have been a member of Churchill's Secret Army, and very humbled to have known and, I hope, been a friend to so many exceptional, courageous and truly wonderful people, many of whom did not 'grow old, as we who are left have grown old'. For they gave their youth, their hopes, their dreams, their joie de vivre . . . so that we might be free.

As I stood in those tranquil cloisters that September evening with the last rays of sunshine dappling the ancient stone walls, sending sunbeams dancing across the lawn, I closed my eyes, and those faces from the past drifted before me. And in the light breeze which lifted my hair and caressed my cheeks I seemed to hear their distant voices whispering:

> When you go home
> Tell them of us and say
> For your tomorrow
> We gave our today.

Roll of Honour of F Section Agents who died in the struggle for the liberation of France

Agazarian, Hon. Flight Lieutenant J. C. S., Royal Air Force Volunteer Reserve. Landed July 1943, on his second mission, as a member of the two-man Gamekeeper team. Captured within a few days. Killed in captivity at Flossenbürg, 29 March 1945. *Mentioned in Despatches; Croix de Guerre avec Palme.*

Alexandre, Lieutenant R. E. J., General List. Dropped February 1944 with Byerly, Deniset and Ledoux (q.v.) to establish and lead the Surveyor *réseau*. Captured on landing. Believed killed in captivity at Gross Rosen, August–September 1944.

Allard, Lieutenant E. A. L., General List. Dropped April 1944 with Leccia and Geelen (q.v.) as a member of the Labourer *réseau*. Captured within a few days. Killed in captivity at Buchenwald, 14 September 1944.

Amphlett, Lieutenant P. J., General List. Dropped August 1943 as a member of the Scullion II coup-de-main party. Captured on the return journey. Killed in captivity at Flossenbürg, 29 March 1945. *Mentioned in Despatches.*

Amps, Lieutenant J. F., General List. Dropped October 1942 with Suttill (q.v.) as a member of the Physician *réseau*. Captured mid-1943. Killed in captivity at Flossenbürg, 29 March 1945.

Antelme, Major J. A. F., General List. Dropped February 1944, on his third mission, with Damerment and Lee (q.v.) to establish and lead the Bricklayer *réseau*. Captured on landing. Believed killed in captivity at Gross Rosen, August–September 1944. *Officer of the Order of the British Empire (Military Division); Chevalier de la Légion d'Honneur.*

Barrett, Flight Lieutenant D. J., Royal Air Force Volunteer Reserve. Dropped March 1944, on his second mission, with Mulsant (q.v.) as a member of the Minister *réseau*. Captured July 1944. Killed in captivity at Buchenwald, 5 October 1944. *Mentioned in Despatches; Croix de Guerre avec Palme.*

Beauregard, Lieutenant A., Canadian General List. Landed February 1944 as a member of the Lackey *réseau*. Captured July 1944. Killed in captivity at Montluc, Lyon (Rhône), 20 August 1944. *Mentioned in Despatches.*

Bec, Lieutenant F. E., General List. Dropped May 1944 as a member of the Headmaster *réseau*. Killed in action near Chemiré-en-Charnie (Sartha), 16 June 1944. *Mentioned in Despatches.*

Beekman, Hon. Section Officer Y. E. M., Women's Auxiliary Air Force. Landed September 1943 as a member of the Musician *réseau*. Captured January 1944. Killed in captivity at Dachau, 13 September 1944. *Mentioned in Despatches; Croix de Guerre avec Etoile de Vermeil.*

Benoist, Captain R. M. C., General List. Landed March 1944, on his second mission, with D. M. Bloch (q.v.) to establish and lead the Clergyman *réseau*. Captured July 1944. Killed in captivity at Buchenwald, 14 September 1944. *Mentioned in Despatches; Médaille de la Résistance Française (Rosette).*

Bertheau, Lieutenant L. E. D., General List. Locally recruited and commissioned as a member of the Author *réseau*. Captured April 1944. Died at Sandbostel, Germany, of treatment received in captivity, 7–15 May 1945. *Mentioned in Despatches; Chevalier de la Légion d'Honneur; Médaille de la Résistance Française.*

283

Bieler, Major G. D. A., Régiment de Maisonneuve, Canadian Infantry Corps. Dropped November 1942 to establish and lead the Musician *réseau*. Captured January 1944. Killed in captivity at Flossenbürg, 5 September 1944. *Companion of the Distinguished Service Order; Member of the Order of the British Empire (Military Division); Croix de Guerre avec Palme.*

Bloch, Lieutenant A. G., General List (served as A. G. Boyd). Dropped September 1941 as a member of the Autogiro *réseau*. Captured November 1941. Killed in captivity at Mont Valérien (Hauts de Seine), 11 February 1942. *Mentioned in Despatches; Médaille de la Résistance Française.*

Bloch, Ensign D. M., First Aid Nursing Yeomanry. Landed March 1944 with Benoist (q.v.) as a member of the Clergyman *réseau*. Captured June 1944. Killed in captivity at Ravensbrück, 25 January–5 February 1945. *King's Commendation for Brave Conduct; Chevalier de la Légion d'Honneur; Médaille de la Résistance Française (Rosette).*

Bloom, Lieutenant M. R., General List. Landed from the sea November 1942 as a member of the Prunus *réseau*. Captured April 1943. Killed in captivity at Mauthausen, 6 September 1944. *Mentioned in Despatches.*

Borrel, Lieutenant A. R., First Aid Nursing Yeomanry. Dropped September 1942 as a member of the Physician *réseau*. Captured June 1943. Killed in captivity at Natzweiler, 6 July 1944. *King's Commendation for Brave Conduct; Croix de Guerre avec Palme; Médaille de la Résistance Française (Rosette).*

Bouguennec, Lieutenant J., General List (served as F. Garel). Dropped March 1943 to establish and lead the Butler *réseau*. Captured September 1943. Killed in captivity at Buchenwald, 14 September 1944. *Member of the Order of the British Empire (Military Division).*

Byck, Hon. Assistant Section Officer M. T., Women's Auxiliary Air Force. Dropped April 1944 with Makowski (q.v.) as a member of the

Ventriloquist *réseau*. Died on active service near Romorantin (Loir-et-Cher), 23 May 1944. *Mentioned in Despatches.*

Byerly, Lieutenant R. B., Canadian General List. Dropped February 1944 with Alexandre, Deniset and Ledoux (q.v.) as a member of the Surveyor *réseau*. Captured on landing. Believed killed in captivity at Gross Rosen, August–September 1944.

Cauchi, Captain E. J. D., General List. Dropped August 1943 as a member of the Stockbroker *réseau*. Killed in action at Sochaux (Doubs), 5 February 1944. *Mentioned in Despatches.*

Clech, Lieutenant M. Central List. Landed May 1943, on his second mission, as a member of the Inventor *réseau*. Captured September 1943. Killed in captivity at Mauthausen, 24 March 1944. *Médaille de la Résistance Française.*

Clement, Lieutenant G., Royal Armoured Corps. Dropped July 1943 with Gaillot (q.v.) as a member of the Parson *réseau*. Captured November 1943. Killed in captivity at Mauthausen, 6 September 1944. *Mentioned in Despatches.*

Coppin, Lieutenant T. C., General List. Landed from the sea May 1942 to establish and lead the Bay sabotage group. Captured April 1943. Killed in captivity, 27 September 1943. *Mentioned in Despatches; Croix de Guerre avec Etoile de Vermeil.*

Damerment, Ensign M. Z., First Aid Nursing Yeomanry. Dropped February 1944 with Antelme and Lee (q.v.) as a member of the Bricklayer *réseau*. Captured on landing. Killed in captivity at Dachau, 13 September 1944. *King's Commendation for Brave Conduct; Chevalier de la Légion d'Honneur.*

Defence, Captain M. E., General List. Dropped March 1944, on his second mission, with O. A. G. Simon (q.v.), as a member of the Satirist *réseau*. Captured on landing. Believed killed in captivity at Gross Rosen, August–September 1944. *Mentioned in Despatches.*

Defendini, Lieutenant A., General List. Landed from the sea February 1944 to establish and lead the Priest *réseau*. Captured soon after arrival. Killed in captivity at Buchenwald, 14 September 1944. *Mentioned in Despatches; Médaille de la Résistance Française.*

Demand, Lieutenant G. W. H., General List. Dropped August 1941, on his second mission, as a member of the Scullion II coup-de-main party. Captured on the return journey. Killed in captivity at Flossenbürg, 29 March 1944. *Mentioned in Despatches.*

Deniset, Captain F. A., Royal Canadian Artillery. Dropped February 1944 with Alexandre, Byerly and Ledoux (q.v.) as a member of the Phono *réseau*. Captured on landing. Believed killed in captivity at Gross Rosen, August–September 1944.

Detal, Lieutenant J. T. J. M., General List. Dropped February 1944 with Duclos (q.v.) to establish and lead the Delegate *réseau*. Captured on landing. Killed in captivity at Buchenwald, 14 September 1944.

Dowlen, Lieutenant R., General List. Landed March 1943 as a member of the Chestnut *réseau*. Captured August 1943. Killed in captivity at Flossenbürg, 29 March 1945. *Mentioned in Despatches.*

Dubois, J. R. A. Landed April 1943 as a member of the Donkeyman *réseau*. Captured November 1943. Believed killed in captivity at Gross Rosen, August–September 1944.

Duboudin, Captain E. G. J., General List. Landed March 1943, on his second mission, to establish and lead the Playwright *réseau*. Captured soon after arrival. Died as a result of treatment received in captivity at Ellrich-Dora, 22 March 1945.

Duclos, Lieutenant P. F., General List. Dropped February 1944 with Detal (q.v.) as a member of the Delegate *réseau*. Captured on landing. Believed killed in captivity at Gross Rosen, August–September 1944.

Finlayson, Lieutenant D. H., General List. Dropped March 1944 with Lepage and Lesout (q.v.) as a member of the Liontamer *réseau*. Captured on landing. Believed killed in captivity at Gross Rosen, August–September 1944.

Fox, Lieutenant M. G. F., General List. Dropped March 1943 to establish and lead the Publican *réseau*. Captured September 1943. Killed in captivity at Flossenbürg, 29 March 1945. *Mentioned in Despatches; Chevalier de la Légion d'Honneur.*

Frager, Major H. J. P., General List. Dropped February 1944, on his third mission, as leader of the Donkeyman *réseau*. Captured August 1944. Killed in captivity at Buchenwald, 12 October 1944. *Mentioned in Despatches; Médaille de la Résistance Française (Rosette).*

Gaillot, Lieutenant H. H., General List. Dropped July 1943 with Clement (q.v.) as a member of the Parson *réseau*. Captured with Vallée (q. v.) February 1944. Believed killed in captivity at Gross Rosen, August–September 1944. *Mentioned in Despatches; Médaille de la Résistance Française.*

Garry, Lieutenant E. A. H., General List. Locally recruited and commissioned to establish and lead the Cinema/Phono *réseau*. Captured August 1943. Killed in captivity at Buchenwald, 14 September 1944. *Mentioned in Despatches; Chevalier de la Légion d'Honneur; Médaille de la Résistance Française.*

Geelen, Lieutenant P. A. H., General List. Dropped April 1944 with Allard and Leccia (q. v.) as a member of the Labourer *réseau*. Captured within a few days. Killed in captivity at Buchenwald, 14 September 1944.

Graham, Sergeant H. H., Royal Artillery. Dropped August 1943 as a member of the Scullion II coup-de-main party. Captured on the return journey. Killed in captivity at Flossenbürg, 29 March 1945. *Mentioned in Despatches.*

Grover-Williams, Captain W. C. F., General List. Dropped May 1942 to establish and lead the Chestnut *réseau*. Captured August 1943. Killed in captivity at Sachsenhausen, 18 March 1945. *Mentioned in Despatches; Croix de Guerre avec Palme.*

Hamilton, Lieutenant J. T., General List. Dropped December 1942 as the only member of the Tobacconist reconnaissance mission. Captured within a few days. Believed killed in captivity at Gross Rosen, August–September 1944.

Hayes, Captain V. C., General List. Dropped November 1942, on his second mission, as a member of the Scientist *réseau*. Captured October 1943. Believed killed in captivity at Gross Rosen, August–September 1944. *Member of the Order of the British Empire (Military Division); Croix de Guerre avec Palme.*

Inayat-Khan, Hon. Assistant Section Officer N., Women's Auxiliary Air Force. Landed June 1943 as a member of the Cinema/Phono *réseau*. Captured October 1943. Killed in captivity at Dachau, 13 September 1944. *George Cross; Mentioned in Despatches; Croix de Guerre avec Etoile de Vermeil.*

Jones, Captain S. C., Royal Engineers. Landed May 1943 with Clech and Leigh (q.v.), on his second mission, to establish and lead the Inventor *réseau*. Captured November 1943. Killed in captivity at Mauthausen, 6 September 1944. *Member of the Order of the British Empire (Military Division); Croix de Guerre avec Palme.*

Jumeau, Captain C. M., Intelligence Corps. Captured April 1943 when the aircraft in which he was travelling on his second mission, to establish and lead the Reporter *réseau*, was shot down. Died at Berling-Buch, Germany, of treatment received in captivity, 26 March 1944. *Mentioned in Despatches; Croix de Guerre avec Palme.*

Lansdell, Lieutenant A. R., General List. Landed April 1944 as a member of the Donkeyman *réseau*. Died on active service in France, 3 June 1944.

Larcher, Lieutenant M. L. M. A., General List. Dropped February 1944 as a member of the Scientist *réseau*; later transferred to Verger *réseau*. Killed in action, with Renaud-Dandicolle (q.v.), near Pierrefitte-en-Cinglais (Calvados), 7 July 1944. *Mentioned in Despatches; Chevalier de la Légion d'Honneur.*

Leccia, Lieutenant M., General List. Dropped April 1944 with Allard and Geelen (q.v.) to establish and lead the Labourer *réseau*. Captured within a few days. Killed in captivity at Buchenwald, 14 September 1944. *Médaille de la Résistance Française.*

Ledoux, Captain J. P. H., Highland Light Infantry. Dropped February 1944 with Alexandre, Byerly and Deniset (q.v.) to establish and lead the Orator *réseau*. Captured on landing. Believed killed in captivity at Gross Rosen, August–September 1944.

Lee, Captain L., M.C., Royal Armoured Corps. Dropped February 1944, on his second mission, with Antelme and Damerment (q.v.) as a member of the Bricklayer *réseau*. Captured on landing. Believed killed in captivity at Gross Rosen, August–September 1944. *Croix de Guerre avec Palme.*

Lefort, Hon. Assistant Section Officer C. M., Women's Auxiliary Air Force. Landed June 1943 as a member of the Jockey *réseau*. Captured September 1943. Died as a result of treatment received in captivity at Ravensbrück, 5 February 1945. *Mentioned in Despatches; Croix de Guerre avec Etoile de Vermeil.*

Leigh, Ensign V. E., First Aid Nursing Yeomanry. Landed May 1943 with Clech and Jones (q.v.) as a member of the Inventor *réseau*. Captured October 1943. Killed in captivity at Natzweiler, 6 July 1944. *King's Commendation for Brave Conduct.*

Lepage, 2nd Lieut. M. A., United States Army. Dropped March 1944 with Finlayson and Lesout (q.v.) to establish and lead the Liontamer *réseau*. Captured on landing. Believed killed in captivity at Gross Rosen, August–September 1944.

Lesout, 2nd Lieut. E., United States Army. Dropped March 1944 with Finlayson and Lepage (q.v.) as a member of the Liontamer *réseau*. Captured on landing. Believed killed in captivity at Gross Rosen, August–September 1944.

Levene, Lieutenant E. F., Royal Artillery. Landed November 1943, on his second mission, as a member of the Donkeyman *réseau*. Captured within a few days. Killed in captivity at Flossenbürg, 29 March 1945. *Mentioned in Despatches.*

Macalister, Captain J. K., Intelligence Corps. Dropped June 1943 with Pickersgill (q.v.) as a member of the Archdeacon *réseau*. Captured within a few days. Killed in captivity at Buchenwald, 14 September 1944. *Mentioned in Despatches.*

McBain, Hon. Pilot Officer G. B., Royal Air Force Volunteer Reserve. Dropped March 1944 as a member of the Musician *réseau*. Captured on landing. Believed killed in captivity at Gross Rosen, August–September 1944. *Croix de Guerre avec Palme.*

Makowski, Captain S., General List. Dropped April 1944 with Byek (q.v.) as a member of the Ventriloquist *réseau*. Captured wounded, and died as a result of treatment received in captivity, at Romorantin (Loiret-Cher), 17–18 August 1944. *Mentioned in Despatches.*

Malraux, Lieutenant C. R., General List. Locally recruited and commissioned as a member of the Salesman *réseau*. Captured March 1944. Believed killed in captivity at Gross Rosen, August–September 1944.

Mathieu, Sergeant R. M. A., French Army. Dropped April 1944 as a member of the Stationer *réseau*. Captured May 1944. Presumed to have died as a result of treatment received in captivity, May 1944–May 1945.

Maugenet, Lieutenant A. A. J., General List. Landed November 1943 as a member of the Acrobat *réseau*. Captured almost at once. Presumed to have died as a result of treatment received in captivity, May 1944–May 1945.

Mayer, Lieutenant J. A., General List. Dropped February 1944 as a member of the Rover *réseau*. Captured May 1944. Killed in captivity at Buchenwald, 14 September 1944. *Mentioned in Despatches; Croix de Guerre avec Palme.*

Menesson, Captain J. F. G., General List (served as J. F. G. Menzies). Landed November 1943, on his second mission, to establish and lead the Birch *réseau*. Captured almost at once. Killed in captivity at Flossenbürg, 29 March 1945. *Member of the Order of the British Empire (Military Division); Croix de Guerre avec Palme.*

Michel, Lieutenant F. G., General List. Landed September 1943 as a member of the Archdeacon *réseau*. Captured almost at once. Killed in captivity at Flossenbürg, 1–15 June 1944. *Chevalier de la Légion d'Honneur.*

Montalembert, Lieutenant Comte A. de, General List. Locally recruited and commissioned as a member of the Satirist *réseau*. Captured August 1943. Killed in captivity at Mauthausen, 16 December 1944. *Chevalier de la Légion d'Honneur.*

Mulsant, Captain P. L., General List. Dropped March 1944 with Barrett (q.v.) to establish and lead the Minister *réseau*. Captured July 1944. Killed in captivity at Buchenwald, 5 October 1944. *Military Cross; Chevalier de la Légion d'Honneur; Médaille de la Résistance Française.*

Newman, Captain I., General List. Landed July 1943, on his second mission, as a member of the Salesman *réseau*. Captured March 1944. Killed in captivity at Mauthausen, 6 September 1944. *Member of the Order of the British Empire (Military Division).*

Norman, Major G. M., Durham Light Infantry. Dropped October 1942 as a member of the Physician *réseau*. Captured June 1943. Killed in captivity at Mauthausen, 6 September 1944. *Mentioned in Despatches; Médaille de la Résistance Française.*

Pardi, Lieutenant P. B., General List. Landed November 1943 as a member of the Scientist *réseau*. Captured almost at once. Presumed to have died as a result of treatment received in captivity, May 1944–May 1945. *Médaille de la Résistance Française.*

Pertschuk, Lieutenant M., General List. Landed from the sea April 1942 on a mission for Political Warfare Executive; transferred to Special Operations Executive to establish and lead the Prunus *réseau*. Captured April 1943. Killed in captivity at Buchenwald, 29 March 1945. *Member of the Order of the British Empire (Military Division); Chevalier de la Légion d'Honneur.*

Pickersgill, Captain F. H. D., Canadian Intelligence Corps. Dropped June 1943 with Macalister (q.v.) to establish and lead the Archdeacon *réseau*. Captured within a few days. Killed in captivity at Buchenwald, 14 September 1944. *Mentioned in Despatches; Chevalier de la Légion d'Honneur.*

Plewman, Ensign E. S., First Aid Nursing Yeomanry. Dropped August 1943 as a member of the Monk *réseau*. Captured March 1944. Killed in captivity at Dachau, 13 September 1944. *King's Commendation for Brave Conduct, Croix de Guerre avec Etoile de Vermeil.*

Rabinovitch, Captain A., General List. Dropped March 1944, on his second mission, with Sabourin (q.v.) to establish and lead the Bargee *réseau*. Captured on landing. Believed killed in captivity at Gross Rosen, August–September 1944. *Mentioned in Despatches; Croix de Guerre avec Etoile de Vermeil.*

Rafferty, Captain B. D., Royal Berkshire Regiment. Dropped September 1942 as a member of the Redwood *réseau*. Established and led the Aubretia *réseau* following capture of Redwood. Captured June 1943. Killed in captivity at Flossenbürg, 29 March 1945. *Military Cross; Croix de Guerre avec Etoile de Vermeil.*

Rechenmann, Captain C, General List. Landed from the sea March 1944 to establish and lead the Rover *réseau*. Captured May 1944. Killed in captivity at Buchenwald, 14 September 1944. *Member of the Order of the British Empire (Military Division); Croix de Guerre avec Palme.*

Renaud, Lieutenant J., General List. Locally recruited and commissioned as a member of the Ditcher *réseau*. Captured June 1944. Presumed to have died as a result of treatment received in captivity, June 1944–May 1945. *Military Cross; Chevalier de la Légion d'Honneur; Médaille de la Résistance Française.*

Renaud-Dandicolle, Captain J. M., General List (served as J. Danby). Dropped January 1944 as a member of the Scientist *réseau*. Later transferred to establish and lead the Verger *réseau*. Died in captivity on or soon after 7 July 1944 of wounds received in action, with Larcher (q.v.), near Pierrefitte-en-Cinglais (Calvados). *Military Cross; Chevalier de la Légion d'Honneur.*

Rolfe, Hon. Assistant Section Officer L. V., Women's Auxiliary Air Force. Landed April 1944 as a member of the Historian *réseau*. Captured July 1944. Killed in captivity at Ravensbrück, 25 January– 5 February 1945. *Mentioned in Despatches; Croix de Guerre avec Palme.*

Rowden, Section Officer D. H., Women's Auxiliary Air Force. Landed June 1943 as a member of the Acrobat *réseau*. Transferred to the Stockbroker *réseau* following capture of Acrobat. Captured November 1943. Killed in captivity at Natzweiler, 6 July 1944. *Mentioned in Despatches; Croix de Guerre avec Etoile de Vermeil.*

Rudellat, Ensign Y. C., First Aid Nursing Yeomanry. Landed July 1942 as a member of the Physician *réseau*. Captured wounded June 1943. Died as a result of treatment received in captivity at Belsen, 23–24 April 1945. *Member of the Order of the British Empire (Civil Division); Croix de Guerre avec Etoile d'Argent.*

Sabourin, Lieutenant R., Canadian General List. Dropped March 1944, with Rabinovitch (q.v.), as a member of the Priest *réseau*. Captured on landing. Killed in captivity at Buchenwald, 14 September 1944.

St. Geniès, Captain M. J. G. de, General List. Dropped March 1944 to establish and lead the Scholar *réseau*. Killed in action near Dôle (Jura), 26 June 1944. *Mentioned in Despatches; Croix de Guerre avec Palme.*

Sarrette, Captain P. F. M., General List (served as P. Sawyer). Dropped December 1943 to establish and lead the Gondolier *réseau*. Accidentally killed near Chiddes (Nièvre), 5 September 1944. *Mentioned in Despatches; Chevalier de la Légion d'Honneur.*

Schwatschko, Lieutenant A., General List (served as A. Shaw). Landed from the sea February 1944 as a member of the Stationer *réseau*. Transferred to the Shipwright *réseau* following capture of Stationer. Killed in action near Eguzon (Indre), 7 June 1944. *Mentioned in Despatches.*

Sevenet, Captain H. P., General List (served as H. P. Thomas). Dropped September 1943, on his second mission, to establish and lead the Detective *réseau*. Killed in action at La Galaube (Aude), 20 July 1944. *Mentioned in Despatches; Chevalier de la Légion d'Honneur; Médaille de la Résistance Française (Rosette).*

Sibrée, Lieutenant D. W., General List. Dropped August 1943 as a member of the Scullion II coup-de-main party. Captured on the return journey. Killed in captivity at Flossenbürg, 29 March 1945.

Simon, 2nd Lieutenant J. A. R., General List. Locally recruited and commissioned as a member of the Stockbroker *réseau*. Killed in action at Sochaux (Doubs), 5 February 1944. *Croix de Guerre avec Etoile d'Argent; Médaille de la Résistance Française.*

Simon, Lieutenant O. A. G., General List. Dropped March 1944 with Defence (q.v.) to establish and lead the Satirist *réseau*. Captured on landing. Presumed to have died as a result of treatment received in captivity at Dachau, August 1944. *Military Cross; Chevalier de la Légion d'Honneur; Médaille de la Résistance Française.*

Sinclair, Lieutenant J. A. E. M., General List. Dropped March 1944 as a member of the Monk *réseau*. Captured on landing. Presumed to have died as a result of treatment received in captivity, May 1944–May 1945.

Skepper, Captain C. M., General List. Landed June 1943 to establish and lead the Monk *réseau*. Captured March 1944. Presumed to have died as a result of treatment received in captivity, on or shortly after 1 April 1944. *Member of the Order of the British Empire (Military Division); Croix de Guerre avec Palme.*

Soskice, 2nd Lieut. V. A., United States Army. Dropped August 1943 as a member of the Scullion II coup-de-main party. Captured on the return journey. Killed in captivity at Flossenbürg, 29 March 1945. *Silver Star Medal.*

Steele, Captain A., General List. Dropped June 1943 as a member of the Monk *réseau*. Captured April 1944. Killed in captivity at Buchenwald, 14 September 1944. *Mentioned in Despatches; Croix de Guerre avec Palme.*

Suttill, Major F. A., East Surrey Regiment. Dropped October 1942 to establish and lead the Physician *réseau*. Captured June 1943. Killed in captivity at Sachsenhausen, 18 March 1945. *Companion of the Distinguished Service Order.*

Szabo, Ensign V. R. E., First Aid Nursing Yeomanry. Dropped June 1944, on her second mission, as a member of the Salesman *réseau*. Captured within a few days. Killed in captivity at Ravensbrück, 25 January–5 February 1945. *George Cross; Croix de Guerre avec Palme.*

Tessier, Captain F. R., Reconnaissance Corps. Dropped January 1944, on his second mission, as a member of the Musician *réseau*. Captured within a few days. Escaped May 1944 and joined Spiritualist *réseau*. Killed in action at Le Raincy (Seine-St. Denis), 26 August 1944. *Mentioned in Despatches.*

Trotobas, Captain M. A. R., Manchester Regiment. Dropped November 1942, on his second mission, to establish and lead the Farmer *réseau*. Killed in action at Lille (Nord), 27 November 1943. *Médaille de la Résistance Française.*

Ullman, Lieutenant P. L., United States Army. Dropped April 1944 as a member of the Stockbroker *réseau*. Killed in action at Valentigney (Doubs), on or about 15 April 1944. *Chevalier de la Légion d'Honneur.*

Vallée, Captain F., M.C., French Army. Dropped June 1943 to establish and lead the Parson *réseau*. Captured with Gaillot (q.v.) February 1944. Believed killed in captivity in Gross Rosen, August–September 1944. *King's Commendation for Brave Conduct; Chevalier de la Légion d'Honneur; Médaille de la Résistance Française (Rosette).*

Wilkinson, Hon. Flying Officer E. M., Royal Air Force Volunteer Reserve. Dropped June 1942 as a member of the Tinker *réseau*. Captured August 1942. Released November 1942 and established the Privet *réseau*. Captured June 1943. Killed in captivity at Mauthausen, 6 September 1944. *Mentioned in Despatches; Croix de Guerre avec Palme.*

Wilkinson, Captain G. A., General List. Dropped April 1944 to establish and lead the Historian *réseau*. Captured June 1944. Killed in captivity at Buchenwald, 5 October 1944. *Mentioned in Despatches; Croix de Guerre avec Palme.*

Worms, Lieutenant J., General List (served as J. de Verieux). Dropped January 1943 to establish and lead the Juggler *réseau*. Captured July 1943. Killed in captivity at Flossenbürg, 29 March 1945. *Military Cross; Croix de Guerre avec Palme; Médaille de la Résistance Française.*

Young, Lieutenant J. C., General List. Dropped May 1943 as a member of the Acrobat *réseau*. Captured November 1943. Killed in captivity at Mauthausen, 6 September 1944. *Member of the Order of the British Empire (Military Division); Croix de Guerre avec Palme.*

SOE F Section circuits in France

This list gives details of circuits or circuit members mentioned in this book. Since 2000, information about the SOE's operations has been widely available, and full details of the circuits and networks listed here but not mentioned in this book can be found online and in the official and other histories. (The complete list of circuits in the Réseau Buck can be found in M. R. D. Foot's book *SOE in France: An Account of the Work of the British Special Operations Executive in France 1940–1944*.)

Acrobat
†A. A. J. Maugenet
Harry Rée – worked with
    Acrobat before taking charge
    of Stockbroker
†Diana Rowden – courier
Jean Simon – organizer
    following Starr's arrest
John Renshaw Starr – organizer
Andre Henri Van der Straton
†John Cuthbert Young – wireless
    operator

Actor
Roger Landes – wireless
    operator

Archdeacon
†J. K. Macalister
†F. G. Michel
F. H. D. Pickersgill – organizer

Asymptote
F. F. E. Yeo-Thomas

Aubretia
†B. D. Rafferty – organizer

Author
†L. E. D. Bertheau
Harry Peulevé– organizer
Jacques Poirier – organizer

298

Autogiro
Georges Bégué – wireless operator
†A. G. Bloch (or Boyd)
Noël Fernand Raoul Burdeyron
    (or Norman F. Burley) – agent
Christopher Burney – assigned
    to assist Burdeyron
Raymond Henry Flower
Pierre de Vomécourt – organizer

Bargee
†A. Rabinovitch – organizer

Bay
†T. C. Coppin – organizer

Birch
†J. F. G. Menesson – organizer

Bricklayer
†France Antelme – organizer
†Madeleine Damerment –
    courier
†Lionel Lee – wireless operator

Butler
†J. Bougennec (or F. Garel) –
    organizer

Carter
Charles Henri Lucien –
    organizer

Chestnut
†Roland Dowlen – wireless
    operator

†William Grover-Williams
    – organizer

Cinema
†Emile Henri Garry – organizer
†Noor Inayat-Khan – wireless
    operator

Clergyman
†Robert Benoist – organizer
†Denise Bloch – wireless
    operator, 1943–1945
Louis Blondet – instructor

Delegate
†J. T. J. M. Detal – organizer
†P. F. Duclos

Detective
†Denise Bloch – wireless
    operator, 1943–1945
Blanche Charlet – courier
Henri Sevenet (aka Henry
    Thomas) – organizer
Brian Stonehouse – wireless
    operator

Digger
Jacques Poirier – organizer

Ditcher
Guy D'Artois – organizer
†Jean Renaud

Donkeyman
Rolf Baumann – teacher

†Jean Dubois – wireless operator
Francis Cammaerts
†Henri Frager – organizer
Peggy Knight – courier
†A. R. Lansdell
Vera Leigh – liaison officer
†E. Levene

Farmer
Arthur Staggs – wireless
  operator
†Michael Trotobas – organizer

Farrier
Juliane Aisner – courier
Marcel Remy Clement –
  assistant
Henri Déricourt – organizer
Andre Watt – wireless operator

Fireman
Edmund Mayer – organizer
Percy Mayer – organizer

Footman
George Hiller – organizer

Freelance
John D. Allsop – instructor
Andre Michael Bloch –
  instructor
Rene Dussaq – assistant
John Farmer – organizer
Denis Rake – wireless operator
Reeve Schley
Nancy Wake – courier

Gamekeeper
†Jack Agazarian – wireless
  operator

Gondolier
†P. F. M. Sarrette – organizer

Headmaster
†F. E. Bec
Charles Sydney 'Soapy' Hudson
  – organizer

Heckler
Paul Goillot – organizer
Henry Riley – organizer

Historian
Nicholas Allington – assistant
†Jean Renaud-Dandicolle (or
  John Danby)
†Liliane Rolfe – wireless operator
André Studler – assistant
†George Alfred 'Teddy'
  Wilkinson – organizer

Inventor
†Marcel Clech – wireless
  operator
†Sidney Jones – organizer and
  arms instructor
†Vera Leigh – courier

Jockey
Francis Cammaerts – organizer
Leslie Fernandez
Xan Fielding

Auguste Floiras – wireless
operator
Christine Granville – courier
†Cecily Lefort – courier
Pierre Martinot – instructor
Pierre Reynaud – sabotage
instructor
Antoine Sereni – wireless
operator

Juggler
†Jean Worms (or Jean de
Verieux) – organizer

Labourer
†E. A. L. Allard
†P. A. H. Geelen
†Maurice Larcher – wireless
operator
Marcel Leccia (or Georges
Louis) – organizer

Lackey
A. Beauregard

Liontamer
†D. H. Finlayson
†M. A. Lepage – organizer
†E. Lesout

Marksman
Elizabeth Devereux-Rochester
– courier
Richard Harry Heslop –
organizer
Owen Johnson – wireless operator

Gordon Nornable – wireless
operator
Geoffrey Parker – medic
Jean Pierre Rosenthal –
organizer
Marcel Veilleux – wireless
operator

Minister
†Denis Barrett – wireless
operator
†P. L. Mulsant – organizer

Monkeypuzzle or Monk
Marcel Clech – wireless operator
†Eliane Plewman – courier
†Jack Sinclair
†Charles Skepper – organizer
†Arthur Steele – wireless
operator

Musician
†Yolande Beekman – wireless
operator
†Gustave (Guy) Bieler –
organizer
†G. B. McBain
†Paul Tessier – assistant

Orator
†J. P. H. Ledoux – organizer

Parson
†G. Clement
†H. H. Gaillot

Pedlar
Nicholas Bodington – organizer

Phono
†F. A. Deniset

Pimento
Anthony Brooks – organizer

Permit
Gerard Dedieu – organizer

Physician
Francine Agazarian – courier
Jack Agazarian – wireless
 operator
†J. F. Amps
†Andrée Borrel – courier
Jacques Bureau – radio
 technician
Pierre Culioli – organizer
George Darling – group leader
†Gilbert Norman – wireless
 operator
†Yvonne Rudellat – courier
†Francis Suttill – organizer
Germaine Tambour
Madeleine Tambour

Playwright
†E. G. J. Duboudin – organizer

Priest
†A. Defendini –organizer
†R. Sabourin

Privet
†E. M. Wilkinson – organizer

Prunus
†M. R. Bloom
†M. Pertschuk – organizer

Publican
†M. G. F. Fox – organizer

Redwood
†B. D. Rafferty

Reporter
†C. M. Jumeau – organizer

Rover
†J. A. Mayer
†C. Rechenmann – organizer

Salesman
Edgar Fraser – Dakota expert
Jean Claude Guiet – wireless
 operator
Philippe Liewer (aka Charles
 Staunton) – organizer
Bob Maloubier – weapons
 instructor
†Claude Malraux
†Isidore Newman – wireless
 operator
†Violette Szabo – courier

Satirist
†Marcel Defence – wireless
 operator

†A. de Montalembert
†O. A. G. Simon – organizer

Scholar
Raymond Aubin – organizer
Yvonne Baseden – wireless
  operator
Rene Bichelot – assistant
Louis Antoine Nonni
†Marie Joseph de Saint-Geniès
  – organizer
Gonzague de Saint-Geniès –
  organizer

Scientist
Claude de Baissac – organizer
Lise de Baissac – courier
André Grandclément –
  organizer double agent
†Victor Hayes – instructor
Mary Katherine Herbert –
  courier
Roger Landes – wireless operator
†Maurice Larcher – wireless
  operator
Phyliss Latour – wireless
  operator
†Paul Baptiste Pardi – landing
  grounds
Harry Peulevé
†Jean Renaud-Dandicolle (or
  John Danby)

Scullion II
†P. J. Amphlett
†G. W. H. Demand

†H. H. Graham
†D. W. Sibrée
†V. A. Soskice

Shipwright
Amédée (Dédé) Mainguard –
  organizer
†A. Schwatschko

Spindle
Peter Churchill – organizer
André Girard
Victor Hazan
Adolphe Rabinovitch – wireless
  operator
Odette Sansom – courier

Spiritualist
Henri Diacono – wireless
  operator
René Dumont-Guillemet –
  organizer
†Paul Tessier – assistant

Spruce or Plane
Robert Boiteaux – organizer
Henri Paul Le Chêne – organizer

Stationer
Jacques Dufour
Amédée (Dédé) Mainguard –
  organizer
†René Mathieu – wireless
  operator
Pierre Mattei – landing grounds
Jacqueline Nearne – courier

†A. Schwatschko

Alexander Shaw – landing grounds

Maurice Southgate – organizer

Pearl Witherington – courier; organizer following Southgate's arrest of Wrestler

Stockbroker

†Eric Cauchi – instructor

Joseph Maetz

Harry Rée – organizer

†Diana Rowden – courier

†Jean Alexander Simon

†Paul Ullman – wireless operator

Surveyor

†R. E. J. Alexandre – organizer

†R. B. Byerly

Tinker

Benny Cowburn – organizer

†E. M. Wilkinson

Tobacconist

†J. T. Hamilton – sole member

Ventriloquist

†Muriel Byck – wireless operator

Emile Counasse

Maurice Lostrie – saboteur

†Stanislaw Makowski – instructor

Pierre de Vomécourt – organizer

Verger

†Maurice Larcher – wireless operator

†Jean Renaud-Dandicolle (or John Danby) – organizer

Wheelwright

Jean-Claude Arnault – assistant

Yvonne Cormeau – wireless operator

Philippe de Gunzbourg – courier

George Reginald Starr – organizer

Anne-Marie Walters – courier

Wizard

Eileen (Didi) Nearne – wireless operator

Jean Savy – organizer

Wrestler

Pearl Witherington – organizer

† – killed or executed while on a mission